MODERN AMERICAN PLAYWRIGHTS

MODERN AMERICAN PLAYWRIGHTS

By JEAN GOULD

Illustrated with photographs

948632

DODD, MEAD & COMPANY

NEW YORK

Library of Congress Catalog Card Number: 66-18791
Printed in the United States of America
by The Cornwall Press, Inc., Cornwall, N. Y.

In
memory of
Phil,
who was so much a part of the scene

ACKNOWLEDGMENTS

I wish to express my appreciation to The Players for allowing me to use the extensive collection of the Walter Hampden Memorial Library in gathering material for this book. I am especially indebted to the late Pat Carroll, Custodian extraordinary of books, paintings, and priceless theatrical memorabilia in the Club, and unofficial historian of a bygone era in the theater. I am equally grateful to the present Librarian, Louis Rachow, for his invaluable assistance in locating bibliographical lists as well as books and back numbers of periodicals containing factual data on the theater in the twenties and thirties. My thanks go as well to the members who gave me personal interviews, including Howard Lindsay and Elliott Nugent, and to the other contemporary playwrights who offered their kind cooperation—to Elmer Rice for checking the factual data in the biographical sketch of himself.

I am also deeply grateful to Yaddo, for granting me a residency during the summer of 1964, when the book was begun. Finally, I should like to pay tribute at this time to the now defunct Huntington Hartford Foundation, to which I was awarded a Fellowship in residence at Pacific Palisades, where the major portion of the work was written.

CONTENTS

ILLUSTRATIONS

Following page 112

Elmer Rice
Susan Glaspell
Eugene O'Neill
Philip Barry
Robert Sherwood
Maxwell Anderson
Sam and Bella Spewack
Howard Lindsay and Russel Crouse
Elliott Nugent
James Thurber
George Kaufman and Moss Hart
Lillian Hellman
Clifford Odets
Thornton Wilder
Tennessee Williams
Arthur Miller
William Inge
Edward Albee

MODERN AMERICAN PLAYWRIGHTS

CURTAIN RAISER

For a long time there was no theater in America. America was a wilderness that had to be tamed first, and then it was a colony, not a country. To these shores came people of many nationalities, most of them seeking refuge of some sort—refuge from religious or political persecution, from justice or injustice. Some sought adventure, some riches, some romance; many merely longed for peace. All, whether they wished or not, became pioneers, whose years were spent in wresting the land from the Indians, in felling the trees, building homes, building soil. Small time for recreation, for entertainment, for literature; and no time at all for an art that combined the three: the theater.

More important, the largest group of pioneers—the Puritans—frowned upon the theater and forbade its appearance as an evil influence; the morality plays of the church itself were not permitted performance because they might contain heresies against the strict, barren religious code the Puritans had set for themselves. Woe betide the man who attempted to represent the deity in any drama, on any stage—a law against it was written into the Constitution when freedom was won.

The theater took a long time to be born in America, a long time to come of age. The novelists early told their tales, and the poets sang their songs, but those who might have written great drama were mute, because the drama involved the people, the public—and where the public was concerned, the government could raise its iron hand.

Some few managed to produce plays from "the other side," pieces like *Ye Bare and Ye Cubb,* presented in 1665, which met with little interference, and succeeded so well that many more followed. To soften the official face of disapproval, the offerings were advertised as "operas," and as such, were accepted by authority and audience alike. As the years went by, more and more of these productions were enjoyed by a greater number of people. A group of professionals, the Hallum Company, came from London in 1750, bringing a fine repertory program, the like of which had never been seen on this side of the ocean. Here and there a solitary journalist began to put forth a few ideas in dramatic form, but they were of little or no importance compared to the plays brought over from England.

As the populace seethed and strained to break loose from the royal leash in the 1760s and early 1770s, voices of indignation were raised and allowed to be heard in the drama. Mrs. Mercy Warren wrote biting "propaganda plays" just before the Revolution, to stir into action doubtful colonists who lagged behind through fear or apathy. Plays like *The Group, The Blockhead,* and others, satirized the Tories and made fun of General Burgoyne's redcoats, calling for a complete rout of British forces. So it was that the infant American drama was born amid the din and howl of revolution, a birth unnoticed by the press of events at the time, but nonetheless significant.

After the battle for independence was won, America was too busy proving itself a nation to nourish and develop the neglected art of native drama. Ben Franklin's essays, his achievements in diplomacy were more important to the newly formed United States seeking to establish a new country among the powers of the world. To curry favor with European nations, translations, adaptations of the works of accomplished foreign playwrights were permitted and even encouraged in the United States. A school of writers sprang up, led by William Dunlop, probably the most prolific adapter of French and German plays in the nineteenth century. In England, a determined Queen was crowned, ushering in the long Victorian era of moral and social standards so thoroughly accepted they became an unwritten code of laws governing the thought of western civilization. No playwright dared to stray outside the pale of respectability set up by these standards if he wished to see his work produced.

Not until another struggle began to shake the vitals of the country around the middle of the century did the dramatists in America seek to represent a true picture of the times, and then it was surrounded by the false frame of melodrama. Slavery and the race problem was already a burning question when Dion Boucicault (actor, writer, producer, of Irish origin) presented *The Octoroon* in 1859, a play which created a sensation, but did little to influence the thinking of people as the novel, *Uncle Tom's Cabin,* had done much earlier. Published in 1852, the book by Harriet Beecher Stowe was enormously popular in the northern states long before it was dramatized, and by the end of the year had been translated into nine languages.

After the Civil War, Boucicault wrote many lurid melodramas of the American scene, which depicted the poor as well as the rich, the disreputable as well as the respectable, like *This Is New York;* but his plots were so exaggerated they were highly improbable, and his conclusions so bound by Victorian conventions—the villain always foiled, the lovers always united in a happy ending—that they were ineffectual if not downright laughable. Victorian audiences did not laugh, neither were they moved nor provoked to thought by these plays; they were merely momentarily entertained. For laughter, they went to see the low comedies of Harrigan and Hart, a team that turned out nonliterary farces dealing with immigrant life in America, for which there seemed to be an inexhaustible supply of material as refugees from many lands continued to pour into the country.

All this time the translators were busy keeping abreast of the dramas containing the latest trends of thought from Europe. The plays of Henrik Ibsen, Anton Chekhov, and August Strindberg came as a startling revelation to American playwrights, particularly the young hopefuls longing for greater substance in the offerings of the American theater. The social changes implied by Ibsen in *A Doll's House, Hedda Gabler, The Wild Duck,* and *John Gabriel*

Borkman, as well as his probing into character, served as a stimulus and challenge to fledgling dramatists eager to try their wings.

One of these was Clyde Fitch, who, toward the turn of the century, began to attempt pictures of more than two dimensions in his plays. His *Beau Brummel* was an excellent portrait of a dandy in the 1890s, but he did not go much below the surface in revealing the motivating influences in his character's behavior. He remained completely conventional so far as morality was concerned and his critical faculty was small. Like the famous "Beau," Fitch flirted with ideas, but never knuckled down to serious consideration of them. He had plenty of opportunity to do so in his historical pieces like *Nathan Hale* or *Barbara Frietchie,* but even in those he found it safer to satisfy the playgoers with the sort of presentation he thought they wanted to see. In one play only—*The City*—did he attempt to expose his characters by showing the corruption in the lives of public officials. But his charge against their malpractices had little vitality.

The impact of Ibsen's dramas was felt by other writers seeking to present the truth in the theater. As early as 1881, Bronson Howard, a young idealist, dealt with the struggle of capital and labor in *Baron Rudolph;* but any effect this work might have had was canceled by his next play, *The Henrietta,* which showed Wall Street in a more or less favorable light, and was perhaps written to appease the anger of the capitalists at the implications of "Baron Rudolph." It has been said (by the critic, Brander Matthews) that Bronson Howard was "born too soon," like many an artist whose vision goes beyond his time. The actor, (James) Steele MacKaye sought to portray the American scene in the written as well as the spoken word, but his lean dramas for justice in cases like the Haymarket anarchist trials lacked any real artistry or strength, and he left the task of fleshing the picture out in detail to his son Percy, who possessed a poetic turn of mind and a prolific pen, which he wielded well into the twentieth century.

Several figures came to the fore in the first decade or so, among them Edward Sheldon, whose play, *The Nigger,* in 1910, was the first to come to grips with the race question since *The Octoroon.* Like the earlier play, *The Nigger* created an immediate sensation, for its plot concerned an ambitious Southern politician, who, on the eve of success, learns that he has Negro blood in his veins—(to him) a discovery that spells disaster and utter ruin. That the play is meant to be an indictment of such an attitude toward the mingling of races and toward the colored race in general is never clearly stated, if indeed Sheldon intended it to be. The drama was a "shocker"; audiences were so stunned by the exposé of the hypocrisy of one man and the irony of his fate that the larger meaning was lost upon them, if it was there in the first place, which is doubtful. Sheldon's next play, *The Boss*, presented the following year, was concerned with the rising trend toward Party boss rule in politics; but it did no more than portray a ruthless politician, who, in accordance with the accepted moral code, was reformed in the end. Furthermore, Sheldon's equally famous *Salvation Nell*, although it described the seamy side of American life, was far from being a realistic picture of the slums or the derelicts the Salvation Army was trying to save. Whether Edward Sheldon would have developed into a thorough realist or strong dramatist and true artist can never be known. At about this time, he was stricken with a terrible disease which paralyzed his whole body, so that he was bedridden for the rest of his life. His brain was not affected, but his condition seemed to have cut off his creative urge; he was content to serve as consultant and "play-doctor" to the ills of other men's works. Many noted playwrights were to travel to his bedside in the years that followed, many producers and directors sought his advice. And many a vehicle that rode to triumphant success on Broadway had been hitched up beforehand at the bedside of Edward Sheldon.

The poet among these early figures in the American drama was William Vaughn Moody, whose principal theme was the conflict between puritanism and passion. In his verse dramas, *The Faith Healer* and *The Great Divide*, he went one step farther than his colleagues in the search for truth. He was daring enough to suggest that a woman could in all honesty love a man who had "violated" her, a concept that took much courage at the time. But he gave in to the sentimentality and prescribed formula of the era, which counteracted the forward movement and kept his work static in spite of his talent and vision.

The sole figure in the first ten years of the twentieth century who might lay reasonable claim to the name of realist was James A. Herne, and then in a single play, *Mary Fleming*. Because of his honest treatment of the problems faced by his half-prostitute heroine, Herne has been called (by John Gassner) "the outstanding realistic playwright before O'Neill." His plays, particularly *Shore Acres*, had wide popular appeal, and influenced a number of writers to try the drama, all the way from the dialect poet Paul Laurence Dunbar to the literary critic William Dean Howells. Herne's sympathy with the downtrodden and underprivileged whom he portrayed in his plays led him to become interested in Henry George and the single tax as a solution to the injustice and inequality of the free enterprise system, and for a time he tried to promote this moderate socialism; but he soon discovered that the power his work gained as propaganda it lost in artistic value.

In all the writing for the theater in America up to this point there was indeed little artistry, and a deplorable lack of the indefinable quality that comes from the spirit of the playwright, the spontaneous poetry of his passion as he embraces the world. However, certain forces were agitating that were soon to bring about a chance for the better in the American theater. Those interested in raising the level of stagecraft found a true artist in Max Reinhardt, whose productions ushered in a new era in this country as well as Europe. In Great Britain, Gordon Craig experimented with the simplification of sets; and when George Pierce Baker, the drama professor then at Harvard, showed slides of Craig's pared-down settings to his English 47 "Workshop" students, they made a profound impression, which undoubtedly influenced the dramatists of the future. The epoch-making New York Armory Show of international art in 1913 was another factor. Young hands like Robert Edmond Jones, Lee Simonson, and Norman Bel Geddes created new physical settings for the life of the drama, which in turn gave rise to greater spiritual achievement. The "little theater" came into existence; sparked by Professor Baker's 47 Workshop, other groups of amateurs banded together to form the Wisconsin Players in Madison and Milwaukee, the Chicago Little Theater (later the Goodman Art Theater), and last but not least, the Provincetown Players, who renovated and remodeled the dilapidated wharf at the tip end of the Cape to make their amazingly successful experiments.

Finally, there was restlessness abroad. Another war was brewing, unperceived by most of the world but nonetheless sensed in its vibrations as part of the general upheaval which brought about a fresh approach, a changed order, and greater growth than the American theater had shown for over half a century.

The stage was set, the cue given, and the modern playwrights promptly made their appearance.

CHAPTER I

---◆---

ELMER RICE

THE FIRST of the "moderns" to enter the limelight by bringing revolutionary ideas to American drama was Elmer Rice. In 1910, he was a pale, thin, red-haired young man who worked in his Cousin Moe's law office. By 1914, in a meteoric rise, he would become the leading playwright of the year.

He hated the law; or rather, he hated the life he led, working in the large downtown firm of which his Cousin Moe, "M.H.G.," was the domineering head. Elmer hated the long hours and going to law school after work or in the evening, the subway ride uptown every night to the second "railroad flat" where three generations of the Reizenstein family had lived in cramped quarters ever since he could remember. He was tired of having to share a room with "Grandpa," although he had loved the old man when he was little, and, as a boy of five or six, he went trudging beside his grandfather to his first school, P.S. 57, on 115th St. They had lived in a flat-house on 90th St. then, where he was born in 1892, and where his infant brother died when Elmer was three. There had never been any more children, so he had grown up as an only child in a household of elders. It was Grandpa who took him to see the first plays he ever witnessed, when they rode in the horsecar down to the German Theater in Irving Place at holiday time, to see the fine actor, Rudolf Christians, present dramatizations of Andersen's fairy tales. Those performances were the greatest treats of his childhood, giving him a taste for the theater which nourished his inner life from that time on, and was now the principal source of spiritual energy that kept him going through the work week, scrimping on the few dollars he earned so that he could take in—usually standing—at least one performance a week. (He always kept his programs—a practice he began when he was twelve.)

At eighteen, Elmer was still fond of his grandfather, devoted to him as he was devoted to his mother, with whom he had a warm relationship. Born Fanny Lion in Warrenton, Virginia, a small town near Baltimore, his mother was the kind of woman who seemed to live only for the care and comfort of those around her, and who could accept, if she did not always understand, the actions of those dear to her. She had almost no social life outside the family, and rarely left the house except to visit old friends occasionally on a Sunday afternoon; yet she was generally contented, cheerful—even optimistic—and serene in her attitude toward life, its sorrows and trials. Through nearly thirty years she looked after the needs of her four men—besides her husband, son, and parents-in-law, her brother-in-law had boarded with them from the time she was married to Jacob Reizenstein—and she hardly ever complained of being "put upon" in any way.

Elmer had found his grandmother, who died when he was small, rather formidable, but he always had a certain fondness for his Uncle Will, a sporty fellow with a hearty sense of humor, a jolly bachelor who stepped out with various women but never married, and who frequently knocked off work to go fishing. The only person in his family whom Elmer had difficulty loving was his father, who was chronically—though intermittently—ill with a frightening disease, epilepsy. Without warning, he would be seized by fits, disturbing to witness, which left him weak and unable to work for days at a time; as a result he could not make a living, even as a part-time cigar salesman, a fact which made him as cranky and complaining when he was well as when he was ill. He criticized his son constantly, picked on him, Elmer thought, yet he sensed that in some dim way his father loved him but was never able to show him affection. They were uneasy together; and, try as he might, the boy was never able to feel more than pity, heightened by moments of anxiety, toward his father.

Without the weekly board-money from Uncle Will and Grandpa (who was "retired"), the family could not have managed; and even so, Elmer had had to give up his education when he was halfway through high school to find a job. Not that he minded leaving the commercial training course he had been forced to take; he had never cared for school anyhow, "never learned anything of the slightest value" to him, he declared later. He was not athletic, mostly because he was so nearsighted he could not play well, a fact that was not discovered till he was sixteen. Luckily, there was a library close to the second flat-house, a haven for a boy who possessed both imagination and brains, but was never stimulated by the conventional paths of learning he had to follow in public schools in the nineties. In the library he could go his own way; it became his "university" and his "shrine." He read everything that struck his fancy—novels, adventure stories, and plays. If he could not go to the theater as much as he wished, he could read plays, from classical drama to Shakespeare and the translations of Ibsen or Chekhov. He devoured books, reading late at night after he came home from work in the warehouse office that hired him as a mail-clerk answering complaints. He persuaded his mother to let him set up a cot in the living room so he could stay up reading long after Grandpa went to bed; and although she consented, she was afraid Elmer was "straining his mind" and ruining his eyes. He was not sure what she meant by the first (and he suspected she wasn't either), but it was eyestrain that led to the discovery of his myopia; and after he had glasses (which opened up a whole new perspective of life for him!), he read more than ever. When he went to the theater, he could see the actors' faces, the details onstage as never before.

He had lasted less than a year in "business," because his employer had to "retrench" in the panic of 1907; so when Cousin Moe (Grossman) suggested that Elmer come to work as a case-file clerk, he had decided to give it a try. Some of the cases he had to keep track of were interesting and there were a number of clients connected with the theater—Oscar Hammerstein for one. He rapidly picked up a knowledge of terms like "affidavit," "pleading," "contract," "judgment," "brief," "transcript," and so on, which were to serve him well as background material when he began to write his own plays. But the job soon became routine, and he realized that he could never earn more than a few paltry dollars unless he became a lawyer. (He put most of his weekly pittance into the family coffer, but if he earned more, perhaps he could go to see more plays.)

After he enrolled and began attending night school, he kept up his reading of literary and dramatic works, even in class: his grasp of the law was quick, for one thing; for another, since students were called on alphabetically, he was prepared for questions when the professor came to the "R's"; and the rest of the time he read some library book hidden behind a law text. Much to his surprise, he graduated with honors, and passed his bar exams easily. He became a junior lawyer with the firm, and his salary went up slightly, but not as high as he had expected.

By now he was engaged to a girl from a family much like his own —an intelligent girl who loved to go to the theater but did not share his passion for everything connected with it. He saw himself settling down to a routine, conventional life in the law profession: struggling, perhaps outsmarting the other junior lawyers to get ahead, raising his family in another railroad flat—and all at once he bolted! He left his Cousin Moe's law firm forever, and announced to his fiancée and family that he had decided to become a playwright.

If his mother had her doubts, she did not show them but accepted his decision with her usual cheerful calm. His girl stood by him for a time, but as months went by and no play of his appeared on Broadway, she became discouraged about the prospect of their marriage, and wrote him a letter breaking the engagement, saying she could not wait any longer. He was angry, he was bitter, but not brokenhearted—only more determined than ever to write a successful play.

He began experimenting with form, seeking to find some new method of dramaturgy that had never been seen on a stage before. From the cases he had handled, the court trials he had attended, he conceived a plot for a murder story, and a unique way of presenting it. Then, like a poet setting out to write a sonnet, he wrote the lines of his play to suit the form he had fixed. The opening scene was in the courtroom, the murderer has confessed killing a man and asks for the death penalty rather than expose his wife and child to degrading publicity, but the state demands an orderly procedure of the law, including defense counsel, witnesses, and trial by jury. As the first witness, the murdered man's wife, takes the stand, the courtroom scene dims out, and the lights come up on a living room scene, where her testimony is enacted. Then back to the courtroom, where the next witness is called; with each one a new scene is enacted, a part of the story unfolded, so that by the end, the murderer's crime is justified, and he is acquitted. Such a construction was a daring departure from the "well-made play" of accepted dramatists; the young playwright wondered whether he could find a producer. To his amazement, the novelty of the piece with its theatrical possibilities was recognized at once by the producing team of Cohan and Harris, who asked him to sign a contract. Together with them, Elmer worked out a "jackknife" set, by which the courtroom scenes could be moved quickly backward and forward.

On opening night, in August, 1914, Elmer sat in a box with his family, half-sick with fright, his face chalk-white beneath his bright red hair. As the curtain went up, he held his breath, one hand clutching the plush-covered rail of the box for support. The audience seemed puzzled by the first blackout, but there were murmurs of pleased surprise when the jackknife stage went into action and the lights revealed the living room. From then on, the seasoned first-nighters were held to the end, when there was a standing ovation, and cries of "Author, author!" It was overwhelming. He could hardly stand to take a bow. He was literally an "overnight" success. The papers the next morning hailed the play as "revolutionary" in the technique of the theater, and referred to Mr. Elmer Reizenstein —a modest redheaded young man—as an innovator, who had brought to the art of dramaturgy "one of the most important modifications in the last hundred years." The play itself was exciting, but it was the manner in which the mystery story was unraveled that heightened the drama and held the audience spellbound as soon as the initial shock had been absorbed.

The young playwright himself had to adjust to the shock of success. One of the first things he did, as the box office receipts began to pour in, was to move the whole family to a large, comfortable apartment, where he could have a room to himself and a place to work in undisturbed. He was twenty-two years old and had never known the luxury of a room of his own; now he reveled in it. The apartment was neither luxurious nor in a "fashionable" neighborhood, but it seemed more than spacious to the Reizensteins after living in a railroad flat for twenty-odd years.

It was hard for Elmer to realize at first that he had suddenly become a figure of some importance in the world of the theater. The success of *On Trial* encouraged well-established playwrights to make innovations of their own, and inspired many young hopefuls to try his technique of storytelling in reverse, which became known as "the flashback" in the motion picture industry. (The "scenario" writer who was hired a year later by a motion picture producer to do the script for a movie version of *On Trial* had not bothered to see the play and began telling the story in straight narrative; when Elmer enlightened him, the writer's face lit up. "Hey, kid, you had a great idea there!" he exclaimed, rushing over to clap Elmer on the shoulder. In disgust, Elmer withdrew from the contract he had signed.)

As *On Trial* continued to play to packed houses, stories of its author and his amazing career appeared in leading magazines as well as newspapers. Anyone who followed the theater could not have failed to read of his triumph, and one day Elmer received a letter from his former fiancée. She said frankly that she had not found anyone else, that she still loved him, and hoped they could now be married. He wondered fleetingly whether his success had anything to do with her change of mind, but decided he must not be so cynical. However, he told her he needed some time to become attuned to the new order of his life before he merged it with another, time to think about his next play, which he had already begun. Nearly a year passed before they were married, and he brought his bride to live with his family.

Meanwhile, the armed conflict that threatened to engulf the

world had broken out in Europe. Like some playwrights, Elmer Rice had the insight to see the brutality and senselessness of war, wherever it occurred, no matter what its cause, and he was strongly opposed to United States entry. His feeling was reflected in his next two plays, *The Iron Cross*, set in Germany; and *The Home of the Free*, both anti-war; both were "killed" by the very thing he hoped he could help to avert. When this country became involved, there was a slight rash of "patriotic" plays, but he was not swayed from his views, and his pacifism was to remain a lifelong conviction.

He continued to write as he felt. In *For the Defense* he drew again on his knowledge of the law; but the play, though it starred the fine actor, Richard Bennett, did not run long. *Wake Up, Jonathan*, written in collaboration with Hatcher Hughes, and featuring the famous Mrs. Fiske, fared better. However, both were disappointing financially, so when an offer came from the Sam Goldwyn office in Hollywood, Elmer decided to try his hand at scenario writing; he had two families to support now, and the high salary would cover his expenses. At twenty-six, he realized that he had never lived more than two miles from his birthplace, never outside the family circle. Moreover, he wanted to see the wide country that he had known only by place-names. Taking his wife and baby, he headed west. Two years of Hollywood, of the synthetic life there, of routine writing assignments that did not really require his talents or make use of them in any measure, was all he could bear. In New York once more, he decided to find a house in the country. Another baby had been born in California; he wanted his son and daughter to grow up in the fresh air and quiet of country life, and his wife agreed.

They rented a place in the Connecticut village of East Hampton, a small house on a rise of ground, surrounded by woods, where a brook ran along merrily in the spring. It was here that Elmer Rice (he had his name legally changed to the simpler one at about this time) wrote the play that was to become a classic of its kind, *The Adding Machine*. The work came about in a strange mysterious manner, an experience that continued to puzzle him through the years. He was sitting on the porch one summer night long after everyone had gone to bed; the house and woods were still, the sky bright with stars. He had intended writing a play about marriage, and wanted to think about it. But suddenly, in a tremendous flash of creative thought that seemed to come from outside himself, there was revealed to him an entirely different play—complete; characters, plot, scenes, all opened up before his brain's eye! Half-bemused, trembling with excitement, he rushed into the house and wrote until dawn. After a few hours' sleep, he got up and started writing again, feverishly. He put down lines and scenes as fast as they came pouring out, using both sides of the sheets of the yellow-paper pad on which he had scribbled in pencil the night before. He hardly stopped to eat, and for seventeen days worked in a white heat, until his children wondered if he had gone daft. When the first draft was completed, he was exhausted, yet elated over his achievement. He scarcely rewrote a line or word, and he had no trouble lining up the Theatre Guild to produce his play.

The Adding Machine, which opened in 1922 and ran well into 1923, was another immediate hit, and created another furor because of its unique form and further innovations in staging. The fantasy of Mr. Zero, for twenty-five years a faithful bookkeeper who is fired when his firm puts in an adding machine, who kills his boss in a frenzy of anger and frustration, who is executed for his crime and goes to heaven where he is put to work on an enormous adding machine, was enacted in seven scenes without a break. It made use of many different kinds of dramaturgy, especially in the heaven scenes and finale, when Mr. Zero's soul is sent back to earth because he fails at the seraphic machine; it has been called both "impressionistic" and "expressionistic," the first of its kind on the American stage. But Elmer Rice was not aware, when he recorded that late-night nocturnal revelation, that he was imitating (or borrowing from) any European school of dramatists. The influence may have been unconscious, a result of the vast range of his reading, but whether this was so or not, *The Adding Machine* was remarkable for its sardonic humor, the universal note of its theme, and for its vision. The play, which has been performed throughout the years, on many stages in many countries, was far ahead of its day. Its indictment of overmechanization is perhaps more timely in the era of automation than in the 1920s.

With his second history-making production in the annals of the American theater, Elmer Rice was regarded as one of its most important figures. He knew everybody, and everybody who knew him liked him. He was extremely reserved, modest about his achievements, and had a quiet sense of humor. He could also show a fiery temper, but this was rare; it flared up mostly when his sense of justice was outraged, when freedom of speech, which he held dear, was challenged—threatened in any way. (In 1916, Elmer had been one of the founders of the Civic Club, forerunner of the American Civil Liberties Union, in which he has long been a member.) Other writers sought his advice, or expressed a desire to collaborate with him on a new play.

One of these was Dorothy Parker, with whom he wrote a sparkling comedy, called *Close Harmony*. Critics who saw the out-of-town previews, thought it could not miss—but it did, and by a wide margin. Disappointed, but by no means downhearted, Elmer declared a holiday, and planned a long-dreamed-of trip to Europe for himself and his family. On the same ship they found a fellow playwright, Philip Barry; and for amusement during the crossing, the two colleagues concocted a spoof mystery play. It was done in a spirit of fun, and completed sporadically through the mail while the playwrights were traveling in different places in Europe. Entitled *Cock Robin,* the final script was a clever, if somewhat contrived murder mystery; and when it was presented in 1928, directed by Guthrie McClintic, was surprisingly successful, all things considered.

The Rice family, Elmer especially, fell in love with the sort of life they found in the various countries they visited. Each one brought fresh delights, not the least of which were the art treasures in museums and churches, which disclosed a whole new realm of pleasure from then on. Returning late in 1927, and while recovering from an emergency operation, Elmer found himself dwelling on the differences between the United States and Europe, comparing the cultures, and trying to discover the forces that produced the outlook—the sort of existence he had always known until a few years earlier—in the country that had fought to become "the land of the free." For the first time he saw the flat-houses and the lives of the people who lived in them with complete objectivity. He began writing a play about them. Taking a typical tenement— not a slum, but a building that housed lower middle class families, mostly working people—he pictured the struggle they all had to wage for survival even in an era of prosperity. The entire action took place in front of the tenement, the inside scenes presented as if the spectator was looking in the window; through the constant comings and goings, the fortunes of the tenants are set forth—the sidewalk battles, the comic incidents, the love affairs, the jealousies and tragedies, all combined to form a drama of human understanding and excitement. There were fifty characters (one of the principals, a stagehand) who made innumerable entrances and exits in the course of the action. In choosing his title, Elmer (still thinking of the figure-filled canvases he had seen in European art galleries) borrowed from the language of painters: *Street Scene,* he called it with eloquent simplicity.

Finding a producer for such a play was almost impossible. Lawrence Langner of the Theatre Guild said it was not a play at all, and other producers who read the script agreed. Moreover, no one wanted to risk a play requiring fifty actors. In his book, *The Living Theater,* Elmer Rice devotes one chapter, "The Biography of a Play," to the story of the first production of *Street Scene,* recounting his own struggle before the opening night of January 10, 1929. He himself had cast and directed the play after finally securing a "has-been" producer, William A. Brady, the only one who would chance it. And even as the curtain went up, no one knew what the outcome would be, but the prospects were dark indeed. Preview audiences were enthusiastic, and so were the first-nighters; reviews were very good; but the question was: would the general public take to such an unusual play? The answer came soon enough, as lines started to form at the box office and the play continued to run even after the depression set in. *Street Scene* won the Pulitzer prize that year. Road companies toured the country with it; movie rights were bought. Elmer himself produced the play in London. As late as 1947, a musical version was written by Kurt Weill and Langston Hughes—a New York City Center presentation.

With the phenomenal success of *Street Scene,* Elmer was spurred on to write and direct a new play nearly every year. More than once he had two plays running on Broadway at the same time. His next hit was an action-packed drama, *Counsellor-at-Law,* set in a background strongly reminiscent of his Cousin Moe's law office. To play the role of the Counsellor he picked an actor he had seen at the Yiddish Art Theater—Paul Muni, who became famous before the end of the run for his superb interpretation of the part, which led to his long career in motion pictures.

As the depression deepened, Elmer Rice, along with other dramatists, was concerned over the "general welfare" of the country, and in *We, the People,* again requiring a cast of fifty, he sought to show a cross section of the population affected by the depression; but its implied censure of the economic system and those who tried to maintain the status quo caused the critics to label it "communistic." Although the audience of liberal-minded theatergoers cheered the play and the actors offered to cut their salaries to keep it running, the manager would not allow the ticket prices to be lowered, so it closed after a short run. Disappointed, Elmer determined to produce his own plays.

When, after David Belasco's death, his famous theater was up for sale, Elmer and his wife figured out a way to buy it, and for several years tried to make a go of it; but the plays Elmer was impelled to write—*Judgment Day,* which dealt with the scandalous Reichstag fire in Germany; *Between Two Worlds,* which compared (and contrasted) Soviet and American life—were misunderstood by the critics and condemned to early closings by their reviews. His sense of justice outraged, Elmer withdrew from the Broadway theater for a time, but he continued to write plays. (He also tried his hand at a novel or two, but it was playwriting that was vital to his very being. "I shall probably go on writing plays until stopped by an act of God or of the public enemy," he remarked to Burns Mantle in an interview.)

He had to relinquish the cherished project of running his own theater all too soon; but shortly thereafter he was recruited for the gigantic task of initiating the Federal Theater Project—a dream perhaps even more dear to him. In a letter of outline to Harry Hopkins, Elmer Rice listed as the first three basic requirements of a national theater:

1. High standards of quality.
2. Low prices of admission.
3. Security and permanence of employment for workers in the arts.

Then he went on to propose allotment of federal funds for the renovation of regional theaters in a hundred cities across the country to serve as community centers for the performing arts. His program also included the coordination of theater and education, with prices as low as twenty-five cents for school children. The wide scope of his plan was never realized, but a great many performing and creative artists benefited by the Federal Theater Project during the short time it lasted. Elmer, who was asked to head the New York Region theater, set his own high standards, and went about fulfilling them with his usual ardor. One of his projects was the weekly dramatization of news events, entitled, *The Living Newspaper,* which proved both exciting and successful. But when the State Department stepped in to censor his news-dramas, demanding deletion of an item about Mussolini's military campaigns at the moment, Mr. Rice, in a passion of rage, denouncing censorship in the strongest language he could muster, resigned his post. *The Living Newspaper* continued briefly, and not long afterward, the entire Federal Theater Project was killed when Congress failed to renew the funds for its allotment.

Bitterly disappointed, disgusted by the short-sightedness of government officials, Elmer returned to a variation of his earlier dream; this time, in collaboration with some of his colleagues—Maxwell Anderson, Robert Sherwood, Sidney Howard, S. N. Behrman, and later, Kurt Weill—he formed the Playwrights Company. The five produced their own plays for the next twenty years (Elmer continuing to direct the offerings he wrote himself), and enjoyed greater success than any of them dared to hope. The plays were chosen and produced with relatively little conflict, including the long-run musical, *Knickerbocker Holiday,* by Maxwell Anderson and Kurt Weill. There was a cooperative spirit that pervaded throughout, perhaps because they were all able, sensitive, yet practical artists. Even the press agent was a talented young writer, Philip Stevenson, whose one-act play, *What It Takes,* dealing with the tragic suicide of an automobile salesman, won the New Theatre League Award, and served as forerunner for Arthur Miller's *Death of a Salesman* twelve years later. Stevenson was afterward co-author of the suspenseful war-drama *Counterattack.* Some of the principles that Elmer could not carry out in the Federal Theater Project were followed by the Playwrights Company, to the benefit of all concerned.

In 1942, after twenty-five years of marriage, the Rices were divorced. Elmer's father had died, followed a few years later by "Grandpa" at the age of ninety-two; his Uncle Will went to live by himself, and Elmer's mother had moved in with him and his family. His wife had always found fault with his mother, an attitude he resented; for a long time she and Elmer had been drifting apart. (For that reason they had bought the Belasco Theatre together, but the project had not drawn them any closer.) Moreover, Elmer had fallen deeply in love with Betty Field, the appealing young actress who starred in his plays, *Two on an Island* and *Flight to the West*, in 1940. (The latter was an exciting drama set in an airplane carrying fugitives from strife-torn Europe, just before American entry into World War II. From the tales of terror revealed during the flight, the play was considered obviously antiwar as well as anti-Nazi; and, although the reviews were good, it did not have a long run.) By 1942, despite the difference in their ages, Elmer Rice and Betty Field were married and had moved into a rambling old house on a hilltop in Stamford, Connecticut; his play of that year was called, appropriately, *A New Life*.

He felt indeed that he had started life anew. He had never known such happiness before; here was someone who could share his total experience, in the theater and away from it, who could be as engrossed in its problems and as thrilled by its triumphs as he. His home was serene; Betty, who had no quarrel with his mother, appreciated the qualities in her that he had always revered. In the next few years, three children were born, and the house in Stamford hummed with new life. It was for Betty that he wrote *Dream Girl*, a biographical play with psychiatric overtones, subtly comedic, based on a series of dreams that reveal the whimsical, often wistful personality of the central figure. Production by the Playwrights Company was assured, and Elmer, as usual, directed; in the title role, Betty gave every indication of a star performance, but unfortunately, she suffered an attack of laryngitis on opening night; she went on in spite of it, and as a result, the play was far from being the hit they had expected, although it ran for a year, and later toured the country, and enjoyed a much longer run in England. As Betty's throat did not improve, the understudy had to take over, and she could not bring to the role the quality that belonged to Betty alone. Both Elmer's disappointment and hers was deep; somehow it marked the beginning of a series of misfortunes over a period of years that led to the breakup of their marriage.

Heartbroken at first, he had the courage to continue living in the Stamford house by himself. (His mother died before the real crisis occurred, his older children were on their own, and Betty took their children with her after the divorce.) Elmer had the inner fortitude to go on writing, working in and for the theater. He had been one of the founders of the Dramatists Guild, instrumental in bringing about many contract reforms; he kept up his activity as a member of the board, and served in other organizations as he had in the past. As a vice-president of the P.E.N. Club, he traveled to international conferences of writers in Europe and the Orient. He taught a course at New York University, out of which came his book, *The Living Theater,* published in 1957. He began writing his autobiography, *Minority Report* (a legal term once more), which was completed and published in time for his seventieth birthday in 1962, and which might well be considered a rich, personal history of the theater in America. Most important of all, most essential to his well-being, he continued to write and direct plays. *Cue for Passion,* based on the theme of *Hamlet,* and *Love Among the Ruins* (produced in 1963) are among his latest. Elmer Rice's capacity for living, for the enjoyment of life, has been large, no matter what his trials; and he remains today the devoted friend of his first love—the theater.

Sidney Howard

Sidney Howard seems to have been born attached to "the silver cord," albeit loosely tied, which was the subject of one of his most eloquent plays. Next to the youngest of six children, he came into the world in the country home of the Howard family near Oakland, California in 1891. Although he went to public schools, camped in the high Sierras, rode horses, and lived an outdoor life along with his brothers and sisters, he was "sickly a good deal as a kid" because of a weak lung; he could never take part in strenuous games or school sports, a fact which galled him and gave him something of an inferiority complex. Perhaps to compensate, his parents paid him close attention when he showed a penchant for the arts and the artistic in nature. They took him on trips to British Columbia and Mexico, and, when he was seventeen, to spend a year in Italy for his health. Both his parents were musicians, and Sidney, who was given piano lessons, inherited just enough of their talent to tantalize him. From his father he also inherited a love of gardening and books. (The elder Howard, a "Handel hound" and a collector of fine editions, saw to it that there was both music and literature available to his children if they were so inclined.)

Sidney's parents gave him a toy theater one year, which kept him happily occupied for many hours and engendered his lifelong interest in producing as well as writing plays. Because of his frail health (which eventually became robust) he was late in starting his college education, but his parents "coaxed" him to complete it, especially since he was already writing plays which showed great promise. He graduated from the University of California in 1915, and "was talked into" going to George Pierce Baker's 47 Workshop at Harvard. Perhaps because he was doubtful to begin with, he did not like Baker's methods in putting across his ideas on the theater. Being impulsive and outspoken, Sidney criticized the Professor sharply, but later "ate his words," when he realized that he was wrong; and he always regretted the fact that he left the Workshop before completing the course. After serving as an ambulance driver in World War I, and, on his return from overseas, as a correspondent on labor strife for such magazines as *The New Republic, Life,* and *Colliers*—a post which provided experience in the school of realistic writing—he turned to his first interest, the theater. He translated D'Annunzio's *Fedre* for Nazimova, whose performances of classical tragedy were at their peak; and, with the critic–biographer, Barrett Clark, whom he met in the same year, wrote a play called, *The Rivet.* (Although it was far from a great play, the collaboration welded the two writers in a literary and personal friendship that lasted a lifetime.)

Sidney Howard's first original play, *Swords,* produced in 1921, failed as a romantic drama, but it brought romance to the playwright in the person of the leading lady, Clare Eames. They were

married immediately after the play closed, and for the next nine or
ten years, until their separation in 1930 and the actress's death in
London the following year, their relationship proved of lasting
benefit to Howard's career as a playwright. "Clare held me hard to
the theater," he confessed to Barrett Clark after she was gone. It
was she who urged him to develop the idea for his first hit play,
They Knew What They Wanted, which won the Pulitzer prize
the year it was produced, in 1924. Set in the Napa Valley vineyards
near his birthplace in California, the play was Sidney Howard's
interpretation of the classical Paolo and Francesco tale, retold in
contemporary terms, with a warm, vibrant earthiness native to the
California scene of his boyhood. Although O'Neill saw the script
of the play (possibly through Barrett Clark) before writing *Desire
Under the Elms,* and although the two plays opened only two
weeks apart, in November, 1924, and ran at the same time on
Broadway, both concerned with the stories of two men and a
woman, there was little similarity between the two. O'Neill's play
is a poetic tragedy, based on the Freudian theme of the Oedipus
complex. Howard's play is a realistic drama, from some aspects a
comedy–drama, and at its height, a melodrama; its poetry lies in
the warmth of feeling found in the American–Italians whom Howard knew so well; its story line had an Italian source. Yet some
people were inclined to equate the two works, to the annoyance of
both playwrights, particularly Howard. When the usually penetrating Robert Benchley blithely referred to both plays as "French
triangles," Howard was highly indignant. "I was outraged for both
O'Neill and myself," he wrote to Barrett Clark. Surprisingly, yet
understandably, it was his own play, and not O'Neill's, that won
the Pulitzer prize. (O'Neill's direful and darkly-colored tragedy
was not yet evaluated as a work of art, and Howard's play had tremendous appeal because of its warmth and down-to-earth realism.
The splendid performance of Pauline Lord, as Amy, also added to
the charm of the play.)

They Knew What They Wanted was followed by *Ned McCobb's
Daughter* in 1925; and the strong, psychological, and widely-dis-
cussed drama, *The Silver Cord* in 1926. Sidney Howard claimed to
know little or nothing of Freud, but his play was a fascinating
analysis of mother-love carried to extremes; and it was a powerful

indictment of the woman who subtly draws "the silver cord" into a strangle-hold and refuses to let go. Whether or not he based his thesis on actual experience cannot be known, but the over-protectiveness of his parents may have presented him with the germ of the idea he developed so forcefully in *The Silver Cord*. It may also have been part of the differences between Clare and him, which began around this time, and reached the breaking point in 1929 when he took their daughter and went to live in California with various members of his family for a year or two. Although she "held him hard to the theater," Clare Eames could not bring herself to share his interests outside it, and as a result, they parted company. Before the rift became final, however, he had written and partially produced *Lucky Sam McCarver,* several adaptations of foreign plays, and the first draft of *Yellowjack* (1928), his stirring, stark drama of the fight against yellow fever. A dramatization of a chapter in Paul de Kruif's book, *Microbe Hunters,* the play was not produced until 1934, when it was highly successful on Broadway, later becoming a favorite offering of repertory companies and college theatres throughout the country.

After the death of Clare Eames, Sidney Howard married Leopoldine ("Polly") Damrosch, one of the five daughters of the famous conductor, Walter Damrosch. In so doing, the playwright linked his career in the theater with his love of music, and was also able to develop his third interest, gardening, for he and Polly bought a farm at Tyringham, Massachusetts, where they both found satisfaction in working the soil. Here their three daughters were born; and here, along with farming, he wrote the first draughts of *The Late Christopher Bean,* 1932; *Alien Corn,* which starred Katharine Cornell in 1933; an adaptation of Sinclair Lewis' novel, *Dodsworth,* in 1934; and *The Ghost of Yankee Doodle,* produced by the Theatre Guild in 1937. He tried to be a playwright and run the farm at the same time, a task that proved fatal: he was killed in a senseless accident—crushed against the wall of the barn by a tractor that went out of control when he tried to start it, September 1, 1940. His friends, and he had many in the theater, were horrified and saddened by the news of his untimely death. He had been a man of great vitality and enthusiasm, often helping younger playwrights—Lynn Riggs, for one—to find a place in the sun. Barrett Clark, who mourned him deeply, wrote of him, "He was a kind of modern knight, a man whose heart demanded that there be decency and justice in the world." Joseph Wood Krutch commented on the "exhilaration" in Howard's plays, calling them "among the best ever written in America."

CHAPTER II

SUSAN GLASPELL

AND

THE PROVINCETOWN PLAYERS

Aᴛ ᴀʙᴏᴜᴛ the time that Elmer Rice was on the verge of revolutionizing the stage technique of the commercial theater in his native city, two starry-eyed, literary iconoclasts arrived from their native city in the corn belt—Davenport, Iowa—to join the little theater movement in the East. They were Susan Glaspell and George Cram Cook, and at that moment they were not aware that theirs would be a history-making contribution to the art of the drama in America: it was their wedding day, April 14, 1913. They had been married by the mayor of Weehawken, had lunch at the Brevoort, and took the Fall River boat for Provincetown to spend their honeymoon summer in a small house at the tip end of the Cape, down the road from a crumbling old fisherman's wharf.

For Susan Glaspell, it was a time of incredible happiness not unmixed with wonder, a tender amazement at the mere fact of their marriage, which never completely left her. She had been born July 1, 1882, nine years later than her groom, in the same city, but under such a different roof that they might always have remained worlds apart except that both had inquiring minds and the courage to question the values and beliefs prevalent in their society. She was the daughter and granddaughter of humble fruit farmers, who, when she went to school in Davenport, borrowed books from the Cook Memorial Library, sometimes attended services at the Cook Memorial Church, and often walked past the Cook Home for old ladies. George Cram Cook, familiarly called "Jig" from the time he went to prep school at Griswold Military College in Davenport, was born and raised in the town whose institutions emblazoned his family name three times over. Since there was no Glaspell Home for the Friendless or anything like it, Susan grew up knowing all about Jig Cook long before he was aware that she existed. She knew that his ancestors, like hers, had been pioneer settlers on the land back of the Mississippi, who built log cabins and became farmers; and she had often heard the legend of the sons and grandsons who became lawyers and bankers to build the thriving town of Davenport. They built for themselves the big, boxlike mansions of brick painted slate gray, adorned with towers and mansard roofs, which her parents early pointed out to her, and in one of which Jig had been born. Susan later came to see the ugliness of those houses, but at the age of seven or eight she regarded them, and the big brick stables for horses and carriages in back, as palatial (if rather formidable) residences.

Later she also learned the legend of the Cabin where the Cooks spent their summers. Jig's mother (whose father had once owned a steamboat on the Mississippi) showed rare taste in having the original log cabin, built by her parents, moved from the backwoods to a place of honor and beauty along the riverbank. In those days, "Iowa people with money for new houses were not bothering about log cabins," and her action was considered "queer." Queer, too, was the fact that you could take a volume of Plato or Ruskin from the bookshelves beside the fireplace in the old, "freshly chinked" log cabin and note that the pages were well-thumbed; that a fine old tapestry hung on those rough-hewn walls; that there were Greek urns in this cabin on the Mississippi, and that conversation might include the mystic rites of India or the music of Beethoven as compared to Bach. When Susan Glaspell was seventeen, a brilliant English student who "wanted to write," she was told by her teachers and various townspeople that she must visit the Cabin and get to know this odd, bright, quick little woman who encouraged the joys of the spirit in her family and friends. Susan had gone there once, invited at the suggestion of one of her sponsors, the summer before she went to the University of Chicago. Slightly skeptical at first, she had come away with genuine admiration for Ellen Cook, for the atmosphere of culture she had managed to bring to this small haven back of the bustling river-town of Davenport, for the warm, unpretentious hospitality she offered, leaving visitors free to read or wander along the reedy bank of the "wide water" if they chose. On that visit, Susan had met Jig Cook for the first time, briefly.

He had been teaching at the University of Iowa, having graduated from there and from Harvard, after a year at Heidelberg and another traveling in Europe, mostly in Italy. A classical scholar, with a passion for Homer and Dante, he was also an athlete, tall and powerfully built; he had a classic profile and head, shock of dark hair (early to turn white) sweeping back from a peak on his high forehead; his eyes, from under dark brows, were at once alive and brooding, often mystical in expression. Susan, who was slight, delicate, wistful-eyed (at that moment), possessed a wit and practicality that saved her from being overly shy. When he came into the room, looking for Renan's *Life of Jesus,* which lay open on the table, she could not help observing, after he had acknowledged their introduction with a preoccupied nod, "Oh, you read it in French!" He looked at her in some surprise, as if he thought her comment strange. "Yes," was his only reply, as he picked up the book and went out.

(His surprise made her smile, and one day, as they were taking a walk in Provincetown, she twitted him about his attitude on that day of their first meeting.)

Four years in Chicago, where she worked her way through college, brought greater confidence to Susan Glaspell. She had chosen to study in the surging, Midwestern metropolis instead of the corn-fed prairie town of Iowa City because she wanted to get away from the unimaginative minds she had known in Davenport, from what Jig called "the Puritanic distrust of pleasure and beauty." In Chicago the first seeds of socialism were beginning to sprout, and Susan found their growth exciting. She went to lectures, forums, and to the theater, where new worlds of thought were unfolded before her eyes in the dramas of Ibsen and Chekhov. She felt a fleeting urge to write plays of her own, but dismissed it because she thought the form was beyond her talent. She would write short stories, or a novel first. When she returned to Davenport with her degree, she took a job as a newspaper reporter. At least she would be writing, recording life.

In those four years, George Cram Cook had turned his back on teaching, had become a philosopher-farmer, tilling the fields at the Cabin to turn them into a truck-farm, meditating as he plowed. Winters he lived alone, writing; a novel had been published by Macmillan. One summer the librarian in Davenport showed him the writings of a seventeen-year-old boy, Floyd Dell, who was look-ing for a job. With an unerring eye for the creative ability of other writers, Jig sensed an artist of more than a grain or two of talent, and offered a summer or two on the farm, working the land, writ-ing, talking, arguing. Young Dell had strong socialist leanings, and before long he and Jig had formed the Monist Society in Daven-port, "for the propagation of our philosophy in the guise of reli-gion, or religion in the guise of philosophy." The Monist Society attracted all sorts of people; anyone who was of a mind to speak out could be heard, and it was here that Susan Glaspell and George Cram Cook came to know each other. Susan, who had a mind of her own now, and was not afraid to show it, would politely refuse to go to church with her parents on a Sunday morning; on Sunday afternoon, she would walk boldly through the main streets of Dav-enport to a narrow side alley and up a dusty stairway to a bare barnlike room over a saloon, where the Monist Society held its meetings. The first time she went she was astonished at some of the faces; here was the postman, "a few of the more fearless club-women," among others—people whose families still drove Grand-mother out to the Old Settlers' picnic; and above all, here was Jig Cook, son of one of the town's leading families. She was stimulated, thrilled when he spoke, welding universalist religion with Greek philosophy and the principles of a socialist economy. Excited, he twisted the forelock of his thick hair into a horn. His eyes, like those of a seer, now flashing, now somber, had the power to pierce and to move people's souls with their fervor. Watching the faces in the hall, Susan saw during those early days how contagious his enthusiasm could be; she was to witness it again, when they formed the Provincetown Players.

She and Jig became friends outside the Monist Society; they went for walks and talked "of all the things there were to talk about." They might have married that same year, except that each had obligations to fulfill. He was engaged to a girl from Chicago; their wedding date had recently been set for some months ahead. Susan had made plans to go to New York for a time, to join the staff of a newspaper there, and then she was going to Paris. (Every young woman with "advanced" ideas must live in Paris during the decade of the "noughties," as they were dubbed by some wit.) But before she left, the two had reached, without word or deed, a point of understanding that made them realize they would not be forever apart; it was sealed between them in a moment of revelation.

So it was five years before they went to the mayor of Weehawken, then boarded the Fall River boat for Provincetown. Susan had found no ties to bind her to the life in Paris; and Jig had discovered that he had made a gross mistake in going through with his wedding plans; when Susan came back to Davenport, he knew there could be no one else. He had finally left his wife and two children, to become, during the time of divorce, a (literary) critic for "The Friday Literary Review" of the *Chicago Evening Post,* along with Floyd Dell, who had quickly "made good." They reviewed both books and plays, the latter events of excitement, especially the productions of the Irish Players. As Susan was to write twelve years later: "Quite possibly there would have been no Provincetown Players had there not been Irish Players. What he—Jig —saw done for Irish life he wanted for American life—no stage conventions in the way of projecting with the humility of true feeling." Jig himself held that there could be "an American Renaissance of the twentieth century," wrought, like the Italian Renaissance (according to Nietzsche), by a hundred creative artists, the core of which might well be the theater.

During the first summer they dreamed and drowsed with happiness; Susan wrote a short story or two; Jig gardened—he loved to work with his hands as well as his brain. Together they walked around the curve of the Cape, and talked of the future. They came to know their neighbor, Mary Heaton Vorse, whose articles and stories championed the underprivileged; twice widowed, she had come to Provincetown with her children in the summer of 1906, and had decided to become a year-round resident, buying the house she had rented—which included the old wharf with the fishing shack at its end. She introduced them to her friends, writers who had followed her lead in getting away from New York— Hutchins Hapgood and his wife, Neith Boyce, Max Eastman, who had recently founded the magazine of protest, *The Masses,* along with Jack Reed and a few others, also part of the Provincetown circle of writers.

The following spring, Susan and Jig bought an old house across the road, which they remodeled themselves, with help from Max Eastman, Wilbur Daniel Steele and his wife Margaret; Jack Reed; Mary Vorse; Floyd Dell, who had followed Jig from Chicago; and Jig's mother, who had come to stay with them. (His father had died a few months before.) They knocked out walls, opened the closed-in staircase, and, when Susan was forbidden to go up and down steps because of sudden heart trouble that summer, Jig contrived and built a tiny elevator for her, with ropes and pulleys, lead pipes and lumber.

In the winter, they lived where their friends did, in New York City's "The Village," where rents were cheaper and tradespeople more friendly to struggling artists than those uptown. Both Susan and Jig were writing most of the day; they formed the habit of having tea before their "glowing coals" in Mulligan Place, and then going to dinner at "Polly's" to meet their friends for a good dinner at low cost; sometimes they would stop at the Washington Square Bookshop, run by the Boni brothers (Charles and Albert), and a hangout for anyone interested in the little theater movement. Here it was that the Washington Square Players came into existence with a spontaneous performance of *Lord Dunsany* one afternoon, using an impromptu paper set created on the spot by Bobby (Robert Edmond) Jones. Jig and Susan attended some of the first performances of the Washington Square Players in the Band Box Theater they finally secured on 57th Street, where Jig uttered the initial "audience collaboration" line—one of the principal features of little theater groups. Sometimes they went down to the Neighborhood Playhouse in the "exuberant pushcart" district to see Biblical plays like *Jephthah's Daughter*, performed with the ardor of ancient Hebrew ritual. When, on rare occasions, they had enough money for tickets to a Broadway play, they "came away wishing they had gone somewhere else." But the experience always made them more determined to create a new kind of native theater, one, Jig said, after seeing *Lysistrata*, that would be comparable to the Greek theater of Aristophanes. Late at night, before their glowing grate in Mulligan Place, he and Susan would talk of what the theater might be.

One night they got onto the subject of psychoanalysis, just then beginning its vogue in the Village. "You could not go out to buy a bun without hearing of someone's complex," Susan said. She and Jig began tossing back and forth bits of conversations they had heard, phrases which suddenly grew into lines of dialogue for a sprightly comedy, which they called *Suppressed Desires*. They wondered if anyone else would ever have as much fun with it as they had in writing it. But when they took the script around, even the Washington Square Players thought the play was "too special." (Fifteen years later it had been given by every little theater and almost every Methodist church; golf clubs in Honolulu; colleges in Constantinople; in Paris and China and every rural route in America. Far from special indeed.)

When summer came, and no one else had put on their play, Susan and Jig decided to put it on themselves in Provincetown. Neith Boyce had a new play, *Constancy*, and her husband suggested that the two could be put on in the Hapgoods' house, which had a larger living room than the Cooks'. Red-bearded Bobby Jones, who had just returned from a year in Europe studying stage design, came to join the Provincetown circle that summer, and offered his services. He enjoyed using his ingenuity in staging. The group had no lighting equipment, so he just "put a candle here and a lamp there." To provide separate "sets" for the two "one-acters," he sat the audience in the Hapgoods' living room so that they were facing the broad seaside porch for the performance of *Constancy*. When it was over, they turned their chairs around to face his setting for *Suppressed Desires*, for which he rearranged the furniture in an alcove-room to represent a Greenwich Village apartment. The audience was so delighted with the initial, wholly casual production of the players that all concerned agreed this must not be the end. Neighbors who had not been asked to the Hapgoods' were hurt. The plays must be given again, if possible in a larger place, so more people could come.

Margaret Steele, who had taken the old fishhouse on the wharf as her writing studio, offered—at Jig Cook's suggestion—to let them use it for the revival of the double bill. With his usual enthusiasm, Jig wrote another comedy, *Change Your Style,* satirizing two rival art schools. Wilbur Steele had written a symbolic political play called *Contemporaries,* and the two were presented as a second double bill "to end the first season. . . ." At both performances, members of the audience brought their own chairs or campstools, placing them in among the oars, anchors, and nets, and around a rowboat stored there. The performance was staged at the far end, in front of the sliding doors that formed the rear wall—once used by the fishermen for hauling in their catch.

That first "season" was enough to fire the imagination and ardor of a visionary like Jig Cook, who saw in it the means of realizing his dream of a Beloved Community, built around the theater. After the summer people had gone, he would go out to the wharf and "step" the fishhouse, measuring the stage space; there were two feet more, he was sure, than he had thought. He would open the sliding doors and stand looking across the harbor, hearing the waves lap the piles below him, yet not listening; he was planning for next summer, for the future; then Susan would see him walking slowly back, "head a little bent, twisting his forelock."

They were back early in spring. Jack Reed was just home from Mexico, where he saw a medieval miracle play that had survived the centuries; he added the fire of his own enthusiasm for the creation of an atmosphere like that of the ancient Greeks, in which, through experiment, a new American drama could be born. He, Jig and Susan, and the Hapgoods talked long and earnestly about their purpose, and, before the other members of the group appeared, had arrived at an "affirmation of faith": "One man cannot produce drama. True drama is born only of one feeling animating all the members of a clan—a spirit shared by all and expressed by the few for the all. If there is nothing to take the place of the common religious purpose and passion of the primitive group, out of which the Dionysian dance was born, no new vital drama can arise in any people."

Faced with such a faith, the other members—now numbering thirty—were glad to make the five-dollar contribution to help convert the old fishhouse into the Wharf Theater. Using all hands available, they hauled out the old boat, oars, nets and anchors, returning them to their respective owners; they bought lumber at the second wharf "up-along," constructing a playhouse out of the shell of a shack, twenty-five feet square and fifteen feet high. The ingenuity that enabled Jig to build an elevator for Susan served him now to devise a stage, only ten feet by twelve, which was in four sections, movable, so they could have different levels, and run it through the big sliding doors at the back if they chose, to give the effect of distance. If they needed a backdrop of the sea, they had only to slide back those doors and the wide bay itself provided the scene—dark water, points of light from passing ships, swept at intervals by the beacon of the Cape lighthouse. With the rest of the lumber, they built backless wooden benches, which, placed close together, would seat ninety people.

Under the name of the Provincetown Players, adopted by a unanimous vote, the group proudly announced a season of four bills of three one-act plays each. The opening bill—a revival of *Suppressed Desires;* a satire by Jack Reed, called *Freedom;* and *Winter's Night,* by Neith Boyce—played to a full house. And before the next bill, through a letter composed by Jig, eighty-seven of those ninety seats had been bought by subscribers at the price of one dollar for the three remaining bills of the season. The people would be associate members. The fine response paid for lighting equipment and sets; the most expensive set at the Wharf Theater cost thirteen dollars. Now they had everything but the plays for the second bill. Wilbur Steele completed a script for a minor comedy entitled *Not Smart,* and several other members had plays in process. They met at the Cooks' for readings, but could not seem to agree on the next bill.

Susan was desperate. She decided to ask the two Irishmen who had taken a shack up the street—the younger one said to be the son of the famous actor, James O'Neill—whether either of them had any scripts. Meeting the older man—Terry Carlin—on the street, she asked, "Terry, haven't you a play to read to us?"

"No," he answered. "I don't write, I just think, and sometimes talk. But Mr. O'Neill has got a whole trunkful of plays." He smiled.

It didn't sound too promising, but Susan could not waste time speculating. "Well, tell Mr. O'Neill to come to our house at eight o'clock tonight, and bring some of his plays."

So, as Susan told the story, "Gene took *Bound East for Cardiff* from his trunk" and the actor, Frederic Burt, read it to the group assembled in the living room, among them Harry Kemp, the "hobo" poet, and his lovely red-haired wife, Mary Pyne, who had just joined the Provincetown Players. O'Neill, who had come to Provincetown at the suggestion of his friend, Jack Reed, was inclined to be wary of little theater groups. His deepset eyes moody, he said with nervous diffidence that he preferred to stay in the dining room during the reading if he might. (He was afraid to hear the lines, afraid to look at the faces of the listeners.)

But the little circle that night listened spellbound to those lines. When the reading came to an end, they rushed to congratuate the playwright; as Susan said: "He was not left alone in the dining room when the reading had finished. Then we knew what we were for." Jig, especially, was excited; here was the dramatist he had been searching for—the one who could justify his faith in a native theater. *Bound East for Cardiff* won a unanimous "Aye!" and went into rehearsal immediately. It was presented two weeks later, leading the second bill of the Provincetown Players, the first time Eugene O'Neill was produced on any stage.

Susan felt that she had never seen a more moving production. Jig played Yank, the dying sailor, who spoke of life as one who knew he must leave it. The small stage looked like a forecastle, and nature provided the perfect scenic effect. "The sea has been good to Eugene O'Neill," Susan wrote ten years afterward. "It was there for his opening. There was a fog, just as the script demanded, fog bell in the harbor. The tide was in and it washed under us and around, spraying through the holes in the floor, giving us the rhythm and the flavor of the sea while the big dying sailor talked to his friend Drisc of the life he had always wanted deep in the land, where you'd never see a ship or smell the sea. It is not merely figurative language to say the old wharf shook with applause." The audience and actors were one—and this was the aim of the Provincetown Players.

And so it would continue: the spectators were part of the Players, were adventurers together, Jig would say, expounding his theory. A day or two after the second bill had been launched, he said briskly, "Now, Susan, I have announced a play of yours for the next bill."

"But I have no play!" she gasped. His answer was calm, positive: "Then you will have to sit down tomorrow and begin one."

Susan protested. It was one thing to have worked out a comedy together with him, but she didn't know how to write a play. She had never "studied it."

"Nonsense," said Jig. "You've got a stage, haven't you?"

So she had gone out on the wharf, sat alone on one of the backless benches, and "looked a long time at that bare little stage. After a time the stage became a kitchen—a kitchen all by itself." She could see where the stove was, the table, and the stairway. She saw the door at the back open, and people all bundled up coming in— perhaps two or three men, and two women who hung back, reluctant to enter— When she was a newspaper reporter in Iowa, Susan had been sent down-state to do a murder trial, and she had never forgotten the sensation she had when she went into the kitchen of a woman locked up in town. She had always meant to write it as a short story, but now "the stage took it for its own."

She hurried in from the wharf to write down what she had seen. "Whenever I got stuck," she recalled, "I would run across the street to the old wharf, sit in that leaning little theater under which the sea sounded, until the play was ready to continue. Sometimes things written in my room would not form on the stage, and I must go home and cross them out." (Observing her, Jig said with satisfaction, "What playwrights need is a stage—their own stage.")

Ten days later, there was a reading of the play at Mary Heaton Vorse's. Susan, working on a revision at home, was late to the meeting, but when she got there, "the crowd liked *Trifles* and voted to put it in rehearsal the next day." So began Susan Glaspell's career as a dramatist in her own right. *Trifles* was an immediate success, and became a lasting favorite with producers of short plays all over the world. In 1962, it was included in a book of eight careful selections, characterized as "this country's most successful one-act plays written in the English language," nearly fifty years after that first production. The editor, Donald Fitzjohn, says in the Introduction, "*Trifles* is the oldest play in this volume, but it is by no means dated. It is not simply a play of detection, in which the two women discover the missing motive for a murder and decide to suppress the evidence. . . . Fundamentally it is a play about compassion; although this is never mentioned specifically."

It was a great summer for all concerned; they "swam from the wharf as well as rehearsed there; . . . would lie on the beach and talk about plays—everyone writing, or acting, or producing. Life was all of a piece, work not separated from play." Susan made notes for further scripts, which eventually became *The People, The Outside, Woman's Honor,* and *Tickless Time.* Another O'Neill play, *Thirst,* was produced. Late at night, after the audience had gone home, the big door had been drawn shut, and the last actor who had wanted to talk shop had left, Susan and Jig would stroll out on the wharf before going to bed. They would talk by themselves, trying to discover why they so intensely wanted to write plays and put them on, what their goals were, and what the future might hold.

Although she should have been prepared, Susan was appalled the day Jig said, "When we go to New York for the winter, we will take our theater with us." She was afraid for him, afraid people would laugh at him, starting a theater in New York—"new playwrights, amateur acting, somewhere in an old house or stable"— and she said frankly that she did not think they were ready to go into New York, she "feared" they couldn't make it go.

"Jack Reed thinks we can make it go," he said. And Susan thought it logical. Those two were the first to believe—adventurers both, men of faith. But she asked, "Where will we get the money?"

His answer was prompt: "Our associate members will subscribe to the New York season. That will be our nucleus." And he was right.

One of the few real satisfactions he had was that members of the 1916 summer audience were members every year thereafter. The glow of his vision was inspiration to all who worked with him. (O'Neill, who rarely expressed admiration for his associates, later called Jig Cook "a really imaginative man, imaginative in every way. He was against everything that suggested the worn-out conventions and cheap artificialities of the commercial stage.") The group met on September 5 to organize and draw up a statement of their beliefs: "that it is the primary object of the Provincetown Players to encourage the writing of American plays of artistic, literary, and dramatic—as opposed to Broadway—merit. That such plays be considered without reference to their commercial value, since this theater is not to be run for pecuniary profit. . . . That the President shall cooperate with the author in producing the play under the author's direction. The resources of the theater shall be placed at the disposal of the author. The author shall produce the play without hindrance, according to his own ideas." They voted to keep the name of Provincetown Players, but O'Neill proposed adding, "The Playwrights Theater," to which all agreed. Jig's enthusiasm for his "discovery" was boundless. "All the world will know Gene's plays someday," he declared. "Someday this little theater will be famous; someday the little theater in New York will be famous. . . . We've got our group of playwrights and they've got to have their stage. Gene's plays aren't the plays of Broadway; he's got to have the sort of stage we're going to found in New York." To Susan, who saw him off as he was leaving for New York to find a theater before the others came from Provincetown, he said reassuringly, "Don't worry!" Then, above the sound of the moving train, he called, cupping his mouth with his hands: "Write—another—play!"

So, dutifully, she completed the script of *The People;* and when she arrived in New York, she found Jig at 139 Macdougal Street, the ground floor of an old brownstone, owned by Jenny Belardi, a stage-struck, easy-going Italian woman, who was delighted at the prospect of having a theater for her parlor-floor tenant. Jig was standing in the midst of shavings, lumber, and bags of cement, ex-

plaining to an Irish cop and a building inspector just why the
partition between the parlors must be torn out, and a steel girder
put in—the "why" and "how" of the Players. "Now here is Susan
Glaspell," he said, as if she had come in on cue. "She is writing
plays." Then, turning to the policeman, "And then there is a
young Irishman, O'Neill—" Eventually, they were allowed to open
the season, not as a theater, because they had no money for a license, but as a private club, supported by subscribers. (A season
subscription could be bought for five dollars, plus four dollars
membership dues.) And by the end of October, the ground-floor
flat at 139 had been converted into a theater, 44 feet long by 15
feet wide, holding 140 seats on tiered wooden benches—this time
with backs—and a stage at the rear, 10½ by 14 feet. The proscenium arch was decorated in bright red colors and hung with a
plain canvas curtain. Lighting equipment was at a bare minimum,
out of necessity: the steel girder had taken most of the treasury
(and Mrs. Belardi had agreed to wait for her $100 a month rent).
There was no space for shifting scenery; there was only a community dressing room. Hard it was "to create one's own beauty,"
as Jig called it, with such primitive tools. "Even knowing we did
it, I am disposed to say what we did that first year couldn't be
done," Susan wrote afterward, still incredulous at their achievement during that initial New York season.

Yet it was not so difficult to understand, because everyone
worked for the sheer love of it. (Jig, as President, and Mrs. Bror
Nordfeldt, the secretary, were the only ones on salary—each at $15 a
week.) No one thought in terms of work-hours spent at the theater
in one capacity or another. Jig practically lived there; on the day
of dress rehearsal, he would go like fury—lifting, pounding, working to finish a set; arguing with a stage manager; he would forget
to eat lunch, and Susan would bring him a bottle of milk to sustain
him while he worked through till curtain-time. His mother, who
was "Ma-mie" to the Players just as she was to Susan and Jig,
pitched in with a will, as assistant stage manager and property
mistress—"making costumes, getting props, even handling them
backstage during performance." Though seventy years old now, she
went around in the same crisp way; and even at twelve o'clock,

after serving through every scene-shift, perhaps having worked since morning, she had to be urged to rest. "I want to die with my boots on," she said.

They opened with *Bound East for Cardiff* at the top of a triple bill, including Louise Bryant's *The Game,* and a comedy called *King Arthur's Socks,* by Floyd Dell. "Gene," who was inclined to shie away from the frenzy of group activity, agreed to supervise the staging of his own play, well aware that the performance would mark his debut in New York. *Bound East for Cardiff* was the hit of the bill in New York as it had been in Provincetown; and, although no critics were present (except as subscribers, for the Players refused to court reviews with free press tickets), word of the remarkable play by James O'Neill's son—and of its staging by the Provincetown Players—soon got around. After the second bill, featuring *Suppressed Desires,* the subscription list doubled, and the Players knuckled down to a haphazard "routine" of writing, staging, rehearsing and acting new plays.

Susan spent most of her time writing. The four plays she had sketched were produced; and frequently she received a check for some article or short story. She was the mainstay of the Cook household, but she counted this as a minor contribution to the theater, glad of the chance to allow Jig to give full time to his dream. She never saw the faults that others saw in her husband—that he was long-winded and pontifical at times, and could be dictatorial at others—and in an argument of policy she stood staunchly beside him.

"The scenery might totter at times," she wrote, "the waits were long, the ventilation bad, and the seats uncushioned, but that audience is already an historic one. For one after another they were seeing those dramas of the sea written by Eugene O'Neill. No one else was producing him then, and I leave you the story of the unfolding of his career, of his growth in power upon that tiny, experimental stage, as justification of the idea of this man George Cram Cook." Allowing for the worshipful eyes through which she saw her husband, Susan Glaspell's statement was scarcely an exaggeration. O'Neill himself admitted, "If I hadn't had the Provincetown Theater, I would have had to write commercial plays like Sam Shipman."

Before the end of the year, the Players received their first recognition as a group, in a review by Heywood Broun, who had been an early subscriber, and was watching their work with interest. He had just switched from sports writer to drama critic on the *Tribune,* and devoted part of his column to the Provincetown Players. Burns Mantle in the *Evening Mail,* and Clayton Hamilton wrote a piece praising the group for its efforts; Hamilton remarked that its plays were "strangely interesting and strikingly impressive."

By the second season, the Players had nine hundred subscribers, and with the increase in treasury they improved the Playwrights' Theater by renting the floor upstairs for cloak room, dressing rooms, scenery storage, business office and "clubroom." Two more salaried members were added—Lewis Ell, as property man and carpenter; and Nina Moise, as "general coach." She had joined the group in February the previous year, and had proven a valuable director, particularly of O'Neill's plays, *The Sniper,* an anti-war play, and *Before Breakfast.* The first bill began with *The Long Voyage Home,* one of four plays Gene had written in Provincetown during the summer; and a comedy by Susan called *Close the Door.* Two days after the opening, O'Neill was featured in a two-column headline, "Who is Eugene O'Neill?" on an inside page of the Sunday drama section of *The New York Times;* the short piece below, only four hundred words long, was nevertheless a milestone in his career as an emerging figure of great potential in the theater, with the Provincetown Players in the role of his sponsor. More of his plays were produced, provided they were "experimentals—" *In the Zone,* which became a classic, was considered too conventional for the group, and was produced by the Washington Square Players with great success. The Provincetowners were not envious or regretful; it was their aim to *cause* better American plays to be written; and if a script employed too many tricks of a Broadway play, it was not for them.

Yet they could not help expanding. For their third season, with the help of $1,000 from a benefactor, the Provincetown Players moved into another building of Mrs. Belardi's, a few doors away, at 133 Macdougal. It had been a stable once, large enough to be turned into much more of a bona fide theater, with a seating capacity of two hundred. Below, a roomy basement became workshop, dressing rooms, and storage area; and above, were clubrooms, even a small restaurant. One of the old hitching rings had been left in an auditorium wall, and around it a set-designer painted the legend: "Here Pegasus was hitched."

Here the rest of the O'Neill sea plays came to life—*Where the Cross Is Made; The Moon of the Caribbees; Ile;* and the other one-acters revealing the mysterious lure of the harsh life of the sea. Here was produced the only three-act play the group ever attempted, *The Athenian Women,* a play against all war, urging the kind of peace that would produce art as the Greeks knew it, written by Jig Cook toward the end of World War I. Here another of his "discoveries" came to light—Edna St. Vincent Millay, with plays written for the Playwrights Theater. And here Susan's gift for dialogue developed, with the production of *Bernice, Inheritors, The Verge,* and *Chains of Dew.* Preparations for each new bill might bring arguments, dissensions, discouragement; "hard things were said to one another in the drive of the last rehearsals, the strain of opening night." But after a first night there would be a party in the clubroom over the theater, and wounds were healed; Susan might see Jig's arm around a neck he had threatened to wring the day before. They all laughed together at past mistakes and became one again, impulse and courage is if they had never been shaken."

Summers were spent at the Cape, writing, working toward the next season in New York. One fall, Susan and Jig decided to spend the whole year writing in Provincetown. O'Neill and his wife Agnes were there, and the four became close friends. That spring, Gene performed an act of friendship that Susan never forgot when the Cooks' beloved dog, Nezer, lay dying of a strange disease he had contracted during the winter. "It was our wedding anniversary, so the O'Neills came up to see us," she related. "No one felt festive, but it was good to have these friends in the house. 'I need help!' we heard Jig cry after he had gone up to see Nezer.

"'I'll do this for you, Jig,' Gene said, and Jig and I left them alone in our house while we went and stayed all night at their house." The next morning they knew that Nezer's agonies were over.

And of a later time she wrote: "One day in 1920, Jig and I

walked across the dunes to the O'Neills'. We were having the big storm with which we often close August on the Cape, and it was a thrilling struggle getting from the town on the harbor . . . to the abandoned life-saving station on the outside shore, now the home of Eugene O'Neill.

"We had come because Gene had a play to read to us—an idea that had been in his head for several years. He used to speak of it as *The Silver Bullet,* but at dinner that night he told us he wanted to call it *The Emperor Jones.* Before the cheerful logs in a room where lifeboats had swung, Gene read us his new play. Then Jig knew he wanted to go back to the theater. He had been wavering. . . . But walking back across the dunes next morning, Jig said he must leave instantly for New York. 'Here is a challenge! This is what I have been waiting for!' His voice, his eyes were electric. 'This marks the success of the Provincetown Players. Gene knew there was a place where such a play would be produced. He wrote it to *compel* us to the untried, to the impossible.' "

Jig's fire for an experimental theater leaped higher than before, sparked by the eight-scene tragedy of Brutus Jones, short-lived "Emperor," as he tears his way through the jungle, fleeing from the people he had tricked into subjection, now pursuing him with the beating of voodoo drums and the silver bullets to kill him. A play of such terror and mystic intensity must be set against a sky dome to give the effect of depth and space. To the other members of the company, this was truly the "impossible" if not sheer madness on Jig's part, especially since the dome he wanted, constructed of concrete and steel, would cost $500, practically the whole treasury. But he kept insisting that it would be worth the risk; he slept in the theater for a month to save expenses. And he would brook no delays; *Emperor* must open the season, the dome must go in at once. He finally went out and bought the materials over the heads of all; then he went to work. One of the writers, Edna Kenton, who came to the playhouse to see if the scripts had come from Provincetown, found him there alone, "standing at the back of the stage, in a morass of steel netting and iron bars and cement. He was making plaster, in workman's clothes, poising himself against expected attack" as he saw her coming.

"There's to be no argument about this," he told her. "I've had enough from everybody. The Emperor has *got* to have a dome to play against." He spoke of the "thick forest at first . . . steadily thinning out . . . scene after scene . . . to pure space. . . ." Afterwards she related,

"As he went on, it began to happen—one of his hours of rare creative fancy, as he stood thinking aloud the values to be found and given from the playwrights' brief directions. . . . I was to see many times over the play that made Gene O'Neill famous, played against the dome downtown, against wrinkled cycloramas uptown, with different casts and directions, but never so clearly as it played itself that morning in the dim little theater, with no voice but one, no audience but one." By the time his concrete dome was complete, radiating light in all directions, capable of lending spectacular effects of distance to any production, the Players who had called Jig Cook mad began to congratulate him. New scenery had to be made, and for this he requested Cleon Throckmorton, who came from Washington "and in five terrific days remade the scenery." (He remained as set designer for the Players.) Before he left Provincetown, Jig had told Susan that he thought the role of the Emperor must be a black man. "A blacked-up white is not in the spirit of this production," he held. And he stuck by his conviction until he found a colored actor, Charles Gilpin, who had recently won brief mention for a small role he had played in Drinkwater's *Abraham Lincoln*. As soon as Jig heard his voice in the lines, he said, "It's a go!" and Gilpin was hired, the first Negro actor to play a leading role in the American theater.

Opening night (November 1, 1920) was "an historic success," acclaimed by the audience with an "avalanche of applause," and by the critic Kenneth Macgowan as "a tumultuously exciting first night." When the uptown New York critics came on the third night they heaped praise on the production as a whole—play, setting, lighting, and acting were lauded in language of superlatives. The Players were inundated with requests for tickets; the subscription list rose to 1500 in a few days. They were pushed into national prominence with offers from Broadway theaters and managers. It was overwhelming, and all too soon was to prove their undoing. Jig, who did not see the play from the house until the third night, was so exalted by the performance that they had an impromptu party in the clubrooms afterwards, at which he said, "Perhaps groups like ours are about to inherit the whole duty of dramatic man." Some laughed, saying that was a large order; he smiled too, but his fervor held. "We ought to make ourselves more equal to the job," he said. He did not mean, however, that they should move uptown, or accept Broadway offers of any kind. And over this question, the group split up. *The Emperor Jones* did move to a Broadway theater on December 27, the day the Provincetown Players opened with another O'Neill play, *Diff'rent*. But their ranks were depleted by the move, and they could not concentrate on the experiments of the Playwrights Theater with the intensity it demanded. With factions warring, the venture lasted only one more year; its final O'Neill presentation was *The Hairy Ape,* but Susan and Jig did not even see the opening night performance. Jig felt that as soon as the Provincetown Players succeeded, they had failed, because they failed to make the proper use of their success, because they allowed the uptown point of view of money and notoriety to fill the air, stifling their former freedom. They would do better to stick to their own "modest and intensely important job," he said, and that was to cause the writing of the best plays that could be written in the United States, and to give each play the best possible start in life. Their purpose could not be accomplished once commercialism took over. Three years before he had declared in writing: "We promise to let this theater die rather than let it become another voice of mediocrity." Now, after endless arguing could not sway the majority, he wrote: "Since we have failed spiritually in the elemental things—and since the result is mediocrity— we keep our promise: We give this theater we love good death; the Provincetown Players end their story here. Some happier gateway must let in the spirit which seems to be seeking to create a soul under the ribs of death in the American theater."

A few days later, Susan found Jig sitting alone in the theater. The curtain was up, the blue light he loved was on in the dome; they sat there, silently thinking over the past seven years, in the place that had meant so much to him, until at last he said, "It is time to go to Greece." They would stay for at least a year.

Before they sailed on March 1, there was a meeting in O'Neill's apartment in New York. It was agreed that the group should be incorporated under the same names, and that the season would end, after the run of *The Hairy Ape,* with Susan's comedy, *Chains of Dew.* Then the theater was to be leased to an outside group for a year while Jig was away.

He was never to return. He died a year and a half later in Delphi, of a strange disease. He and Susan had settled in the ancient mountain village among the Greek peasants, who had grown to love him with a devotion that amounted to worship. He learned their language, adopted their dress, let his hair and beard grow long, and walked among them as a wise and honored man. He translated his play, *The Athenian Women,* into modern Greek, built an outdoor amphitheater, and put on a Biblical play with a cast of natives. He and Susan had raised a little mongrel, which they called ToPuppy, training him to be "wise," the villagers said. The dog became a victim of a deadly disease called glanders, and, although Susan and Jig tended him carefully, as they had Nezer, they could not save him. The night the animal lay dying, Jig commented, as they tried to ease him, "No Gene O'Neill to help us this time." A few hours later Jig was stricken with the same disease, which, in very rare instances, according to the doctor, is communicated to people. And not many days afterward, Susan, mute with grief, allowed the peasants who had so loved him to perform the burial rites for her husband in the graveyard at old Delphi. The Greek government decreed that a great stone from the Temple of Apollo be placed as a headstone over the grave of George Cram Cook—a tribute never paid to anyone in Greece before.

When Susan, still under the shadow of his death, returned to New York, she found that O'Neill, Kenneth Macgowan, and Robert Edmond Jones had reorganized the Provincetown Players, changed the name to the Provincetown Playhouse (dropping the "Playwrights Theater") and, in a complete reversal of policy, had opened with a European play, Strindberg's *The Spook Sonata.* Outraged, she lost no time in letting them know that they had no right to such action; and, since they had forsaken the primary principle set forth by Jig Cook, they had no right to continue to use the name Provincetown. But Gene finally convinced her that the name was not an insult, but a memorial to Jig. He suggested a plaque for the playhouse, with the inscription: "To the memory of George Cram ('Jig') Cook, poet of life, priest of the ideal, lovable human being, to whose imagination and unselfish devotion this Playhouse owes its original inspiration and development for free creative expression."

If Susan felt privately that O'Neill's words were written merely to placate her, she wisely said nothing, but took him at his word; she went to their old house in Provincetown, where she spent the next two years writing her own memorial to Jig, telling his life story and the story of the Provincetown Players in a book which she called *The Road to the Temple*. It was published in 1927, by Frederick A. Stokes Company, publishers of Jig's novels.

Once that labor of love was completed, and she was satisfied that she had done full justice to the achievements of Jig's brilliant but blighted career in the theater, she set about writing a full-length play. She had always been interested in Emily Dickinson's poetry, in the way it had been hidden by the poet, not to be revealed to the public eye until after her death, and then only after fierce family controversy. Susan Glaspell's play, *Alison's House*, brought to life the startling discovery of Emily Dickinson's "Letter to the world" by her sister Lavinia, the dilemma it posed for New Englanders disciplined by Puritan repression; the conflict it produced between Lavinia and her brother Austin and his wife—all but thinly disguised—was exposed in the tense situation, the tight, dramatic dialogue that was Susan Glaspell's particular strength as a playwright. (She used economy of words and implied meanings as effectively as O'Neill employed an exciting overflow of phrases to expound the thoughts and emotions of characters.)

In spite of Gene's almost contrite attitude now that Jig was dead, Susan felt that he had betrayed her husband and that the plaque, with its extravagant inscription, was suggested only in a moment of repentance. She did not want her play to be presented in the Provincetown Playhouse, which, by 1926, could be hired by anyone who wanted to produce a play. Over on 14th Street a new group had taken up the torch—the Civic Repertory Theatre, recently organized by the actress, Eva LeGallienne, was gaining steadily, if at times uncertainly, under the power provided by the experimental theater, fresh enthusiasm, and a cash subsidy. It was to this enterprising workshop that Susan submitted the script of *Alison's House,* which was accepted with alacrity, but production was not scheduled until the end of the 1930 season.

The opening night performance received universal praise from the critics, and the run was extended for two weeks more. After twenty-five performances, they were about to close the season when word came that *Alison's House* had won the Pulitzer prize! The award came as a surprise to everyone, including Susan, even though the reviews had been uniformly—and highly—favorable; hers was not a play of popular appeal; although intensely dramatic, it was not sensational. Now, however, the company decided to move the production to Broadway; Eva LeGallienne, who had directed *Alison's House,* played the role of Emily's sister because it was thought her name would be a Broadway attraction. Susan, who still held staunchly to Jig's concepts, to his scorn for commercial theaters, did not care whether her play had a long run or not. She had justified his faith in her ability by writing a prize-winning play, and that was all that mattered. *Alison's House* did not last on Broadway; it was not for the general public. But, like *Trifles,* Susan Glaspell's full-length play proved to have enduring appeal for little theaters throughout the country; like *Trifles,* it re-creates the life of a character who never appears—in this case, one who has just died, a circumstance more subtle than the usual Broadway play, more likely to attract producers in art rather than commercial theaters. For at least ten years, *Alison's House* was a favorite of little theaters, and it is still frequently presented by colleges and universities.

For a time, Susan worked with the Civic Repertory Theater, hoping it would prove "the happier gateway" Jig had spoken of; but her heart was no longer in the movement, which continued to fall far short of his ideals. She retired from the theater and returned to writing novels, a number of which were published before she died, July 17, 1948.

Susan Glaspell could hardly be called a playwright in the fullest sense of the term; her output was extremely small. Yet of all the writers—O'Neill excepted—who furnished scripts for the Provincetown Players in the seven years between 1915 and 1922, she was the only one whose name has endured as a playwright, whose works are still produced. Beyond that, Susan Glaspell and her husband, Jig Cook, will remain the outstanding figures of the Provincetown Players, the only little theater group that fostered the development of America's first dramatist of stature.

CHAPTER III

———◆———

EUGENE O'NEILL

W<small>HEN THE</small> Provincetown Players "discovered" Eugene Gladstone O'Neill, he already had lived through more adventures and survived more misfortunes than many people experience in a lifetime, and he was only twenty-eight years old. The son of the famous actor, James O'Neill (sometimes called "Monte Cristo" after the role that gave him his enormous following in the theater), the future Nobel prize-winning dramatist began life in a hotel room on October 16, 1888. His parents were staying at the Barrett House, a family hotel catering to theatrical people, on Broadway at 43rd Street. It was an appropriate setting for a writer who, willy-nilly, was to be connected with the theater all his life, and who was, in a sense, always homeless, despite the many residences he was to own at one time or another.

O'Neill has been called, like Melville, an Ishmael among men of his time and profession, but his wanderings began much earlier: before he was two months old, he was traveling from one town to another with his parents, on a cross-country tour of *The Count of Monte Cristo*. His mother nursed him "in the wings and in dressing rooms," he said more than once, with some bitterness. She had to put him in a bureau drawer on two pillows for a cradle. He was fed, dressed and put to sleep in hotel rooms and trains. He was inclined to scoff at actors like John Barrymore, who boasted about having been born in a trunk. Since his first seven years were spent in being trundled about all over the country, Eugene O'Neill knew whereof he spoke, when he concluded disparagingly, "I can't see that a theatrical life on the road is such a marvelous thing."

He might have been less acrid if he had not suffered from deep loneliness on those tours. His mother detested the life, and traveled with her husband merely out of an aggrieved sense of duty; from the time Eugene was born, she was not well, and only medicine with pain-relieving drugs seemed to make her existence bearable. She was still mourning the loss of a second son, Edmund, who had died three years before, at the age of one and a half. He had caught the measles from the oldest child, James, Jr. ("Jamie"), who was sent to boarding school at Notre Dame, Indiana, shortly after the baby died. (Eugene was barely three months old before he was taken to Notre Dame, not far from the "one-night stand" the company was playing, to be shown off before ten-year-old Jamie and his classmates; the latter were far more interested in the boys' actor-father, whose glamorous presence carried over to offstage appearances.) As soon as Eugene was old enough to walk, he was put in the care of a nurse, Sandy, who took sole charge of keeping him occupied and entertained while the O'Neills were on tour. Mrs. O'Neill, the former Ella Quinlan, a small-town girl from Ohio, never adjusted to the unconventional life of a traveling theatrical troupe.

Although Sandy was undoubtedly fond of small Eugene, her ideas of diversion, except for an occasional excursion to an aquarium, zoo, or circus, consisted of filling his head with horror tales—the latest murder stories in the news—or visiting the popular "waxworks" museums of the day, where he stood in terror before the effigies of hideous criminals and misshapen creatures. An impressionable child, endowed with a vivid imagination, he frequently was wakened by nightmares, only, perhaps, to be "soothed" by Sandy with another lurid tale. He never could come close enough to either of his parents to confide the inner fears and fancies brought on by the morbid entertainment provided by his nurse and most constant companion. (On trains he would talk to a friendly conductor, and in hotels he usually knew the porters, but he rarely came into contact with other children.)

If his mother withdrew within her shell of sorrow and her own private realm of religion by going to Mass alone every morning, Eugene O'Neill's father was removed from him by the stage, and the world of shoddy make-believe it engendered. He later called his father "Monte Cristo" in mocking tones, but at the age of two or three he found it confusing, difficult to distinguish between the swashbuckling, and the melodramatic Count, who brandished a sword in one scene, and rose, dripping with salt and sawdust on his tattered clothes and long beard, in another. To realize that both of these were one and the same man who patted Eugene on the head and told him to get out of the actors' way in the wings, or held his mother's hand now and then, trying to wheedle a smile from her, was indeed a puzzling problem. But by the time he was five or six, Eugene had learned all the tricks of the backstage wizards. He knew that make-up and costumes could change his father into different characters. He knew that the deafening applause was necessary to "drown out the noise of the mechanical storm being manufactured . . . behind the swinging profile of artificial waves." He was bored by the long, ranting speeches, and by pretty actresses who wanted to hug him.

He was always glad when the tour ended and the family, including Jamie, who came from boarding school, would spend the summer together in the harbor town of New London, Connecticut. Here James O'Neill had bought a small, pink clapboard cottage on a lonely curve of land that led to the lighthouse marking Long Island Sound. Here Eugene felt the first inclination toward a love of the sea that was never to leave him, as he climbed on the high sandstone rocks that overlooked the picturesque harbor, where square-riggers still might be seen at anchor between whaling voyages, lying alongside wind-jammers, and the bustling Sound steamers. If his brother Jamie went off on his own pursuits (telling him he was too young), Eugene would be content to stay on the rocks by himself—dreaming, drawing pictures of the ships, watching the sea gulls wheel and dip into the water. Reading, which Sarah taught him at a very early age, proved to be a blessed means of escape for him on tour, and was a pleasant pastime in New London when left to his own devices. He would take a book to the rocks with him and sit there for hours, lost in some story, and mulling it over afterwards while he watched the harbor sights. In New London, too, his father seemed more of a human being and less of a chameleonlike giant who took on different guises to suit the setting. One summer James bought a miniature train for Eugene; it ran on tracks around the yard by means of a coal-burning engine, large enough for Eugene to sit in and steer. He stoked it himself, fetching and carrying the fuel and ashes in a coal scuttle from the kitchen. Running his railroad was one of the few childhood joys he had.

By the time he was seven, he was beginning to accept the idea of life on tour in the winter, followed by the more relaxed summer months in New England. His delicate lovely mother was still remote, but his father, who always made such a show of heartiness and conviviality that it had no meaning, had moments of genuine warmth and true interest in his sons during the summer months. Jamie, whom Eugene regarded with the hero worship of a much younger brother for an older, was gradually allowing him to explore the coastline in the O'Neills' boat, along with him and other adolescents. Both boys learned to swim at an early age and became expert swimmers.

Eugene knew that each fall his few pleasures would end for another year, a difficult fact to face. Just before his seventh birthday, he was suddenly confronted with an even more severe exile: he was sent to a Catholic boarding school by himself. It was true. Jamie would be only four miles away at a prep school in the same area of the upper Bronx, on the banks of the Hudson; but that was small comfort in terms of daily companionship—Jamie might as well have gone back to Notre Dame. If Eugene had felt lonely in the strange, wandering scheme of life he had known for half of every year up to this time, he now felt desolate, completely lost in the rigid schedule, the sudden melee of new faces, noise, the nuns who "knuckled the boys on the bean" if they didn't know their catechism. And he never got used to it. In the six years that he attended St. Aloysius, he always went through the same dread at returning in the fall, the same stifled outbursts in his pillow the first few nights, so that not even his roommate, Joe McCarthy (three years older), would know his feeling of utter desolation.

He liked Joe well enough, but he never caught the group spirit, never joined in sports or pranks. The boys, who called him Gene, were inclined to call him "sissy" for his standoffishness, but when one of them attempted to do so, Joe punched him in the nose. Gene was grateful for his roommate's protection, but he did not bother to change his ways. Any free time he had was spent in reading all the books he could lay his hands on, some, like Anatole France, way over his head. Kipling's adventure stories fascinated him, and he would talk about wanting to go to sea. He was mediocre in most of his studies, but shone in Reading, and once he consented to take part in a school play, his only "outside activity." He wrote long letters to Jamie while the other boys were building snow-forts or, in the spring, were shouting in glee as they jumped into the hay mounds of fresh-cut grass.

Gene O'Neill dutifully learned his catechism, dutifully went to Mass every Sunday, partly because he thought piousness might bring him closer to his mother, partly because he thought it might supply the warmth he sorely needed; but after two years, at the age of nine, he remarked to Joe McCarthy, "Religion is so cold." Although he took Communion three years later, and then attended another Catholic school, the De LaSalle Institute in New York City, for two years, he did not find the solace he was seeking. His mother grew worse; she could not get along without the aid of drugs and had to be sent periodically to a sanitarium. His brother Jamie could not withstand the strain; although he was a brilliant student, he began to lead a wild and dissolute life; his letters to Eugene were cynical, corrupting, bewildering at first, until Eugene discovered that Jamie had been as troubled as he about their mother's illness, their father's false heartiness, their queer, cold family life. He made up his mind he would accept no more of the religious training, the rigid schedule and narrow outlook of Catholic schools.

At fourteen he enrolled in Betts Academy in Stamford, Connecticut, where he spent the next four years in comparative freedom and far less misery than he had known before. He found that he could read as much as he liked or go for solitary walks without being considered peculiar; or, if he wanted to join his schoolmates, he was welcome. He was attractive, tall, slender and lithe; although his luminous dark brown eyes were often brooding, they could also light up with a sense of fun. If he felt like it, he stood as ready as the next one for contriving tricks to play on professors or means of sneaking out after hours. Betts was one of the early liberal academic schools that allowed the student to go at his own pace, to follow his own bent within the broad field of the classics and sciences. He was taught to observe the world around him closely, and then to record his observations in "well-systematized notebooks."

The latter proved to be invaluable training for Eugene, who soon developed a sharp eye for detail and an ear for dialogue, both essential to the dramatist. The habit of keeping an organized notebook remained with him always, serving him well in outlining plays, in jotting down bits of talk from every walk of life he encountered, colorful phrases to be used in character development. At Betts he discovered, and devoured, the tragic novels of Tolstoy and Dostoevsky, the brazen decadence and brilliant cynicism of Oscar Wilde, and the great sea stories of Jack London and Joseph Conrad. It was Conrad, more than any other writer, who made him long to go to sea himself. In New London, during the summers, he hung around the docks waiting for the square-riggers to come sailing in with stately grandeur, as they still did occasionally in 1904 and 1905. He struck up conversation with captain and crews, hoping to hear tales of romantic voyages. He would linger there for hours listening to the old salts, drawing out their stories with his questions.

His mother disapproved of his consorting with sailors, considered coarse and uncouth company; but his mother disapproved of almost everything he and Jamie did by this time, so he paid little heed. She complained that neither the boys nor their father spent much time at home in New London, yet she did nothing to create a home life for them. The two brothers were openly in league against both parents, yet they allowed their father to dominate their lives in some respects because they were economically dependent on him; and beneath the antagonism toward their mother lay a deep loyalty. Jamie, who had been asked to leave college because of his flagrant disregard of rules, had joined the *Monte Cristo* company as an actor in a minor role. Overshadowed by his father, he revolted by continuing his wild ways and casting his influence over Eugene when they were together. To New Londoners, the O'Neill sons were a pair of *enfants terribles* from a theatrical family, and their parents did nothing to dispel the impression, seeking to hide the twisted, tragic family relationship.

Following his graduation from Betts, Eugene O'Neill entered Princeton, but he stayed less than nine months, having learned very little more of intellectual value to him than he had discovered on his own in the works of Wilde, London, Conrad, and, later, in Ibsen. Most of his free time was spent in the taverns in Trenton, and many of his weekends were spent in New York. When Jamie was not on the road, he continued the liberal education of his "kid brother" in the ways of the world, including the underworld of the Tenderloin district. Eugene passed on this questionable wisdom to his few cronies at Princeton when he occasionally brought one of them into New York for a weekend. He also treated them to performances of Broadway plays, since he had free access to most of the theaters in town through his father. The sole benefit he derived from his months at Princeton was an early play, *Abortion,* written in 1913, in which he sought to crystallize his ideas of undergraduate life in "ivy-league" colleges.

The five years in between were fraught with hair-raising escapades on a downward path that nearly spelled his doom. For a time he worked as a clerk in a mail-order jewelry firm in which his father had invested some of the *Monte Cristo* earnings. While Eugene chafed at such a chore, he broadened his intellectual horizons in trying to get away from the limitations of it. He haunted Greenwich Village, then in its heyday as a haven for radicals, and, in the Unique Book Shop, run by the well-known anarchist, Benjamin Tucker, Eugene discovered the writings of Nietzsche. They were to have a profound influence on him, particularly *Thus Spake Zarathustra,* which became his Bible. He copied passages into his notebook and learned them by heart, as he had memorized his catechism. His job as mail-order clerk lasted less than a year, after which he persuaded his father to give him a small allowance, allegedly to try his hand at poetry, sharing a studio with a couple of artist friends, Ed Keefe and George Bellows. The three led a harum-scarum existence, packing in as much entertainment as their scant pocket money would allow; when that was gone, they could always take in a play in one of the thirty theaters along the Rialto. (The one exception Eugene made was *Monte Cristo,* when his father's company was playing in town—for him it would be a waste of time, he told his friends!) On Saturday nights they were on the town from dusk till dawn, usually in the Tenderloin district, at the Haymarket, once a theater, now a gaudy restaurant and variety hall. Here Eugene found the types of women that were to people his plays a little later, beginning with the down-trodden Rose Thomas in *The Web,* and progressing to the defiant and complex heroine of *Anna Christie.* (Now he wrote a sonnet, called "The Haymarket," which sang mournfully of "the young girl" whose "drunken tears fall down her painted face" as she "sobs her sad, sad history—and lies!") Here Bellows, who became a leader in the "ashcan" school of painters, found plenty of subject matter for later canvases. Once in a while the three would-be rakes became stagedoor johnnies, ogling the curvaceous, dazzling Ziegfeld Follies beauties; or, if they could afford it, took out some of the chorus girls whom Eugene had met through Jamie.

When nothing else offered, they attended society affairs, Sunday afternoon teas or supper parties (particularly when they were hungry after a long Saturday night and there was nothing in the studio to eat). At one of these, Eugene met Kathleen Jenkins, a sparkling debutante who was bored with the conventional young men of her set, and was fascinated by the famous actor's son who had more than a touch of the poet in his nature. The mercurial Eugene, by turns dark and brooding, sardonic and cynical, scholarly, gentle and sympathetic, spelled mystery and enchantment to Kathleen. And as Eugene, heartened by her admiration, quoted verses from *Childe Harold,* or spouted the nihilistic philosophy of Nietzsche, or shyly showed her poems that he had written, her feelings for him grew more and more romantic. Within a few weeks he realized with a start that she was in love with him; and his need for the love he had never known from his mother was so strong that he had no will to discourage Kathleen's adoration, although he was by no means in love with her. If she had been one of the sleazy girls from the Tenderloin, it would have been an easy matter, but Eugene could not bring himself to break off the first friendship he had ever had with a "nice girl." Sorely troubled, he finally turned for help to his father, who, instead of offering wise counsel, flew into a rage, denouncing Kathleen as a fortune hunter and, worse yet, a Protestant. His sons must marry Irish Catholics or remain bachelors. He ended the tirade by saying that he would arrange to have Eugene join an expedition to Honduras, prospecting for gold along with an engineer he had hired to look after another one of his investments.

Eugene agreed, figuring that the plan would prove an adventure as well as an escape. But some obstinate quirk in him, resentment, doubtless, against his father's dictatorial methods, made him seize on Kathleen's madcap suggestion of an elopment the week before he was to leave. They took the ferryboat to Hoboken and were married by an Episcopal minister in Trinity Church on October 2, 1909. (In two weeks Eugene would be twenty-one, but he gave his age as twenty-two just to make sure of getting the license.) At the moment he felt only that he was playing an ironic prank on his father before leaving the country.

The expedition was a fiasco; life in the steaming jungle was a living hell for Eugene O'Neill. The humid oppressive heat, the hords of insects which nearly ate him alive, and the strange, sickening food was revolting, frightening. At night when they made camp, the jungle held a thousand terrors: the "Formless Fears" he described so graphically in *The Emperor Jones* rose out of moss-bearded trees and eerie sounds to threaten his sanity. The search for gold along an unnavigable river was back-breaking and futile. After six months he came down with malaria, suffering chills and fever for several weeks; he finally became so ill that he was sent to the United States embassy, and from there back to New York. Still weak and suffering from malaria, he was assailed by glaring headlines in a *World* news story which announced the birth of a son, Eugene Gladstone O'Neill, 2nd, to Kathleen, thereby revealing their runaway marriage. At the height of his fever he had received a letter from her, he recalled, but he had not been able to grasp its contents at the time; and now, before the full impact fell upon him, he was whisked off by his father, who swore his son had been tricked, and set his lawyers to seek a divorce immedi-

ately. Eugene was appointed stage manager of *The White Sister,*
a rank melodrama then touring the country, with his father in the
supporting role of a bishop.

Hardly aware of what had happened, Eugene was rushed into
the helter-skelter routine of a traveling theatrical troupe for the
first time in nearly fifteen years. As a member of the company, he
could see, as never before, the shoddiness of the make-believe, the
tawdriness of a profession that passed itself off as an art. He
scorned his father for accepting anything less than the lead, for
appearing in a vehicle so maudlin as to make *Monte Cristo* seem
restrained by comparison. He was bored with his post, which was
hardly more than assistant ticket-taker. He did not even have the
company of his brother, for Jamie had finally secured a leading
role in a play called *The Traveling Salesman,* and was on the road
by himself. Their mother was constantly under medication or in
the sanitarium. Eugene had time to regret his hare-brained marriage to Kathleen, but the mere thought of facing his responsibility frightened him. Outwardly sardonic and sophisticated, he
was inwardly baffled and bewildered by life. To escape from the
problems he found insurmountable, he turned to reading, as he
had done so often before. He could be carried away by the sea
stories of Conrad. When the tour ended in Boston, he had just
finished rereading *The Nigger of the Narcissus,* a story that affected him deeply.

A Norwegian-based barque, the *Charles Racine,* had just put in
Mystic Wharf, and as Eugene, under the spell of Conrad's compelling yarn, wandered along the docks talking to her crew, he was
seized with an overwhelming desire to sail before the mast. Before
he quite knew what he was doing, he had signed on as ordinary
seaman, and when the *Charles Racine* set sail for Buenos Aires,
Eugene O'Neill was aboard. (He went with his father's approval:
with Eugene out of the country, James could arrange for the divorce more easily, and he felt that life at sea might "make a man"
of his second son.)

As the "old hooker" cast off from land and bounded into the
open sea, Eugene cast off the burdens that had been weighing upon
him and for the first time in his life, felt free. Like Melville, he was
struck with wonder at the mysterious beauty, the rhythm and poe-

try of the surging waves; a "wild delirium" coursed through his veins when he had to run aloft during a hard blow. And, like Conrad, he felt at peace with God, at last, when he was far from land; he experienced a sacred ecstasy in the limitless stretches of sky and water, a religious calm such as he had never known. Unlike either Melville or Conrad, however, young O'Neill felt at home with the men as well as the ship rolling in the vastness of the deep. He was not, like Melville, repelled by the lusty and often lurid tales of love told by the sailors over and over again; on the contrary, Eugene listened eagerly and took note of those yarns unconsciously for later use. From his nights at the Haymarket, he could join in with a few stories of his own. He felt a camaraderie, a kinship with sailors such as he had never felt with his classmates at Princeton, or even his artist friends. "I look on a sailor man as my particular brother," he said. And when he wrote about them, O'Neill was not, as he said later, like Conrad, "detached and safe at the wheelhouse of the vessel, looking down at his men on the deck and describing their activities." He added emphatically, "When I write about the sea, I want to be on the deck with the men."

Moreover, when the ship landed in Buenos Aires (and in further voyages, when they put in at various ports), Eugene was with the men when they headed for their various haunts, searching for entertainment and romantic adventure. In Buenos Aires, their favorite spot was an infamous saloon on the waterfront, the Sailor's Opera. Its mood and madhouse-atmosphere was more like a wild bacchanale, as Eugene once described it: "Pickled sailors, sure-thing race track touts, déclassé Englishmen, underlings in the diplomatic service, boys darting around tables leaving pink and yellow cards to red plush paradises, and entangled in the racket was the melody of some ancient turkey trot banged out by a sober pianist. . . ." Some old sailor might get up and unroll a yarn, another might do a dance, or there would be a heated discussion between, say, Yankee and British sailors as to the respective prowess of their ships. And, if nothing else promised, "a bit of harmless fight" usually could be depended upon as the inevitable star feature to round out the evening's entertainment.

Sometimes he accompanied his comrades to the suburb of Barracas, where they took in pornographic motion pictures that were "mighty rough stuff. Nothing was left to the imagination . . . of course the sailors flocked to them." But Eugene was perceptive enough to realize that this was only another means of alleviating the loneliness of the sailors' lives. Most of them, like himself, had become disillusioned early in regard to religion and society, and sought relief from private sorrow in public perversity. He could see that "save for the usual exceptions, they were not vicious men. They were in the main honest, good-natured, unheroically courageous men trying to pass the time pleasantly." Yet, as much as he liked the crew, he did not sail with them on the return voyage of the *Charles Racine.*

His decision to stay in Buenos Aires came when a young Britisher he met at the Sailor's Opera suggested that they share a room in a pension together for a time. The son of a nobleman, handsome to the point of being "almost too beautiful," he reminded Eugene of Oscar Wilde's description of Dorian Gray, even to the flowery name. He had fallen into disgrace with his family and fiancée because of his drinking, and had come to South America seeking a new life, but he was not making much headway, and he thought if he and Eugene pooled their resources and efforts, they might both return to a more respectable level of existence. Eugene had blown most of his ship's wages the first night at the Sailor's Opera, but he was willing to give the plan a try. He attempted one job as a draftsman unsuccessfully, followed by several miserable weeks at a meatpacking center, and finally went to work for the Singer Sewing Machine Company, where he lasted no longer than he had at the other places. It was a farce for him to attempt to hold down a humdrum job and he knew it. His companion was not having much success either, and they parted, Eugene signing on board a tramp steamer to South Africa. The voyage was so unpleasant on the cattle boat (which carried mules) that he rarely spoke of it afterward, and he was not allowed into South Africa because his wages did not amount to the $100 necessary to enter. Back in Buenos Aires he lost track of his English friend, who was to turn up, with the far-from-flowery name of "Smitty," in three of O'Neill's best-known sea plays—*Bound East for Cardiff; The Moon of the Caribbees;* and *In the Zone.*

At the moment, his pockets soon empty after he returned from South Africa, Eugene spent the next few months "on the beach"— in this case, the waterfront docks and—if he was lucky—the park benches of Buenos Aires. Again, unlike Melville, who recorded his bizarre experiences across the sands of the South Seas in *Omoo*, Eugene was less a beachcomber than a bum, one of the derelicts who huddled for shelter in a waterfront shack and begged food from the galleys of incoming ships. When his existence had sunk so low that he felt almost secure in the fact that it could go no lower, he began to write poetry again, and to make some notes of his experiences. (As yet he had no thought of being a dramatist, but something impelled him to write down the faint outlines of scenes that were to shape his plays.) Although the pulse of his creativity was feeble, weakened by the harsh pace of dissipation, it was still strong enough to lead him aboard another tramp steamer, the S.S. *Ikalis*, bound for New York. The crew was "mixed," the forecastle dank and crowded, the food (as usual) abominable, yet the *Ikalis* was destined to become famous as the S.S. *Glencairn*, the setting for the most successful of his one-act plays of the sea. Several of the sailors he shipped with on this voyage became the central characters of the sea plays. Yank, in *Bound East for Cardiff*, Olsen, in *The Long Voyage Home*, and Driscoll (whose name he did not even change), a powerful, redheaded Irishman, were all shipmates he hobnobbed with on land and at sea. When the *Ikalis* docked in New York, he went along with them as a matter of course to "Jimmy-the-Priest's," a waterfront dive which served him first as the setting for the opening act of *Anna Christie*. Squalid, a combined saloon and flophouse, it was the scene of many a tragic end to the wandering, restless life of the sailor. Men who had drunk from the dregs took their last swallow here. Presided over by the crafty proprietor, called mockingly "Jimmy-the-Priest" because of the chalk-like pallor of his skin and his china-blue eyes, the "disinherited" sat around summing up the past, comforting each other in their common misery, arguing bitterly at times, and at times philosophizing in dreary resignation. Thoroughly a part of the scene, Eugene could not reproduce it until many years later when he wrote *The Iceman Cometh*; until he was far enough away in space and time to see it objectively; and until he was mature

enough to grasp the significance of these wretched lives in relation
to the world outside, and to the history of man. The place was so
indelibly impressed on his mind that he could describe it in detail
more than thirty years afterward.

He made one more voyage, this time to Southampton and back
on a merchant ship as an able seaman. He did not like the duty,
and found the voyage irksome compared to those on a sailing vessel. (He had been talked into signing on by Driscoll, who was a
stoker, proud of his strength in feeding the furnaces of the steamer;
but Eugene missed climbing the ratlins to loose or make fast the
sails. He missed the poetry of bounding along on a ship in full
sail. He was, however, more than satisfied with his rank as "able
seaman," and kept his discharge papers till the end of his days.) On
his return, he stayed at Jimmy-the-Priest's again, stubbornly resist-
ing support from his father, who had arranged the divorce from
Kathleen. That whole procedure seemed to him more sordid than
his murky existence at Jimmy-the-Priest's, but when he fell ill from
malnutrition (and "rotgut"); when he tried unsuccessfully to take
his life with sleeping pills, he was forced to go back to his father's
peripatetic roof: *Monte Cristo* was touring the country as a vaudeville attraction on the Orpheum circuit.

The company was in New Orleans when he managed to catch up
with it, and his father, after scolding him roundly as if he were a
small boy, gave him a minor part in the cast. He would have only
a couple of lines to learn, but when he objected on the grounds
that he was no actor, his father insisted. Jamie, whose attempt at
independence had petered out after *The Traveling Salesman*
closed, was playing the Count's son, and could help Eugene. This
was James O'Neill's way of keeping his sons under his domination,
of preventing either of them from becoming a threat to his career,
which was fast going to pieces. The mere fact that he had to put
Monte Cristo on the vaudeville circuit spoke for his dwindling
popularity, and the shortened version made the play ridiculous, but
the once-heralded actor pretended in stubborn pride that he still
considered it a fine vehicle for his talent.

Eugene, particularly, was embittered at being under his father's
thumb again, embarrassed at having to read lines that had little or
no meaning. He hated them so he could hardly memorize his

"part," if such it could be called. He felt inferior, deflated, humili-ated. He and Jamie, who had deteriorated, at the age of thirty-four, into a confirmed alcoholic, did all they could to detract from the production, both to show their contempt for the vaudeville version of the play and to aggravate their father. Eugene, influenced by Jamie, was often led on to do things he later regretted. Yet, in spite of everything, he was all unconsciously absorbing a knowledge of stagecraft, the essentials of acting and line delivery—even down to breathing intervals—that was to give his own plays the indefinable quality of "theater." Because of this experience, or exposure, to his father's profession, he knew instinctively what was "good theater" and what was not.

When the tour was over, he landed a job with the New London *Telegraph,* which, though it lasted only ten months, taught him the habit of writing, wrestling with words and phrases for a concen-trated period of time each day, a discipline he had not known be-fore. He was not a competent reporter in that he was apt to over-look the basic newspaper data—"who, what, when, where and why" —in favor of the artistic aspect of a story, the larger meaning or social significance of some event or catastrophe. The managing editor might despair of young O'Neill's report of a murder, in which he neglected to give the name and address of the victim, the time and place of the deed, etc. But there was enough of the spark of genius in his description of the bloodied body on the floor, the poverty, and filth of the hovel, to bring Eugene praise from the publisher, who had the insight to realize that James O'Neill's sec-ond son might amount to some thing one day. And when Eugene began to submit poems of a satiric nature, clever parodies that showed he possessed a sharp political sense, the publisher, noted for his liberal views, encouraged his efforts by accepting them for the poetry corner of the paper. Eventually, Eugene took over the column, which included light verse, short features and anecdotes, running it in addition to his reporting, keeping himself occupied and away from the drab, dreary family life in New London. The vaudeville tour had finally finished *Monte Cristo,* and no new play was in sight for his father or brother. His mother was home from the sanitarium, but she did not seem to be much better this time, and when the whole family was together, the strain was unbearable. In addition, Eugene was haunted by feelings of doubt and regret, not to say guilt, over his marriage and divorce, and the son he had not seen. All during the summer of 1912, the four O'Neills tried to maintain a semblance of normal relations with each other, but when they were together, there was nothing but haranguing, accusation and recrimination. It was twenty-four hours in this crucial summer of 1912 that Eugene chose to dramatize in his revealing, analytical record of the O'Neills' tragic history, *Long Day's Journey into Night.*

His health broke when he contracted a cold he could not shake, a racking cough that would not leave. By December, it was definitely diagnosed as tuberculosis. He had to resign from the *Telegraph,* and, after some wrangling over the expense with his father, he went to take the cure at Gaylord Farm in Wallingford, Connecticut. The long rest he was forced to endure when he arrived, faced with the possibility of death if he did not observe the regulations of the sanitarium, brought him to grips with the value, the true meaning of life. Followed by outdoor exercise as soon as he was able, and coupled with the kindness and understanding of the nurses and doctor, the treatment at Gaylord proved to be his salvation. During the months he had to spend in bed, he not only read omnivorously, but he pondered and meditated on classical drama; he had time to relate his own sorry search for love to the ideas he found. The psychology of sex struck him full force in the modern European plays—Ibsen, Wedekind, and particularly Strindberg. In the last he saw the inner struggle of man laid bare as no American dramatist had ever dared to show it. The thought of *Monte Cristo, The White Sister,* or any of the plays produced by the commercial theater in America, made him cringe when compared to Strindberg's stark, dissecting drama. Then, as his strength came back, he realized that he could write plays of truth and honest passion— whether or not anyone produced them! His poetry was nothing, a mere pastime, an outlet for bitter humor, tomfoolery. Suddenly, as if by revelation, he knew that he must write plays. He had absorbed (almost by osmosis) from his father a knowledge of the theater which most embryo playwrights did not have. He would use it to good advantage. By the time he was released from the san-

itarium—pronounced cured, after six months—he was determined
to write for the theater—not out of lust for money, but out of his
agony and anguish, his experiences of the past few years, and the
experiences of those whose lives had been thrown with his.

Eugene was told by the doctor that he must observe the conva-
lescent routine for at least another year, so he persuaded his father
to let him stay in New London when the O'Neills left for their
apartment in New York in the fall of 1913. He could room and
board at the Rippins'—a British family who ran a restaurant in their
home, where the O'Neills took dinner more than half of the time
in New London. Rather doubtfully, his father agreed to the plan,
and Eugene settled down to a strict schedule of outdoor exercise,
reading, and writing plays. (He swam every day, even in the icy
temperatures of January; he wrote steadily for hours, sending out
manuscripts as soon as they were finished, to one producer or another. During the long evenings he read, sometimes till one or two
in the morning.) In the year he spent at the Rippins', he turned
out a fair portion of the "trunkful of plays" he brought to Provincetown: eleven one-acts, and two full-length plays. The dialogue
was stilted, the situation sometimes contrived, but his earnestness,
his honesty of purpose and his anguished heart came through, even
in those early awkward attempts. One of those who sensed the
seeds of greatness in him was Clayton Hamilton, the essayist and
drama editor of the *Bookman,* who was spending the spring in New
London, not far from the Rippins'. When Eugene, with deep fear-
fulness, asked him to read his efforts, it was Hamilton who advised
him to develop the theme of the strange lure of the sea in his plays,
the life he had known on the *Ikalis.* The critic pointed out that the
sea had been the subject of poetry in Masefield; of novels in Melville and Conrad; but no one had dealt with it in drama until now.
O'Neill, he felt, had the power to do it justice.

Eugene, who admired and respected Hamilton's opinion, needed
little urging; using the nucleus he had, he went to work. His father,
who also respected Hamilton's word, was finally convinced that his
errant son was serious about playwriting. In a burst of generosity
(and because he did not want it said that he had not recognized
Eugene's ability), he offered to have some of the plays privately
printed. The little volume, entitled *Thirst,* received a glowing

review by Hamilton in the *Bookman,* but no one else mentioned it; and few copies were sold. Eugene had trouble giving them away. Still determined, he persuaded his father to send him to Harvard in the fall to attend George Pierce Baker's 47 Workshop. Baker was in his late forties in 1914, approaching the peak of his career. He limited his two seminars, one at Radcliffe and one at Harvard, to twelve students, known as "Baker's Dozen." An advanced seminar was further limited to four men and four women, the best from the previous year. Eugene considered himself lucky to be accepted.

He was, however, remote, usually silent, and quite casual in class. His classmates, including the poet, John V. A. Weaver, rarely saw him smile. When he spoke, it was mostly in monosyllables. Yet he showed a shrewd grasp of theater knowledge, and his comments on student manuscripts, delivered in an offhand way, could be biting, often hilarious. The girls in class found him irresistible. They were always calling for "Gene," but he showed little interest in any one of them. He was intent on learning to write plays, not according to Baker's dictates, but his own. And Baker, recognizing young O'Neill's originality in spite of his faults, invited him to come back for the advanced seminar the following year.

His father, however, in a fit of thriftiness which often succeeded his bursts of generosity, decided one year at Harvard was all he could afford to give his son. Eugene, angry, disappointed, and defiant once more, took up with three artist-friends—George Bellows, John Sloan, and Art Young, who allowed him to share their apartment in Greenwich Village. Their favorite haunt was the "Hell Hole"—their nickname for the bar of the Golden Swan Hotel. It was a dingy, ramshackle saloon, on only a slightly higher level than Jimmy-the-Priest's, but it drew artists, intellectuals, a wide variety of "Bohemians" within its swinging doors. They mingled happily with truck drivers, teamsters and gangsters, spouted poetry along with radical politics and entered into any brawl with heady enthusiasm. One of the Hell Hole's most loyal inhabitants was Terry Carlin, anarchist, nihilist, raconteur, and Irish wit, who managed to get by on his gift of gab. He asked for little except his Irish whiskey, and he usually got it, if not from one patron of the Hell Hole, then from another. Gene took an immediate liking to Terry, who was to influence his philosophy, and the course of his life, more than any other man. Terry, who knew and was admired by many literary notables of the time, including Theodore Dreiser, Jack London and John Reed, introduced Eugene as his "protégé," promoting his work whenever possible. It was Terry, whom Eugene the dramatist immortalized as Larry Slade in *The Iceman Cometh,* who insisted that Eugene submit his work to some group producing plays. And so it was that they had come to Provincetown, where the first O'Neill play was produced at the Wharf Theater.

Once started, Eugene O'Neill's desire to write plays drove him to turn out one manuscript after another, expressing his thoughts as well as he could in words. He felt, as his friend Terry once remarked, that "words only conceal thought and do not express it"; but in his longing to divest himself of the torment within him, Eugene poured out an endless stream of words, as if from a miraculous pitcher. If his style brought him the judgment of being "repetitious," it also revealed his passion for truth—his overwhelming need to dissect his own double nature as well as the duality in mankind generally. And repetition brought the rhythm of the sea, of the universe, to his prose.

Two years after the sea plays had been presented by the Provincetowners, the budding playwright received his first wide critical attention in print, when *Smart Set* published *The Long Voyage Home,* and George Jean Nathan (one of the editors, along with H. L. Mencken) became his lifelong friend and sponsor. It was this publication in the November issue of *Smart Set,* 1917, plus the accompanying check for $75, which finally convinced Eugene's parents that he must have some ability. The fact that so prominent a critic as Nathan heralded their son as "the first great talent in our native theater," could not fail to impress both the elder O'Neills, although his father never understood why he chose such depressing themes, why his plays almost always ended in tragedy. (His answer, which he repeated to an interviewer in 1922, was: "Sure I'll write about happiness—if I happen to meet up with that luxury!" Moreover, he experienced a kind of exaltation in tragedy, a feeling akin to the heroic figures of classical tragedy, which somehow was communicated to his audiences, and brought him their lasting devotion, no matter how much they might debate his merits as America's leading dramatist.) His father came to rehearsals of the New

York productions in the Provincetown Playhouse; and although he might sound off against the new technique in acting and directing, as well as the subjects of Eugene's plays, he began to offer a grudging praise, and to take pride in his son's growing reputation. Even his mother came out of her shell to comment, "Imagine Eugene's getting seventy-five dollars for one of his plays!" His brother was by turns proud and jealous of Eugene's initial successes.

During the fall and winter season in New York, Eugene continued to haunt the Hell Hole with his cronies. They usually slipped into the barroom through the entrance on Sixth Avenue and Fourth Street, just under the "El," and left it only when they felt a dire need for coffee or food, when they would repair to Polly Holiday's or Romany Marie's, several blocks up the Avenue. Now and then some of the Provincetowners threw a party in the Hell Hole, and on one such occasion, Eugene met the young woman who was to become his second wife—Agnes Boulton, a fairly successful writer of short stories. She possessed a fragile beauty, and an inflated opinion of her own work that intrigued and challenged Eugene. He monopolized her all evening, escorted her to her hotel, and left her open-mouthed by announcing, "I want to sleep with you every night for the rest of my life!" It was more than a year before they were married, and then the ceremony was performed by a Protestant minister, instead of a Catholic priest; but they received the blessings of Eugene's father, who admired Agnes' work, and thought she might have a leavening effect on his son's. His approval went so far as to include the purchase of the abandoned coast guard station on the tip of Provincetown. It had been made into a home by Mabel Dodge Luhan some years earlier, and was coveted by many of the Players as an ideal hideout for an industrious playwright. The gift was a complete surprise to Eugene and Agnes, who moved into their first real home shortly before their first child, Shane, an eight-pound boy, was born in the fall of 1919.

Eugene, briefly elated by the birth of his son, was so immersed in the wave of artistic creativity that surged within him, accompanied by the aggravating problems of getting his first full-length play, *Beyond the Horizon*, produced, that he hardly took notice of the baby. (When he did, he was struck with a feeling close to terror at the responsibilities of fatherhood, a reaction he never overcame in regard to either of his children by his marriage to Agnes.) Time and again for months the three-act script, which concerned two brothers whose separate tragic fates are foreordained, had been on the verge of production, but it was gathering dust in George Tyler's office, and Eugene, his brain bursting with ideas for other plays already outlined in his notebooks, did not know where to turn next.

Then one day he learned that Richard Bennett, bored with playing the lead in Elmer Rice's *For the Defense,* had picked up the neglected script in Tyler's office, began reading, and was so taken by the drama that he was ready to catapult it into production. He wanted to play Robert Mayo, the younger of the two brothers, and he offered to give matinee and several evening performances of the O'Neill play, alternating it with *For the Defense.* Eugene did not care for the arrangement, but he was sick to death of striving and struggling, so he consented. *Beyond the Horizon* opened late in 1919, and was so successful that it pushed *For the Defense* off the boards. Early in 1920, the play that came into the limelight almost by accident, brought Eugene O'Neill his first Pulitzer award, and established his career as the foremost American playwright. His father, still puzzled by his second son's peculiar genius, was nonetheless gratified by the recognition, and ran true to form by claiming that he "knew all along Eugene would make it."

With a curious mixture of pique and amusement, Eugene accepted his father's attitude cynically, and took little satisfaction in having shown them all that his talent was more than a figment of his imagination. But when his father suffered a broken leg in an accident, Eugene, his harsh feelings softened, visited him in the hospital. His mother, miraculously, found the strength to cast off her drug addiction at this time, and Jamie, following her example, gave up drinking. For a brief period of months, the four O'Neills came closer to family harmony than they had ever been. But in July, Eugene, at work on the final draft of *The Emperor Jones,* received word that his father, who had recovered sufficiently to walk with a cane, was in the hospital again, this time with an illness that proved fatal. The conflict he had always felt toward his father would not allow him to grieve openly, yet he felt that Fate had dealt him personally a severe blow just as he was on the threshold of fulfillment in his career as a figure of importance in the theater.

His mother, surprisingly, took hold of her husband's affairs with an aplomb she had never shown while he was alive. She and Jamie went about settling his debts and handling his numerous investments with a vigor that was astonishing in both of them. Jamie, sticking to his pledge, accompanied her everywhere. Eugene could concentrate on his writing without the interruption of family troubles or squabbles. His respite, however, was to be short-lived. A year and a half later, his mother was taken ill in California, where she and Jamie had gone to see about selling some orange groves his father had bought. She died in the hospital, and Jamie, bereft, weak-willed without her, returned to the numbing solace of drink even before he brought her body back across the country. Eugene, meeting him at the station, was shocked and pained at his brother's condition, at Jamie's sodden confession of the means he had used to blot out their mother's death during that cross-country journey, paying some "pig" (his word for prostitutes) fifty dollars a night to help him forget. Eugene, for all his fondness for barrooms and drinking bouts, never touched the bottle while he was at work on a play; his long abstinence during his battle with tuberculosis had shown him that he could not write unless his mind was clear, unblurred by alcohol. The sight of Jamie, stumbling and incoherent, a wretched, broken figure at forty-two, filled him with pity and revulsion at the same time.

He tried to help the brother he had once adored (and who also might have had a brilliant career), but Jamie was beyond help. Their mother, more than their father, had been the cause of his dissoluteness and his recent reform during her life. Now by her death, she was inevitably the cause of his reversion to complete degradation. For a year and a half a distracting worry to Eugene, Jamie was in and out of sanitariums, trying to pull himself from the stupor of alcoholism, but he could not. He died in a hospital room, suffering from a severe case of delirium tremens. Eugene, whose stature had increased with the stunning success of *The Emperor Jones,* and who was in process of staging one of his most powerful plays, *The Hairy Ape,* buried his brother in sorrow not unmixed with relief and a sense of the futility of life. In less than

three years he had lost all three members of his family. He was
alone now—he felt alone in spite of the fact that he had a family of
his own. He had become attached to the very wranglings he abhorred, and now felt lost. His offering to the memory of Jamie, *A
Moon for the Misbegotten,* was, like *Long Day's Journey into
Night,* many years in forming; but the ideas for the majority of his
plays sprang from the fires of conflict that burned in the family
constellation of the O'Neills. *Desire Under the Elms,* considered
by the critic John Gassner his finest, "most consistently wrought"
play, written shortly after Jamie's death and produced in 1924,
dealt with the struggle of two brothers and a domineering father.
Time and again, in one form or another, the theme of his family
complex crept into O'Neill's plays.

One of the few satisfactions of his life was his own father-son
relationship with twelve-year-old Eugene, Jr., who was sent to visit
the playwright in Provincetown in the summer of 1922. (Kathleen
had married again, and the boy had been brought up in a normal,
healthy household on Long Island.) Eugene was pleasantly surprised to find that his first-born was bright, winning, and apparently outgoing. Tall for his age, good-looking and well-set-up, he
was interested in sports; but he also had some knowledge of his
father's plays, and a very evident admiration for him. It was the
first of many visits that were to increase in a feeling of closeness
between them through the years. Young O'Neill was to become a
brilliant Greek scholar, professor, and authority on Greek drama
at Harvard; on more than one occasion the father would look to
the son for information, or confirmation of his dramatic material.
Yet this, too, was to end in tragedy, when the son committed suicide in 1950, three years before his father's death, perhaps because
he lived in his father's shadow, in spite of the name he made for
himself in his own field.

Small wonder that O'Neill was called a "black Irishman," that
he considered happiness a "luxury" he never met up with.

As success followed success, he enlarged his scale of living; he
bought a rambling house in Ridgewood, New Jersey, and then a
fortresslike palace in Bermuda, both of them away from the world
of men, in his search for the ideal life. But he abandoned them
both, and with the second, he abandoned his second wife and their

children—his son Shane, and his daughter Oona, born a few years after Shane. He and Agnes had quarreled constantly out of a sense of rivalry—professional jealousy which neither of them could overcome. Eugene felt he needed a woman who would devote her whole life to him, who would give him the tender care he never received from his mother, combined with the sexual love of a wife and the understanding of a friend.

He found her in the actress, Carlotta Monterey, renowned for her beauty, her power over men. Because of her, Eugene entered into psychotherapy with Dr. Gilbert Hamilton, and within six weeks he was cured of his alcoholism, an unexpected and extremely rare result. It was at this time, 1927 and 1928, that *Strange Interlude,* the psychological drama of novel-length proportions that startled American theater audiences, commanded to be written, and he could not rest until it was out of him. With Carlotta, whom he married in 1928 after finally securing a divorce from Agnes, he roamed the seas in search of the perfect spot to settle, but though their personal happiness was great, they never found the place to match it. Not in the cold elegance of the castle on the Riviera; not in the Orient; not in the Spanish villa they built on one of the Sea Islands off the coast of Georgia; not in the great house in northern California, nor in the (relatively) small one in Connecticut, where passion and illness led to brutality in both of them. Yet Eugene could not leave Carlotta, and in the end they were living in a hotel apartment in Boston. The irony of it struck him full force as he lay dying, and his last words rattled with typical biting, half-humorous realism: "Born in a hotel room, and—goddammit—died in one!"

Because of Carlotta he had cast off his friends early in his third marriage: the Provincetowners ceased to hear from him, and even his beloved Terry Carlin saw him no more (although he provided for his friend with a small stipend till the end). He specifically cut off his children Shane and Oona in a new will written shortly before his death. Except for those who were necessary to his career —the executives of the Theatre Guild, the critic George Jean Nathan—his son Eugene, whom Carlotta liked (and occasionally, out of duty, the other children), he saw no one for months at a time because of his third wife.

Yet he wanted her to shield him, to provide the quiet, smooth-running household so that he could write—write, write, write his plays. As much as he experimented in the theater, Eugene O'Neill was one dramatist who never deviated from his métier: he never wrote anything but plays, and he wrote them alone. He never collaborated, and, after the collapse of the Playwrights Theater, he never joined another group. The Theatre Guild produced his plays, but he scarcely participated in the productions, and only rarely attended rehearsals. He did not even want his plays to be filmed, although a few of them were. (He refused to see *Anna Christie*, with Greta Garbo as Anna.) He never translated other men's plays.

Without stopping to realize his tremendous output from 1918 until 1928 (the years he was married to Agnes), years which witnessed two of his three Pulitzer awards, and his development from naturalism with symbolistic overtones to religious mysticism, and, finally, to psychiatric drama, Eugene felt that it was because of Carlotta he was able to carry out his creative urge. Because of her he could achieve his classic tragedy, *Mourning Becomes Electra*, in 1930. His dedication to her on the flyleaf of the manuscript is almost embarrassing in its emotionalism. She allowed him to go at his own pace, however fast or slow it might be. She placed no obligations on him, and let him set his own schedule. He spent the hours from seven-thirty early morning till one-thirty at his desk. The afternoon was given over to outdoor exercise, tennis or swimming.

He wrote first drafts of his plays in microscopic longhand. When the first draft was copied, he corrected it for the second, and so on, sometimes making a third or fourth. Often fearful that he had gone stale, he would put a second or third draft aside for days or weeks before taking it up again. After the successful run of *Mourning Becomes Electra*, which won him his third Pulitzer award, he began working on *Days Without End*, his complex religious drama, which combined the techniques of *Strange Interlude* and *The Great God Brown*, with its duo-character, John Loving, to be played by two actors, one called John, the other Loving. Eugene, an agnostic from the time he stopped going to Mass at fifteen, was still seeking redemption, and the theme of *Days Without End* was redemption through faith. He had finished a second draft of the play in 1932, and, unsure of its resolution, voted himself a ten days' rest. He promised Carlotta they would spend the time loafing together. But he had no sooner started on his vacation than a new play, of an entirely different nature, came to him out of a dream. He woke up one morning with the complete plot and all the characters of *Ah, Wilderness!* clearly outlined in his mind, clamoring to be set down in his notebooks.

He tried to go back to sleep, but while he lay half-dozing, the whole comedy unfolded before him, from the opening to the final scene. After wrestling with his religious drama, he was almost resentful of a play so simple, so clear-cut, deposited in his brain by his subconscious overnight! And try as he would, he could not get it out of his mind. So he had spent the next fifteen days—for it took no more than that—writing a first draft with his usual frenzied concentration. Putting it aside then, he resumed work on *Days Without End* immediately, as if he had taken the planned rest. Carlotta raised no objection. She realized that he must write as the demon spirit of creativity in him commanded. (The fate of the two scripts in terms of success was in inverse ratio of the work that went into them. Eugene was surprised to find on second look that *Ah, Wilderness!* needed very few changes. He submitted it casually along with the reworked, and, to him, much more important *Days Without End.* One reading of *Ah, Wilderness!* by the Theatre Guild committee led to a unanimous decision to produce the comedy at once. Six weeks later, it opened with George M. Cohan in the lead, a smash hit, and one of the longest runs in Guild history. *Days Without End,* however, barely made the subscription list—fifty-seven performances—its complicated and heavily symbolic devices a severe handicap to its success.) It was Carlotta who proposed at this time the O'Neill collection of manuscripts at Yale University (where George Pierce Baker had gone in 1929), and she who arranged its establishment.

Many honors came to Eugene O'Neill, including the Litt.D. degree from Yale; memberships in the National Institute of Arts and Letters, the American Academy and the Irish Academy of Letters; and culminating in the Nobel Prize for Literature in 1936. By then he was already suffering from the creeping neurological disease (akin to Parkinson's) which eventually shuddered his whole body; he could not be present at the official ceremonies and had to arrange for a private presentation; but the award gave him a wry satisfaction. He stayed away from the world of Broadway for nearly two decades, but all the time he was writing for the theater. He became deeply engrossed in delineating the doom of the Irish in America through a series of historical, psychological dramas dealing with a family of Irish immigrants from 1775 to 1932, which he intended to call *A Tale of Possessors Dispossessed.* During the twelve-year period from 1934 to 1946, he poured most of his decreasing energy into the cycle, only to destroy the greater part of it shortly before his death. He felt that he had failed to achieve his purpose; and, judging from the fragments that remained—*A Touch of the Poet,* and *Hughie*—he was probably correct. Moreover, when he interrupted the cycle to wrestle with the story of his own family, his own life, he merged victorious twice out of three times: in 1939, with *The Iceman Cometh,* and in 1942, with *Long Day's Journey into Night,* both of which measured up to if not surpassed his early work in masterful probing of the human being. (Even the third play, *A Moon for the Misbegotten,* written in 1941 out of remembrance of Jamie's last years, for all its faults, came closer to truth and artistry than *A Touch of the Poet.*)

Eugene O'Neill died as he (largely) had lived—in frustration and anguish, mental and physical anguish. For all his delving, he had not solved the mystery of man's eternal struggle with himself and an overwhelming universe. The closest he came to a solution was his belief, stated so forcibly in *The Iceman Cometh,* that man must cling to his illusions or perish.

To the last, he was an unpredictable enigma. The man who could be gentle, easily entertained, boisterously humorous and warmhearted, could also be by turns diffident, oversensitive, excitable, meditative and brooding. He was forever puzzled by the problems that confronted him; zealously industrious once he began to write; and, if possible, too prolific for his own peace of mind.

Volumes of a critical nature, negative and positive, have been written about O'Neill, but whether the comments have been favorable or unfavorable, all have granted that his effort to create

art for the theater was Herculean. One of his most ardent propo-
nents, John Gassner, who makes the point that O'Neill won his
reputation twice—once in the twenties and once in the fifties, after
his death—sums it up in a few sentences. O'Neill, he observes, was
"virtually the only American playwright to confront ideas on more
than an elementary level, and to wrestle with them 'tragically'—
'heroically'." (And earlier) ". . . if he failed to write tragedy (as
plainly intended) he achieved a noble tragic mood . . . in a context
of exciting drama."

It is significant that Gassner, Harold Clurman, and George Jean
Nathan (and one might even add the acid Eric Bentley)—all emi-
nent writers on the theater—agree, in their books on drama in the
fifties, that O'Neill is our outstanding dramatist. Whatever his
faults, and all agree there are many, he is "the one American playwright who has consistently written as an artist."

CHAPTER IV

———◆◼◆———

PHILIP BARRY

I F Eugene O'Neill evoked the epithet "black Irishman" in terms of mood, then Philip Barry might be called "Celtic" for his sly humor, his sense of whimsy, and shades of ancient Irish mysticism. Just as O'Neill's outlook was stormy and dark, Barry's was bright and sunny. No greater contrast is to be found among the figures of the American theater than the one between these two Irish-American playwrights. Yet there are certain similarities in their work which indicate that emotionally they were not so far apart.

Like O'Neill, Philip Barry was born of Irish Catholic parents, but under a different star—that of June 18, 1896—and a vastly different family constellation. His grandfather and father, who emigrated from Ireland when the latter was nine years old, somehow found their way to Rochester, New York, and were well established in business by the time Philip came along, the spark of his Celtic ancestry showing in his shining eyes. He was the youngest of an ebullient circle of brothers and sisters, and as such was favored and teased, petted and picked on at the same time. In his effort to be heard over the uproar and confusion of a large family, he stuttered at times, and often took refuge in the daydreams of a fertile imagination.

At the age of nine, bored with the routine reading in Rochester's parochial schools, he began writing his own stories—to the
dismay of the nuns, who expected him to learn his catechism and
write his sums instead of stories. Not that Philip Barry was a bad
boy or a poor student, but he was disturbing to the nuns. He was
good-natured and quick enough in certain subjects, but he did not
"apply himself" to his studies. He squirmed and wriggled in his
seat, and whispered jokes to those around him—a disrupting influence and sore trial to the good sisters' patience. He himself summed
up his education in Rochester with succinct humor: "I was only
bright in spots," he claimed with modest pride, "and was expelled
for being a general nuisance."

However, he did manage to graduate from high school in 1913,
and convinced his parents that he had the brains for higher education. He longed to write, and felt that an eastern school like Yale
would give him a broader background than the municipal or
Catholic college he was expected to attend, like his brothers before
him. His parents were doubtful. His mother, especially, took a dim
view of his desire to become a writer. His father was more sympathetic, but warned Barry that he should also learn a profession that
would give him a decent living. Both parents finally consented to
his going to Yale in the hope that he would be ready to settle down
in Rochester once he got his degree and had had a taste of being
away from home.

Philip, on the other hand, felt that he was escaping from the
commonplace, the deadly dullness of the city of his birth. After his
first taste of campus life in the east, he resolved to return to Rochester as little as possible, a vow he kept for the rest of his life. His
college career was not brilliant, but it was rewarding in more ways
than one. He was enrolled as a political science major, studying for
the diplomatic service, but it was in the required course of freshman composition that he shone. He found he could express himself
freely without being frowned upon or misunderstood. As an elec-
tive he chose a playwriting course one year, which gave him ample
opportunity to indulge his flair for comedy, for fantasy. He turned
out a number of one-act scripts, one of which was accepted for production by the Yale Dramatic Club.

Genial, handsome, with an infectious smile and keen blue eyes,

"Phil" Barry made friends easily, and his ingratiating manner led to his appointment by the State Department at the outbreak of war in 1917, when the Army rejected him (perhaps because of some irregularity in his heartbeat). He served as a clerk in Washington, and as attaché to the American embassy in London from May, 1918, until February, 1919; but he found the diplomatic career he had been training for "very dull indeed." He had to sit at a desk all day doing code work, and often he had to stand in line all evening shaking hands at stuffy receptions. Moreover, his initial success at playwriting had spoiled him for anything else. He could not keep from it.

During whatever spare time he had in London, he wrote a three-act play, dealing with psychoanalysis, a subject he had become fascinated by in his reading for a psychology course at Yale. He called his first full-length drama *No Thoroughfare,* and when he returned to the University, he sent the manuscript to Elsie Ferguson, the famous actress. She was not interested, and sent a flat rejection, which caused him to put the manuscript away for all time. (It was never performed or published.) Since his undergraduate work had been interrupted by the war effort, he completed his A.B. degree at Yale in June of 1919, and went right over to Harvard to study at George Pierce Baker's 47 Workshop. It was a well-known fact that O'Neill, whose sea plays were bringing about a fresh awakening to art in the theater, had benefited enormously from mere contact with Baker, and Phil Barry was eager to find out for himself what the Professor's methods were. He wanted to learn everything he could about the theater in general, as well as playwriting.

He was not disappointed. He found Baker and his "dozen" an exciting, stimulating circle. Unlike O'Neill, he entered into workshop activity with a will, for the backstage business of the theater was new to him, and he approached it with the awe-struck, enthusiastic eyes of the novice—not with the jaded vision of an unwilling professional, disillusioned from childhood, as Gene O'Neill had been.

To Phil Barry the whole experience was exhilarating, and so rewarding that he stayed an extra year, absorbing as much knowledge of the theater as he could—acting, stage direction, and set designing. All the hours he could squeeze in, in addition to playwriting, were spent in learning the fundamentals of technical skill to give him greater understanding of the problems that arose in his plays. Characteristically, he said with self-disparagement that he "wrote some, acted hard, and shifted scenery brilliantly" while he was at Harvard. But in point of fact, he was one of Baker's outstanding students, and his play, *A Punch for Judy* was among the most successful comedies ever produced by the Workshop disciples.

It was followed by the more substantial *You and I,* which won a prize just before Barry left Harvard. A three-act comedy of marriage, it represented a revolt against the twin careers of matrimony and business, and was based in part on his own dilemma. He had met and fallen in love with Ellen Semple, whom he married in 1922, but only after a prolonged debate over his ability to support a wife who was used to a high standard of living, and over the demands his career would make on him after they were married. When *You and I* won a prize for the young playwright, it also won him the hand of the beautiful society girl with whom he was so much in love.

Last but not least, the little comedy of marriage won for Phil Barry his first Broadway production. *You and I* was produced at the Morosco Theater in 1923, touted as a Harvard prize play, which may have been responsible for its relatively long run of six months, a remarkable showing for an embryo dramatist. (*A Punch for Judy* was given two performances at the Morosco in 1921, and a revival production by Knowles Entrikin in his experimental theater at Scarsdale-on-the-Hudson in 1927. Although the 47 Workshop brought forth a number of playwrights who later gained prominence, few saw the scripts they had written in class professionally produced. O'Neill's work under Baker's tutelage was considered too awkward and poorly structured for production.)

Encouraged by his initial success, Barry followed it by a play that disguised his own life even less than the first. Called *The Youngest,* it concerned the youngest son in a large family, who feels inferior to his sisters and brothers because they boss him around, and, aided by his mother, make fun of his longing to be a writer. In rounding out his plot, the youngest member of the Barry family dramatized one of his childhood daydreams: the father dies and in his will unexpectedly leaves everything to the youngest, who is thereby elevated to the highly enjoyable position of being sole heir, sought after by the others. In his new status he acquires confidence in himself, winning their respect (as well as the girl who first encouraged him). His conclusion is that "a man's greatest victory is over his own family."

There were early signs of Barryesque humor in the lines, of whimsy in the situations. In one scene, balloons filled the stage as the hero and his girl harked back to their childhood. The play had only a brief stay on Broadway, but Phil Barry was not one to be thrown off his course so easily. In addition to his wife, he now had a son to support—Philip Semple Barry—but he would not countenance the thought of going back into the diplomatic service, or earning his livelihood any other way but playwriting. He loved the theater, and had already made fast friends among those who, like himself, were struggling for a foothold—Robert Sherwood for one; the tie between them was to prove lifelong.

Barry's next attempt was not only a definite improvement in style and technique, but it marked the beginning of his tendency toward experimentation in the theater. Like his colleagues, he had caught the fever of innovation; he was, in fact, highly susceptible, with his imaginative, fanciful mind, coupled with his capacity to question, as well as to accept, human behavior. For Philip Barry was not a shallow playwright, nor entirely a comedic one, though he was labeled both by various critics. His artistry was to lie in the high comedy of manners he was able to create when he combined his gifts, but that would take a few years.

Meanwhile, his third offering, *In a Garden,* was a result of self-examination, plus the ingredient of fantasy when he allowed his imagination to carry his penchant for tearing apart people's feelings and personal relations to an improbable conclusion. In the play, a novelist and a playwright who have the same tendency to dissect human relations that Barry possessed, conduct an experiment which backfires. The playwright, at the suggestion of the novelist, re-creates the garden setting of a former romance of his wife, assuming that by repetition the lost love will lose its glamour. Instead, through a series of miscalculations in regard to the reactions of everyone concerned, he is left without a wife. Tired of his constant analyzing, his meddling and manipulating, she forsakes him just as he was about to retire from his profession in order to have time to "live." She realizes that he will never stop being a puppeteer. "I can almost feel the tug of each separate string, making me jump this way, that way," she says at one point. And so she breaks the strings.

It may well have been that Philip Barry was suffering from certain qualms regarding his own practices, or those of any writer in "using everything, everybody, cutting them up and putting the pieces together again." In making this observation, Lissa, the wife in the play, who goes on to say, "I've even seen myself, dressed up in another person—walking across the stage in your plays . . ." may have been voicing the views and complaints of Ellen Barry, Philip's own wife. But in any case, he had created a play that showed a marked advanced toward the cleverness and grace which were to characterize his work later on. The fine line of demarcation between reality and the dream-world of the theater that emerges from *In a Garden* with the sure touch of a Pirandello, gave promise of the high comedy to come.

The period of the twenties, following the First World War, was fraught with upheaval as a "lost generation" tried to accustom itself to the monumental changes that mechanized warfare had brought. The machine was replacing people in factories and horses in the street. Model T Fords, "flivvers," raced through rural routes and small towns, and in the cities, along with heavier "machines" like the Packard, Marmon, Pierce-Arrow and Rolls-Royce, the streets began filling up with delivery trucks to replace the wagon as well as the horse-drawn carriage. The street cleaners, who patrolled New York cities with their canvas bins—called "white wings"—sweeping up the manure, a familiar sight during the boyhood of the playwrights who became prominent in the twenties, had all but disappeared.

When Elmer Rice gave voice to his version of a bewildered generation's protest over the upheaval of change, he did it "expressionistically," in *The Adding Machine,* produced so successfully in 1923. Philip Barry, whose awareness of the temper of the times was no less keen, chose to do the same thing with sheer fantasy, in a tender and hilarious satire called *White Wings.* In his play, there is not only a street cleaner, but a horse—Joseph—who strenuously objects to the monsters that are pushing him off the street. Joseph was one of his most delightful characters, and, although there were backstage problems in fabricating a horse, he was one of Barry's favorite creations. (Joseph, in his antics and neighing indignation, might be compared with Lewis Carroll's animals in *Alice in Wonderland,* or with the creatures of the Irish poet, James Stephens.) In spite of its serious overtones, *White Wings* has been called Barry's "most appealing, gayest comedy." Opening-night performances received good reviews, and the audience for the most part came away with the tears of laughter mixed with pathos streaming down their faces. Congratulations from colleagues came pouring in; the actors and those connected with the performance expressed their joy in doing it.

Yet the play, produced early in 1926, lasted only three weeks. Possibly because of its undercurrent of social consciousness, or because its fantasy, as described by the critics, was difficult for the unimaginative to grasp, *White Wings* did not attract large audiences. And the producers, unwilling to take the chance that the enthusiasm of those who saw the show would gradually bring greater audiences, decided to close, to the dismay of theater people generally, let alone the playwright himself. Some of his friends urged Phil Barry to try to force the producers to keep the play going, but he was too much of a gentleman, in the best sense of the word. It was not in his nature to hound the financial powers-that-be for favors. He accepted their decision gracefully, and turned to another idea he had been considering in his mind for an entirely different sort of play.

Still experimenting, he began work on a religious drama, the story of John the Baptist. In *White Wings,* he had displayed thorough originality by means of whimsy; in the new play, he was to reveal a feeling for poetic mysticism that was no less a part of his make-up. Again, unlike O'Neill, Philip Barry had never suffered torment over his Irish Catholic upbringing. He may have questioned its concepts, searching for spiritual values of greater scope, but he never thought of leaving the church of his fathers. Moreover, he had married a Roman Catholic; so in general, he had never had to endure the writhings of religious conflict, never sought redemption, as O'Neill did in *Days Without End,* because he had not repudiated his early teachings. One reason for his writing *John* just at this time may have been that he needed the comfort of religion: the Barrys had received the severest blow of their married life—the loss of their infant daughter. The joy occasioned by her birth—for both of them had dearly wanted a daughter —was soon afterward turned into grief, which was never entirely erased. (They eventually had a second son, Jonathan Peter, but never another daughter.) It may have been to soften his grief that the playwright chose a religious subject.

Philip Barry's struggle was principally of an artistic nature—the desire to fulfill his yearning toward the serious as well as the comic in art. And with the play *John*, he began the long, uphill battle, which he never quite won, to express himself artistically both as the disenchanted and the believer. The religious drama (to be performed with the utmost simplicity, according to his stage directions) was in five acts and a single setting almost bare of stage furnishings. As an "experimental piece," it was produced by the Actors' Theater early in 1927, about a year after *White Wings*. But the public did not care for the mystical outpourings of a playwright who had just begun to win a name for himself as a modern skeptic, as an urbane writer of witty commentary on human emotions. In spite of its poetic aspects, *John* could not sustain the interest of the audience, and was withdrawn after ten performances.

Although he was rather stunned by its total failure, for even his kindliest critics had small praise for the Biblical drama that was his first attempt at serious writing, Phil Barry was not one to brood over the sad fate of *John*. Instead, he and Ellen decided to take a trip to Europe. It was a curious coincidence that the lack of success of their most recent plays should have brought Philip Barry and Elmer Rice together on a ship bound for Paris, and certainly it was a lucky happenstance for both of them. As they began to commiserate with each other, their sense of fun took over, and they started to hunt for an idea that would make a sure-fire hit. So *Cock Robin* was born. And if, after they parted company in Europe, Elmer felt that Philip placed an unfair burden of completing and polishing the mystery play on him, he was justified.

For by that time Philip Barry was already involved in writing the play that was to come much closer to the mark of a Broadway hit—*Paris Bound*. He was especially interested in the reactions of the young to the frenzy of the "jazz age," in the number of couples on shipboard—and in Paris—who were seeking a quick divorce, at the slightest refraction of rules, scarcely giving marriage a chance to succeed. In seeking out the reason for this divorce fever that appeared to be spreading among the lost generation, he found himself examining the values in the private relationship between man and wife; and he came upon an original idea, one that made his play more than a mere domestic comedy. *Paris Bound* dealt with the theme of infidelity in an entirely new way: it suggested that "casual adultery is too trivial a reason for destroying a marriage," as one critic put it. Quite unconsciously, Barry had reached the realm of high comedy—of the true comedy of manners—in *Paris Bound*.

In a series of scenes that shone with sparkling dialogue he exposed the false virtue in assuming that one misstep is grounds for divorce. The comedy, with its bright and breezy lines and fresh point of view, was as welcome on Broadway as a spring zephyr, and it established Philip Barry as a "dashing, debonair, sophisticated author of smart plays, with dialogue distinguished by biting wit," according to one critical estimate of his work. A few, like Richard Watts, who preferred the serious side of Barry, objected to the smartness of the lines, labeling them "occasionally meretricious" and glib; but reviews were generally glowing, and soon the box office had to put up the SRO sign for most performances.

Barry, pleased but not wildly elated, followed his first hit with another, considered by many his loveliest comedy, *Holiday*. In it, he returned to the minor theme of *In a Garden*—that of early retirement from making money in order to have time to live. Now he developed the idea, expanding it to include an indictment of materialistic values, and combining it with another of his recurrent themes—the father-daughter relationship wherein the domineering father is paradoxically dependent on his daughter. The play was an even greater success than *Paris Bound*, and increased the author's reputation as a witty, urbane, and polished playwright. Yet the quality that captivated his audiences, not immediately recognized, was Philip Barry's tenderness toward human nature, his tolerance for its frailty and weaknesses, his acknowledgment of human dignity and grace, in spite of those faults. His wit was not lacking in warmth, nor his accusation in understanding. It was not without basis that *Paris Bound* has been compared to Shaw's *Candida* for its combination of penetrating objectivity and affection. The people in Philip Barry's comedies are neither sentimental nor conventional, and in accomplishing their aims, they do not spill over or stray too far outside the pale. With seemingly little effort, Barry managed to stand on firm ground between O'Neill, at one end of the extreme, and S. N. Behrman or Elliott Nugent at the other.

He could not, however, remain on so narrow a plot. He strove to be remembered for more than the comedy of manners (no matter how skillful) which was his forte. Still plagued by the struggle between good and evil for men's souls, which had prompted him to write *John,* he set about employing his sense of fantasy in a serious vein. The result was his unique, almost mystic, psychological drama, *Hotel Universe.* In the setting of an ancient time-haunted chateau in southern France, he brought together six unhappy souls, wandering through the dark abyss of uncertainty in their lives; four are on the verge of suicide. By means of a two-hour-long one-act, done in a series of scenes, he sought to discover, by examining the six characters psychologically, the source of their unhappiness, the mystery of the universe within the mind.

Starting with a game, "Under the Piano," initiated in a bantering mood by one of the guests who acts out his childhood fears and fancies, the play explored the catalystic effect of the past on the present—the relationship of childhood to adult life, and the liberating effect of reliving childhood scenes. As each character in turn plays "Under the Piano," he or she acts out early joys and traumas, and so gains the insight to face the problems of the present with renewed strength or purpose. A recent estimate of *Hotel Universe* cites it as "one of the truly original masterpieces of modern American drama," which "may be called psychoanalysis transmuted into a work of art." And again: "With the warm humor lacking in *Mourning Becomes Electra* and the subtlety lacking in *Strange Interlude,* Barry created in *Hotel Universe* possibly the masterpiece of psychoanalytic drama." However, the critics of 1930 found

Barry's fanciful, analytic *tour de force* difficult to understand, baffling in its shifting time sequences, and confused in its philosophical content. Few, if any, grasped its significance as psychoanalytic drama, perhaps because of Barry's subtle artistry in applying modern science to the theater. Because the audience could easily identify with the characters, *Hotel Universe* had a surprisingly good run, considering the adverse criticism. It was later filmed, as were *Paris Bound, Holiday,* and most of Barry's box office successes.

Carrying out his theory in *Holiday,* the playwright did not exactly retire, but he took his family to live in the French resort at Cannes, on the Riviera. On his trip to Europe in 1927 (when the idea for *Hotel Universe* first came to him) Phil Barry had been charmed by the group of literary lights gathered together by Scott Fitzgerald at Cannes, and now he rounded out the circle. Here he wrote his next two plays—*Tomorrow and Tomorrow* and *The Animal Kingdom.*

Because of certain similarities, *Tomorrow and Tomorrow* was dismissed by some as a lesser *Strange Interlude;* but the drama it unfolds was based on the Bible story of Elisha and the Shunammite woman. Philip Barry had no desire—or need—to imitate O'Neill; but the allegory of the man of God who fulfills the longing of the childless wife of the Shunammite for a male offspring appealed to him for reasons of his own. He wanted to bring out into the open a third theme from *In a Garden.* Mentioned only in Lissa's wistful lines: "I wish I had a star.—Or a baby. But I shan't ever have either. Sad, isn't it?", the problem of the barren woman was suggested all through the play from the beginning. *Tomorrow and Tomorrow* offered a solution by means of the Biblical story, in terms of the twentieth century. Following the trend of the times, Barry presented Elisha in the guise of a psychoanalyst teaching a lecture course and assigned to the home of a prominent but childless couple during his stay in a small college town. Inevitably, he has an affair with the wife, and in due time after he leaves, a son is born.

The resolution of the play, not completely satisfactory, emphasized again Philip Barry's conviction that it is better to hold a marriage together as long as possible; that the ties that bind are not based totally on sex (indeed, that infidelity may be justified in certain cases); and finally, that unless there is utter incompatibility, divorce is to be avoided.

Tomorrow and Tomorrow was produced on Broadway in 1931, with Herbert Marshall and Osgood Perkins playing the respective roles of the psychoanalyst and the husband. Both splendid actors, they contributed not a little to the immediate success of the play, which, perhaps because of its Biblical origins, did not have Barry's inimitable touch of humor. A straight, serious drama, it was interesting largely because of its theme. Although in no way sensational, the central idea (related, it is true, to that of *Strange Interlude* but not derived from it) was provocative enough to give many people a jolt concerning the accepted values in marriage. Perhaps out of curiosity, perhaps because of the changing attitudes, the play had a surprising popularity in the hinterlands—on tour and in resident stock company productions. By no means superficial, it was less complex, less deeply probing, and much less devastating in its indictment of human behavior than *Strange Interlude*. Barry, who understood human anguish, did not himself suffer from untold torment and guilt as O'Neill did, and as a result, audiences were more at ease and sympathetic toward humanity in watching his play than O'Neill's.

The Animal Kingdom, which was produced in 1932, presented still another aspect of marriage, the spiritual relationship between man and wife; and again, because of its novel situation and fresh approach to human values, proved to be one of Barry's outstanding successes. In this play, the wife, who is beautiful and seductive but entirely lacking in comprehension or sympathy with her husband's interests, becomes in effect the "other woman." His mistress, herself a painter, who understands and encourages his artistic leanings, assumes the role of a wife. The husband, who, up to a certain point, allows himself to be seduced by the woman he has unfortunately married, leaves her in the end for the one he feels is truly a wife. The drama, essentially serious, contained wit as well as wisdom in its perceptive scenes depicting the subtle forces involved in the success or failure of a marriage.

The Animal Kingdom was produced by Gilbert Miller and the actor Leslie Howard, who played the role of Tom—the husband. When he read the play in manuscript, he was so taken with it that he agreed to become co-producer. The depression had made production of plays a doubtful risk for want of backers to begin with, and low box office receipts once it was on the boards. But the venture was an unqualified success, professionally and financially.

The depression years were lean ones artistically for Philip Barry. The social revolution, the awakening of the masses in basic industry, was less significant to him than the effect of that upheaval on the young—the changes it wrought in their sense of values. The three plays written from 1933 until 1938 were not fully realized examples of his art. *The Joyous Season,* in 1934, a Christmas play, revealed traces of Barry's Celtic mysticism and religious background in its history of a second-generation Irish family in Boston. The central figure was a nun, whose Irish Catholic mysticism motivates the action. The lines held much of the playwright's feeling about his religion, combined with his modern psychological approach to emotional problems, and an occasional flash of his elfin humor. This time it is a nun who leads her wealthy but snobbish and disillusioned brothers and sisters back into the past of their childhood to change their neurotic, cynical attitudes. By suggesting that they all return to their old home in the country (symbolically named "Good Ground") for the holiday, she helps them to rediscover the happiness of the earlier, simple life as against the cynicism of the proud Back Bay family they have become. In so doing —and not through theological preachments from her cloistered existence—the nun (superbly played by Ethel Barrymore) helps her family to revise their present values, and to give them a fresh start toward a life of fulfillment. Her answers to their neurotic problems are a little too *pat,* too quickly and simply accomplished. The return to childhood did not recall—as in *Hotel Universe*—any of the traumatic experiences of growing up but only the fond memories of an earlier time and a simpler mode of living. *The Joyous Season* was undoubtedly an attempt on Barry's part to reconcile his Roman Catholicism with his affinity for psychoanalysis; but it was too esoteric an attitude for most people, and did not get across the footlights.

Bright Star, his next offering, another variation of the same theme, belied its title. The drama of the political reformer who goes back to the New England mill town of his past in the hope of bringing about social changes, but finds only bitterness because of his frigid heart, was lacking in the luster people had come to expect of Philip Barry's lines. Dark and somber in mood, except for the brief sparkle of an occasional perceptive observation like, "The inability to love is just about the finest torture there is," *Bright Star* shone but dimly and went out soon after its appearance on Broadway.

Spring Dance, produced in 1936, although it had the freshness and charm of Barry's wit, was slight of texture, and not, strictly speaking, his creation. The vehicle had been a Vassar prize play written by two students, which he took over and refurbished when called in by the producer. However, it remained little more than a surface comedy of college manners.

The young actress making her Broadway debut, Louise Platt, did much to enhance the lines with youthful zest, but the substance was not there. Miss Platt was uncertain of her ability to play the brash comedic role she was called upon to portray; and one day when he was attending rehearsal, she asked Barry for his interpretation of the character. He explained, and, with his customary kindness and considerateness, made her feel much more at ease.

Nearing forty now, he was in appearance—and manner—every inch the polished gentleman. Always immaculately turned out, he resembled the successful insurance man or, more accurately, the suave diplomat in the foreign service he might so easily have become. His hairline had receded just enough to give him the distinguished high forehead, and his keen eyes still sparkled behind the glasses he had begun to wear. Sorrowed by the death of his infant daughter, whom he never forgot, his face frequently wore an expression of gentle gravity; but in general he was still genial and known as one of the most amiable, pleasant playwrights in the profession. He was a member of the Authors' League, where he was active (but not militant) in organizing the Dramatists' Guild. He belonged to the exclusive Century and Players' clubs, qualifying for both as a man of letters and distinguished dramatist. When he was in New York, he sometimes stopped by the bar at the Players' in Gramercy Park at cocktail time, where his quiet wit and easy elegance made him a popular and welcome addition. Any inner conflicts he had were self-contained, but his burden did not make him bitter toward the world of man—and the universe—as O'Neill was.

However, as the thunderous thirties rolled ominously along, he became increasingly alarmed over the spread of totalitarianism, which he saw at close range, since the Barrys still spent half the year in Cannes or Paris. He feared for the "city of lights" long before France fell into darkness under the goose-stepping feet of Hitler's hordes. One cause of the disinterest and dilution of lines in Philip Barry's depression plays was his preoccupation with the international scene, which he expressed first in a different medium —his only novel. A fantasy, called *War in Heaven*, it demanded to be dramatized almost before he had finished the manuscript. The result was his equally fantastic, and deeply probing psychological drama, *Here Come the Clowns*. In it, the playwright used the same means he employed in *In a Garden* and *Hotel Universe*—the acting-out of the past—to make his characters discover the truth about themselves and redirect the course of their lives accordingly. Completed in 1938 and produced in 1939, it preceded *The Iceman Cometh* by several years, yet the similarities are astonishing, especially since the dramatists were writing on different continents, and O'Neill had not been heard from in six or seven years.

Here Come the Clowns, set in a seedy café (almost as seamy as Harry Hope's saloon in *Iceman*), brings together a motley assortment of entertainers, all on the ragged fringe of show business. The café is owned by a former female impersonator, an effeminate man called Ma Speedy, and his patrons quite naturally include a magician, a midget, a ventriloquist and his dummy, and other cronies, one of whom is a chronic drunk. Another is a gentle, kind, deeply suffering Irishman—Clancy—who still mourns the death of his daughter, which took place many years before.

Whether Clancy is meant to be a partial self-portrait of Barry or not, it is significant that the Irishman should be the one who mourns the early loss of a daughter and who discovers, in the self-examination led by the wise magician, that he has been searching for a God-image all his life. (It is Clancy who is accidentally and fatally shot in the scramble for truth; but he dies happy, serene in the knowledge that he had been given a free will to look after himself, and that therefore God cannot be held responsible for the neglect and sad state of man.) As each one in the group goes through the therapy, he sights what is the truth for him; but, like O'Neill's characters in *Iceman*—and unlike Barry's in *Hotel Universe* and *The Joyous Season*—this sorry circle of clowns is too depraved to derive much help from the discovery, or to act on it. Although he does not state it as definitely as O'Neill, Barry seems to be saying that man is not strong enough to live without his illusions. The conclusion was his moment of cynicism after Munich. And when he returned from France with his family in 1939, he expressed the belief that there was much more inspiration for the artist in the United States than in Europe.

Here Come the Clowns was received with a mixture of bravos and bewilderment. Some of the critics, like Richard Watts, praised "the deep sensitivity and brooding compassion" of the play. Others called it morbid, vague, poetic, philosophical, religious, and antireligious. Few saw that it was deeply psychological, or that it was an extension of the theme of *In a Garden* and *Hotel Universe*. In any case, the play was not one to attract a large audience, and it closed after a relatively short run. Perhaps its greatest importance lay in the fact that it clarified the playwright's feeling about religion—the relationship of God and man—for himself if nobody else, and as such, spoke his maturity.

Since France—and Cannes—had lost its charm as a writer's haven, the Barrys bought a house on Jupiter Island, Hobe Sound, Florida, where Philip spent the winter months working, as he had on the Riviera. Perhaps because he had purged himself of his spiritual doubts and fears in *Here Come the Clowns,* perhaps because he was writing once again on home ground, or perhaps because he saw that the country was emerging from the depression with a new set of values, he was able to create his finest comedy of manners—*The Philadelphia Story*. Again, it was a play with serious overtones and penetrating psychological insight, for all the rapid-fire cleverness of its dialogue, its racy antics and bright laughter. And once more it was a mouthpiece of tolerance for human frailty, a well of compassion for the emotional conflicts of young and old.

The play, which probably represents the peak of Barry's art in his most familiar realm—the comedy of manners—combines the themes of two earlier works into a single composition that fairly sings in the felicity of its lines. Taking one of the ideas from his happiest hit, *Holiday*—the dependency of fathers on their daughters —the playwright proceeded to fuse it with the central motif of his much less successful offering, *Bright Star*, and that was the inability to love. But in *Story* he handled the latter with such grace, subtlety and zest, such affection for his character, Tracy Lord, that it brought the glow of real illumination to a subject that had once been regarded as "taboo" in the theater. When the drama came of age in the twenties, with the advent of psychoanalysis, frigidity was presented on the stage, but with a heavy hand—or so light a touch it was negligible. By the late 1930s, the American audience had grown sufficiently aware of the analytic method to recognize and understand the heroine's problem.

Furthermore, Philip Barry's presentation and solution was so deftly done—and so perfectly realized in the performances of the actors—that the public embraced it even as the critics hailed *The Philadelphia Story* with delight. Tracy Lord, as her name suggests, is a "virgin goddess," the proud daughter of a wealthy socialite family, who has been worshiped on a pedestal but not loved, because she has not been able to give love herself. As Barry develops the plot, he weaves in his shrewd observations on the changing attitudes of the young, wrought by the social upheaval of the thirties. Mike, the budding writer and political liberal, says with none-too-gentle irony, "The prettiest sight in this fine, pretty world is the privileged class enjoying its privileges," as he looks around at the extravagant preparations for Tracy's wedding. A product of the era that saw the Newspaper Guild come into existence, Mike is a character that Barry could not have created in the twenties. Tracy, for all her cool high-handedness, is basically warm, highly intelligent, and sensitive enough to be flexible in her judgment of human beings. "The time to make up your mind about people is never," she decides, for she realizes that she herself had deeply hidden impulses that might never have come to light. And she sees that people can and do change, both in their beliefs and their behavior.

As soon as *The Philadelphia Story* had settled down to its long Broadway run (to be followed by a highly successful film version), Barry began work on a new play, once more using the theme of the emotional dependence of fathers upon their daughters. But now, for the first time, he wrote from the point of view of the parent instead of the child. He certainly was not old—only forty-two—but his sons were growing up, and his daughter, if she had lived, would have been grown by now. It was time for him to stop writing about young people as if he were still in their shoes.

Like O'Neill, Philip Barry kept copious notebooks—small, pocket-sized—so he could slip them into his jacket if he felt like it. He started jotting down notes in one, under the heading "Daughter." But he followed with the surprising fragment: "The man of forty-two, at the end of his soul's rope, recovering from attempt at suicide." Then he began to develop the concept of the highly successful man—a lawyer—who has wrung the most he can out of his profession, who is divorced and lonely; his son has refused to become a lawyer (as the father had tried to force him to do) and has left home to go into the theater; and his daughter, to whom he has been too close, if anything, is about to marry a British colleague of his, a man twice her age, a "perhaps less benevolent despot. . . ." And it is this fear, combined with jealousy, which drives him to the point of attempting suicide. Mentally disturbed at times, he hears voices in the garden, calling to him from below. The character of the daughter, whom Barry decided to name Miranda, perhaps recalling *The Tempest,* was, like Tracy Lord, quick, intelligent, objective, "unemotional," to use her word. She loves her father deeply, but claims there is "nothing Freudian" in their relationship. As he envisioned Miranda, the playwright was probably thinking again of the daughter he had only been allowed to glimpse. His friend Sherwood was to write later: "I believe that in Phil's fanciful imagination this daughter lived and grew, and one may see his concept of her in girls that he wrote, especially Tracy Lord and Miranda Bolton."

When Barry had worked out a plot and a solution to the conflict of his characters, he put aside the first draft of the play until he could think it through carefully. He talked it over at various times with Bob Sherwood during the next ten years, but he did not complete the final draft until early 1949, and then he waited with revisions until casting should begin.

In between, he wrote three plays: *Liberty Jones,* in 1941; *Without Love,* in 1942; and *Foolish Notion,* in 1945. He also did an adaptation of J. P. Aumont's *L'Empereur de Chine*, in 1947, which he entitled *My Name Is Aquilon*.

The first two efforts, written during the war out of his deep anxiety for the future of the free world, were too concerned with ideological purpose to allow the art of his gleaming commentary to shine. In the third play, *Foolish Notion*, written right after the war, Barry again displayed his gift for tongue-in-cheek dialogue, for fantasy and originality in analyzing human behavior. His title, based on Robert Burns' lines to see ourselves "as ithers see us," gives a clue to the structure of the play, which consisted of five scenes, four of them fantasies. They are the enactments of imaginings in the minds of four central characters as they try to picture what the fifth—a veteran named Jim—will be like, and what will happen when he comes home from the war, bringing a girl he loves. The fifth and final scene brings the play back to reality with the actual arrival of Jim, and is of course quite different from any of those imagined.

In analytic terms, the comedy was a clever and perceptive study of "projection," wishful thinking, and "regression into the past." The dialogue shone with Barry's usual sharp banter, but was by no means shallow, and possessed his underlying warmth and affection for his characters, his tolerance for their incorrigible habit of complicating their lives. Produced with Tallulah Bankhead in the role of the actress-wife, the play should have been a success, but for some reason did not have the expected long run. Like his other fantasies, it was not thoroughly understood by the critics or the general public. The title itself was unfortunate, since most people did not get the reference to Burns and so missed the point.

The adaptation of the Aumont play was a flat failure, even though the French actor-playwright came over from Paris to star in the production.

It was disheartening, but Phil Barry was determined to keep on trying to blend his gift for high comedy with his equal but unrecognized talent for soul-searching drama, so that there would be no mistaking his intention. His next attempt would be the play he had been working at for eleven years, off and on. He had the feeling when he read over the last draft and began making final revisions that he had come closer to his goal than he had ever been before. If he was right, it would open up a whole new world of theater for him. He decided to call the play *Second Threshold*. He and Ellen had the script copyrighted in 1949, and went to New York to line up a producer. Revisions would depend largely on the casting.

Philip felt the tag-end tiredness he usually experienced when he completed a play, but he kept right on working, hoping for fall presentation. There were the normal aggravations and delays connected with casting. By the end of November, it looked as though he would not see production of this play on which he was pinning his hopes until spring. . . . But he was never to see *Second Threshold* performed.

On December 3, he suffered a heart attack, and a few hours later he had crossed the threshold from which he could not return. Ellen and the boys were beside his bed when he died. He was only fifty-three years old.

It was a little more than a year before Philip Barry's last play was produced, January 2, 1951, and by a strange coincidence, at the same theater—the Morosco—as his first play, thirty years earlier. As soon as she had recovered from the initial shock, Ellen Barry consulted their old friend Bob Sherwood about the possibilities of producing *Second Threshold*. Although Phil had discussed the project with him, Sherwood had not read the completed script, and he did so now. As he turned the pages, he was increasingly excited, moved by the sad melancholy of the central figure (middle-aged Josiah Bolton), yet at the same time entertained by the wit, vigor, and zany antics of the young people in the play—the daughter, Miranda; the son, Jock; the forthright young doctor; and the pretty co-ed.

Stirred into action, Sherwood was able to secure an immediate hearing for the play, and soon after, a producer, Alfred de Liagre, Jr. The Barrys' son, Philip, Jr., was production associate. Opening night reviews were generally good, but not enthusiastic. Clive Brook in the role of Josiah Bolton gave an impeccable performance, and the play ran about three months. Later estimates, however, agreed that in *Second Threshold* Barry had created a work of theater art fusing both his talents, perhaps not in the equal measure he had striven for, but one which realized an unequivocal merging of high comedy with the moving drama of human sorrow.

Most of the critical comment assumed that the title, as well as the drama, indicated that *Second Threshold* was Philip Barry's "swan song," his *Tempest,* and that he must have sensed that the end was near when he chose his title. But in a revealing Foreword to the published version of the play, his friend Sherwood voiced the opposite view. He began by explaining, "The work of revision that I did was in the nature of carpentry rather than creation. . . . What I have done on this play has been generously described as 'a labor of love.' I venture to protest that, despite my affection for Phil and Ellen Barry, it was no such thing. I was impelled solely by a sense of professional obligation. . . . I was often urged to change the title, which was considered puzzling, and the word 'threshold' difficult to articulate. But I couldn't bring myself to change it, for I firmly believed that it was on a second threshold that Phil Barry was standing when he died. I believe that had he lived to see this one through, he would have gained a new confidence, a new understanding of the qualities that were his, a new ability to employ them all. All of the American theater mourns his loss, and the absence of all that he did not live to write."

Later evaluations proved that Robert Sherwood was not alone in his estimate of his friend's gifts. Among others by prominent critics (including Gassner and John Mason Brown), perhaps the greatest esteem came in the summing up by David Sievers: "Certainly it falls far short to dismiss Barry as a witty writer of high comedy of manners, bantering, facile and superficial. . . . Beneath his flippancy was a sensitive and deeply spiritual writer coming to grips with the psychology of his times and expressing a yearning for maturity and emotional wholeness. No other American playwright was able to transmute the raw elements of unconscious life into a work of art so delicate, so subtly ingratiating, and so fresh in form, as did Philip Barry."

CHAPTER V

---●---

ROBERT SHERWOOD

As Robert Sherwood sat writing the revealing, elegiac foreword to his friend Phil Barry's last play, it was as if the spirit that guided his hand was even then giving the sign that "having writ," the Moving Finger would soon move on to Sherwood himself. For this dedicated playwright-citizen of the free world would be gone less than five years hence—worn out with a life devoted beyond the call of duty to his country and his convictions.

Born in the same year as Barry—only two months earlier, on April 4, 1896—Robert Emmet Sherwood had much the same conflict: in his love for the theater, he was divided between creating serious drama and high comedy, between intellectuality of purpose and pure entertainment. He came by his ardor naturally. His father, Arthur M. Sherwood, a successful investment broker, had a veritable passion for the theater, and was prevented from going on the stage only by his tremendous height (a physical trait his son was to inherit). Robert's mother, Rosina—born Emmet—Sherwood, was a descendant of the fighting Irish patriot whose name she bestowed on her son. A first-rate painter and illustrator, she did not allow her role as housewife and mother to interfere with her career,

99

and so was able to appreciate, to encourage, the artistic tendencies Robert began to show at an early age.

Like Phil Barry, Bob Sherwood started writing stories as a small boy, but fortunately was applauded instead of being frowned upon by his mother and sisters. At seven, he was editor of a hand-printed magazine called, *The Children's Life,* to which he was the main contributor, and his sisters the sole subscribers. A year later, he gave up his post for a more important project; he was rewriting *A Tale of Two Cities* because he disagreed with Dickens on the ending, which he considered a letdown after the excitement of the rest of the novel.

The Sherwoods had been living in New Rochelle at the time of Robert's birth, but had moved into Manhattan when he was two, so he was city-bred if not city-born, and took more than childish interest in all that New York had to offer—particularly the theater, to which his father introduced him while he was still in kindergarten. He soon became a connoisseur, and by the time he was eleven (in 1907), he had a play of his own, entitled *Tom Ruggles' Surprise,* ready for production, but it never came off. At thirteen he grew interested in American history, submitting an essay on Lincoln to a nationwide contest; it did not win, but planted the seed that flowered years later in one of his finest dramas.

After attending public school in New York City, the budding playwright was sent to Milton Academy, from which he graduated in 1914, the tallest boy in his class. At seventeen, he stood well over six feet, and was still growing. His great height was exaggerated if anything by his lanky body and elongated face. On the gym floor he loomed high above the other boys, and could no doubt have been the star basketball player of all time, but sports did not interest him to that extent. He was a ringleader in prep-school pranks, however, and showed such talent for getting into scrapes that he was once accused of setting a building on fire.

During his first two years at Harvard, where he enrolled in the fall of 1914, he lived up to his reputation as a scapegrace; but his high jinks, which led him to the verge of expulsion more than once, were properly channeled in his junior year, when he became Editor of *The Lampoon.* His father had been a founder of the magazine that soon became famous as an organ of satire on everything from politics to commercial publications. As editor, young Sherwood found the perfect outlet for his antic spirit in the parody of *Vanity Fair,* considered one of the cleverest issues ever brought out by *The Lampoon.* (Even Frank Crowninshield, editor of the real *Vanity Fair,* was impressed by the similarity between the two publications, and made a note of Sherwood's name.) Again in his father's footsteps, Bob joined the Hasty Pudding Club, but concentrated on writing instead of acting in plays as his father had.

It was evident from the first that he had a definite flair for dialogue, for crackling wit and action comedy. The annual Hasty Pudding show that year was *Barnum Was Right,* by Robert Sherwood, his first play to shine across the footlights. Then, before he could follow with a second offering in his senior year, America entered the war in Europe. He tried to enlist at once, but was rejected because of his great height, which by now was six feet and seven inches in his stocking feet; in a column of fighting "doughboys" he would be an easy target. Full of patriotic fervor, however, he was determined to get into the battle "to make the world safe for democracy." He joined the Canadian Black Watch without much trouble, although he was rather dismayed by his uniform. He was not going to let it stop him, however, and he was probably the tallest man ever to wear kilts!

He was a victim of the horror at Vimy Ridge, and, like most of the soldiers who survived, he never fully recovered from being gassed. Later he was wounded in both legs, a casualty which sent him to a hospital in England for a long time.

He was in a ward full of the wounded and dying, his bed between an Australian who had been terribly burned, and a South African Jew who had a machine gun bullet lodged in his spine and knew he would never walk again. The mixed gallantry and despair of the two men, one on either side of him, served to distract Robert's mind from his own pain, and also to drive home the fact that whatever heroism there might be, it could not compensate for the sheer horror of war. As the three of them lay on their backs in the hospital ward, day after day, calling back and forth to each other when they felt up to it, exchanging combat scenes and past histories, the misery, the senseless destruction of modern warfare hit young Sherwood full force. He swore he would debunk the history books that glamorized war, that he would put his future efforts into bringing peace, a lasting peace to the world. But he could not leave his hospital bed until months after the armistice was signed.

He stayed in England for a few weeks, regaining his strength at a place in Surrey; in the serenity of the surroundings, his inner calm returned, but that did not lessen his determination to denounce the mass murder, the needless tragedy of battle in the name of democracy, or whatever the name of the cause might be.

Back in New York once more, in the fall of 1919, he realized that before he could rouse the world to the dangers of self-destruction, he would have to have a job. Since he wanted to write, preferably for the theater, he applied for a job as drama critic on *Vanity Fair*. Frank Crowninshield, remembering the remarkable *Lampoon* issue of his magazine, offered Sherwood a post as motion picture critic, a new field, but related to the drama. Robert Benchley and Dorothy Parker were reviewing plays for the magazine, so Crowninshield could not promise much in drama, but if Sherwood were interested in the motion picture reviews— Bob was. He started work immediately. He would write plays on the side.

Still suffering from all he had been through, physically and spiritually, he set himself the task of returning to a normal life, working through the pain and weakness he felt at times, as if they did not exist. As a result of the gassing, he was to suffer all his life from tic douloureux, a facial neuritis which would seize him unawares with excruciating pain. As he grew stronger after the war, the seizures came less frequently; but toward the latter part of his life, when the pressures of World War II and public office were upon him, the attacks increased again to an unbearable pitch. Few people ever knew of this wretched ailment that put him through intermittent but severe trial. Only those close to him knew that his dour countenance was more often than not caused by physical pain of one sort or another. He was given to long silences, sometimes between sentences or words, or even syllables, which later became famous along with his "unsmiling, macabre laugh" as part of his eccentric personality, but in those long pauses he might be containing himself against a sudden spasm.

Yet the humor and high spirits in Bob Sherwood were irrepressible, and he was generally known for his good nature. He was shy, but with the people who became his fast friends, he would relax; he could often be the life of the party if he felt well enough. Besides Phil Barry, whom he met in 1921, when he reviewed Barry's first play, two close friends Bob made at this time were his colleagues, Robert Benchley and Dorothy Parker. (When there were several Broadway openings on the same night, he would cover a play occasionally for the magazine.) The three usually had lunch together, when they mulled over the problems and hazards of writing in general and playwriting in particular. Miss Parker, who was not yet known for her clever light verse, was nimble with words and dialogue, yet her attempts at playwriting did not seem to be successful. Benchley, too, kept trying his hand, but usually fumbled. Of the three, Bob Sherwood had had the most experience in playwriting and production, and this principally because of *Barnum Was Right* and the Hasty Pudding shows. Dorothy was selling short stories, but had no luck at all with plays. The three creative critics would discuss and analyze current Broadway productions, trying to figure out what made a hit. Like-minded, they tore plays apart with a good deal of relish.

In 1922, the drama critics of New York staged a show for charity, and it fell to Bob Sherwood's lot to put over a blues song. He was doubtful of his own ability, but he had a remarkable chorus, consisting of Lenore Ulric, Margalo Gilmore, June Walker, Helen Hayes, Winifred Lenihan, and a very young, pretty actress by the name of Mary Brandon. A niece of Booth Tarkington, Mary had come to New York with hopes of making as great a name for herself on the stage as her uncle had done in his books. Bob was attracted by her starry-eyed eagerness early in rehearsals, and long before the gala performance they were in love. What he had considered a misfortune became his "luckiest break" because of Mary. As he said later, he "picked her to be his leading lady" in private life, and they were married shortly after the show was over. (There were many notables at the wedding: Booth Tarkington; Phil and Ellen Barry, whose marriage took place the same year; and Douglas Fairbanks, who was an usher.)

They found a small apartment in New York, but Mary thought they should have a house in the country, especially if they were going to have children, and this fired the future dramatist's playwriting ambitions so that he doubled his efforts. He kept his job on *Vanity Fair* for bread and butter, however. One day Dorothy Parker burst into his office at the magazine and all but exploded. (Diminutive, bright-eyed, and high-strung, she was apt to lose her temper as quickly as she coined a phrase or quip.) She had just been fired! Benchley, hearing the disturbance, had come into the office, and the spunky little writer, when she could speak, regaled her two startled listeners with the facts: She had written a criticism which offended a Broadway producer. He protested to Mr. Crowninshield, who called her into the office and spoke to her about it; she must be less flippant in the future. She shot back at him with spirit (she hardly remembered what she said, but it was to the effect that she would write as she "damn pleased") and was told to "get out and stay out" by the irate editor.

Shocked by her story, Sherwood and Benchley went in turn to object to Frank Crowninshield's rash edict, "rising manfully to the defense of the critic, and the right of woman to speak her own mind." But he was adamant, and they both quit their jobs in protest. They were not called back.

It did not take Bob Sherwood long to find another post, this time on the old *Life* magazine, where he initiated the first regular motion picture column. He was inclined to give movies the same consideration as plays, and his criticism was of such a high order of intelligence that he received a phone call one day from Carl Sandburg, complimenting him on his column. It was the beginning of a long literary friendship, and one that rekindled the playwright's interest in Abraham Lincoln. Before long, he became Editor of *Life,* a position he held for the next three or four years. From there, he went to *Scribner's* as Literary Editor; he also reviewed plays for the New York *Herald.* All this time he was writing plays, experimenting with different forms—and reading, reading enormously in history, and Shaw's modern treatment of it, in plays like *Caesar and Cleopatra, Androcles and the Lion, Man and Superman,* and other works that debunked the heroism of war heroes and presented the formidable personages of history with a casual intimacy that stripped them of glamour and added a human touch.

From the Roman history courses in his schools years, Robert had formed a juvenile hero worship of Hannibal; but now, disillusioned, he decided to divest the general's act in abandoning the siege of Rome of some of its nobility. Partly influenced by Shaw, he sought to account for a celebrated historical fact by finding the woman behind it. In Bob Sherwood's delightful, tongue-in-cheek version, it was Amytis, wife of Fabius Maximus, who, feeling neglected and unfulfilled, managed to slip into the enemy camp and seduce Hannibal; in the process, she makes him see how senseless the destruction of Rome would be. In a sword-play exchange of words, she jabs at his stature as a general: "I want you to believe that every sacrifice in the name of war is wasted. When you believe that, you will be a great man," she tells him earnestly. And again, when he speaks of Fabius as "cruel," she counters: "You say he is cruel. Is there any soldier who is otherwise?" There were many passages in which Sherwood spoke his hatred of war, mostly through the mouth of Amytis.

Since so much depended upon her lines—clever and charming, at times brittle, but with underlying warmth and deadly seriousness— it was important to find just the right actress for the role of Amytis. When Jane Cowl opened in *Easy Virtue,* Bob and Mary Sherwood attended the performance, and both agreed that Miss Cowl would make a superb Amytis, if she were interested in playing the role. Bob decided to find out. He met the actress soon afterward and presented his idea so persuasively that she was not only interested but enthusiastic. She arranged a meeting with her producers, William Brady, Jr., and Dwight Deer Wiman, which turned out happily for all, especially the young playwright. Brady and Wiman accepted the script at once, and *The Road to Rome,* starring Jane Cowl and Philip Merivale, made theater history as the smash hit of 1927.

The surprise success made his job at *Scribner's* unnecessary, so he resigned. He wanted to devote all his time to playwriting. He now had a daughter, Mary, and a house in the country, and, although he might still need his weekly salary, he did not want to rely on it. He would strive harder to write good plays if he knew his living depended on it. His country house was in Surrey, where he had purchased a large rambling home, fulfilling the dream of nearly ten years before.

Here he wrote *Waterloo Bridge,* this time an anti-war romance, which brought out the psychological and emotional damage suffered by a young girl who is about to jump off the bridge as a result of her war experiences. She is saved by an American soldier, a battle-haunted veteran, and his act brings them both to the edge of disaster before the plot is resolved. The play was well received in England where the audiences could understand and identify with the heroine, but Broadway theatregoers seemed indifferent to the plight of the sensitive young girl; a decade had passed since the armistice was signed, and in the United States the effects of cannon fire were forgotten in the blare of gangsters' machine guns or wailing saxophones in an age of prohibition and jazz. (Some years later, close to World War II, the play was made into an artistic and touching film, for which Sherwood wrote the screen play, improving the plot in the process.)

The Sherwoods spent much time in Europe in the "old-world" city of Vienna, which had not lost the charm of a bygone era. It was there that the mischievous idea for *Reunion in Vienna* came to Bob Sherwood. A lively comedy concerning a psychoanalyst, his most attractive wife, and her former lover, it was a subtle satire on the science that came to light in Vienna, and, with its founder, was in its heyday at that time. Literary figures from England and America came to the Austrian capital to be analyzed by the great doctor Freud or his disciple, Jung. Whether Sherwood saw his friend Phil Barry in Vienna or not, there are unmistakable signs that they discussed psychoanalysis as they often exchanged ideas on various subjects for plays, and they were both in Europe in the thirties. *Reunion in Vienna* combines the themes of *In a Garden* and *Tomorrow and Tomorrow,* but treats them with jaunty humor and gentle joshing to imply that even the great Freud might be human enough to lack insight into his own family. The play presented, as the playwright himself phrased it, "Science hoist with its own petard," and established its author's unmistakable flair for high comedy. Produced by the Theatre Guild in 1931, with Alfred Lunt and Lynn Fontanne in the starring roles of Rudolf and Elena (the former lover and the analyst's wife), the play ran for over three hundred performances before it showed any indication of slowing down.

The success of *Reunion in Vienna* posed the same problem for Bob Sherwood that Phil Barry had to face after *Paris Bound* and

Holiday—the question of being considered a serious or comedic writer. In addition, Sherwood had to contend with his underlying purpose in *The Road to Rome*—the spread of pacifism, born of his deep hatred of war. He was to be more adroit than Barry in fusing his disparate urges and talents, but they caused him no less conflict, amounting at times to intellectual anguish as he wrestled with weaving ideas into plot and dramaturgy.

By an interesting (and ironic) coincidence, the Sherwoods were separated not long after *Reunion in Vienna,* and in 1934, the playwright went to Reno to establish the six weeks' residence necessary for a divorce. In the first four of those six weeks, he wrote the penetrating and highly charged work that, in his words, was an "attempt to show the passing of an epoch in terms of melodrama and assembled characters"—*The Petrified Forest.* For some time he had been concerned with the dying civilization he had witnessed in both Europe and America, and his leading character was the frustrated, suicidal representative of the degenerate era that followed the war. He realized that he would have to camouflage his basic concept in order to make it acceptable. As he demanded of Lucius Beebe in an interview the day after production, "do the great run of theatergoers peel off bank notes to see an Indian fighter, a millionaire, and an American Legion symbolize the passing of a world order? They do not. They come to see two parts of highly improbable and sentimental romance stirred, like a Martini, with one part gun-play." He concluded with a humorous shrug, "The trouble with me is that I start with a big message and end with nothing but good entertainment." (Burns Mantle called such talk "typical Sherwood belittling of a rare talent that successfully combined sane thinking with exciting writing," and hailed him as "a melodramatist who, in place of pretending to despise the hokum of our theatre, frankly embraces it with noble purpose and to fine effect." His remarks may have been in reply to the critic who accused Sherwood of "perpetrating hokum of the highest type on the American public.")

Hokum or no, *The Petrified Forest* was chilling melodrama bordering on true tragedy, and was an overnight success when it appeared on Broadway early in January, 1935. Leslie Howard, as Alan Squier, the unfulfilled intellectual of a decaying society on the road to a second world war, and Humphrey Bogart, as Duke

Mantee, the fascist dictator of the underworld, both gave unforgettable performances, and drove home the full import of the lines to those who had the wit to grasp them. Sherwood had been reading Jung, and his protagonist carries, among his meager possessions— which include besides shirt, underwear, socks and toothbrush, a passport and an insurance policy—a copy of Jung's *Modern Man in Search of a Soul*. As he talks to Gabby, the refreshing young girl in the gas station on the Arizona desert—the play's locale—he makes some remarkable observations in the course of his oblique expression of his love for her. Like a kindhearted but dispirited mentor, he tells her, in speaking of man's so-called conquest of Nature: "They've dammed it up, and used its waters to irrigate the wastelands. They built streamlined monstrosities to penetrate its resistance. They wrapped it up in cellophane and sold it to drugstores. They were so certain they had it subdued. And now—do you realize what it is that is causing world chaos? . . . It's Nature hitting back. Not with the old weapons—floods, plagues, holocausts. We can neutralize them. She's fighting back with strange instruments called neuroses. She's deliberately afflicting mankind with the jitters. . . ." That his speech is applicable to the state of the world thirty years afterward is almost eerie testimony to Robert Sherwood's uncanny prescience.

His fears in regard to the world "jitters" were reinforced when he returned to Europe after his divorce. The Sherwoods had met Marc Connelly's ex-wife, Madeleine Hurlock, in their travels on the continent, and Bob had taken an immediate liking to her. Now they were married in Budapest, the city of so many cross currents of culture. It was while he was honeymooning there that the idea for his next play, *Idiot's Delight,* was suggested by a troupe of American cabaret performers appearing in the capital. For purposes of plot structure he brought the cabaret dancers (led by an ex-vaudeville promoter) into a collision with the formidable starting-point of the Second World War. At a tourist resort in the Italian Alps where they are performing, they became involved with a munitions maker, a German scientist, a French Communist, a variety of Italian Fascists, and a sprinkling of passive noncombatants. Among the widely mixed group, they represented almost every angle of the war threat; and through these diverse characters, it is analyzed with humor, excitement and mounting tension. In a postscript to the play, Sherwood wrote an impassioned plea for sanity and peace: "If decent people will continue to be intoxicated by the synthetic spirit of patriotism, pumped into them by the megalomaniac leaders, and will continue to have faith in the security of those lethal weapons sold to them by the armaments industry, then war *is* inevitable; and the world will soon resolve itself into the semblance of an ant-hill, governed by commissars who owe their power to the profundity of their contempt for the individual members of the species.

"But I don't believe this will be so. I believe that a sufficient number of people are aware of the persistent validity of the Sermon on the Mount, and they remember that, *between 1914 and 1918, twelve million men died in violence* to make safe for democracy the world which we see about us today. That awareness and remembrance can be strong enough to resist the forces which would drive us back into the confusion and the darkness and the filth of No Man's Land."

Whether the theatergoers who witnessed the opening night performance of *Idiot's Delight* in 1936 grasped his "big message" in its entirety is doubtful; but it is certain that they received "good entertainment" and came away delighted. Again the Lunts starred in the play, which was hailed by the critics and held up as a happy combination of high comedy and true drama. A perfect vehicle for the Lunts, it displayed their talents to the full for a rousing, zestful performance, a highly intelligent interpretation of the lines. The 1936 Pulitzer prize was awarded unanimously to *Idiot's Delight,* but came as something of a surprise to Bob Sherwood, who was not inclined to take recognition of his accomplishments for granted. He was always doubtful of getting his message across the footlights. Much of the time he felt as if his was the "voice crying in the wilderness," although the comic element in his make-up usually sprang up to dispel his gloominess.

He was forty years old now, and, when he was in New York (for he still lived in Surrey during the summers), he moved in theatrical circles—a Don Quixote of Broadway, exceedingly tall and somber, with his woeful countenance (darkened further by a heavy mustache he had grown a few years before) and incredibly elongated head. Certainly he was battling the windmills about half the time. He championed the playwrights against the producers' high-handed practices; and, more dynamic than his friend Phil Barry, was one of the leaders in the Dramatists' Guild. With Elmer Rice, he initiated the formation of the Playwrights Company, which took place a year later. (He wanted Barry to be a member; but Elmer, recalling his experience with *Cock Robin,* was doubtful, and Phil was not one to force his way, so Bob wisely did not press his affiliation.) When they were in the throes of organization, wondering about the success of their venture—"on tenterhooks," someone said, which led to a request for a definition of the phrase, Bob supplied it quickly: "The upholstery of the anxious seat." It was this agility of mind and his spirited attitude toward the issues of the moment that endeared Bob Sherwood to his colleagues and made his intervals of silence negligible.

Although he hated large gatherings, he enjoyed small parties among close friends, and was known to furnish a solo song and dance with little persuasion. (His imitation of Ted Weems, with top hat and cane, followed by a tap routine, was one of the gems of back-stage celebrations.) Certainly he was no hermit like O'Neill, nor did he need solitude—with a capital "S"—to write; the back country or seaside setting was not necessary to his creative process. He did not, in fact, like the country as such. (His home in Surrey was rustic, but not isolated.) He preferred the city at times, found himself stimulated by the clamor and bustle of Manhattan; if need be, he could write in an office, as he did a few years later. Although he traveled extensively, he did not seek the uninhabited nooks and crannies of the globe, but nearly always the large centers—London, Paris, Vienna, Budapest—where he could mingle with the world.

For relaxation, following *Idiot's Delight,* the playwright turned out *Tovarich,* a sheer comedy and slight spoof of the effect of the Soviet Revolution on the white Russians who managed to escape. He had encountered a good many of the deposed nobility in the capitals of Europe, engaged in any kind of work (usually domestic) to earn a living, and all kinds of intrigue to bring about a counter-revolution in their country. *Tovarich* (Comrade) took a poke at class distinctions and also at the ideology that leveled them all into one, the proletariat. It was a tremendous moneymaker on stage and screen; and part of the proceeds was used by the author to further his campaign for aid to Britain, for the spread of democracy in the face of dictatorship.

For some time, possibly on his return from Europe with the script for *Idiot's Delight,* Bob Sherwood had begun to feel more optimistic about the future of his own country and its form of government. The interests of the common man, the feeling of brotherhood among the working class that emerged from the New Deal, stirred his respect and renewed faith in democracy. (He became an ardent New Dealer, and broadened his activities beyond the proscenium arch. Besides being President of the Dramatists' Guild, he was involved in slum clearance and a municipal housing project in New York.) In his admiration for the leadership of F.D.R. and the ultimate effectiveness of the democratic process, Sherwood found himself dwelling again on the towering figure of Abraham Lincoln. His close contact with the work and theories of Carl Sandburg on the Great Emancipator led him to a closer study of Lincoln, particularly in the early years when doubts and fears must have assailed him. The result, after some discussion of the subject with the poet-historian, was his masterful biographical drama, *Abe Lincoln in Illinois,* a play that revealed the earnestness, the true seriousness of Robert Sherwood. His portrait of the young lawyer-politician struggling to overcome "the civil war going on inside himself" (because of his feeling of inferiority despite his strong convictions against slavery) was subtly shaded and three-dimensional, yet drawn with the utmost simplicity. And in the very plainness, the homeliness of its writing, lay much of the play's eloquence, the quality that gave it the aura of a classic—an American classic. Again Sherwood gave the formal textbook figure the human touch and so made him real. He depicted an Abraham Lincoln wise but not yet strong, wavering before his political fate, harking "to the whispers of the women behind him—his dead mother—" It required the strength of a Mary Todd to inspire him with the drive to act upon his convictions and assume the leadership his country sorely needed.

Produced in 1939, with Raymond Massey giving full realization to the role of Lincoln, the drama was accorded universal acclaim, including the Pulitzer prize for that year. Lincoln's eloquent lines denouncing slavery, his ultimate resolve to move forward to meet the challenge, represented Sherwood's dawning realization that an intellectual with an ounce of common sense as well as brains could embrace a purpose—and, if he had creative ability, could be no less an artist. The playwright's purpose was clear: to stop the spread of fascism, the darkness of dictatorship that was swiftly closing down over all of Europe, placing both England and America in imminent danger.

He began to take an active leadership in Union Now, the organization headed by Clarence Streit urging concerted action by democratic countries against dictatorship. From the first Sherwood had been an advocate of the unified effort, and also of aid to Britain, but now he assumed the responsibility of official posts, and doubled his work on behalf of both causes. In an attempt to draw a parallel between the dying civilization of ancient Greece and the current crisis in Europe, he wrote a play called *Acropolis,* but it was a failure because the picture was too remote from the terrible events taking place in the fall of 1939. While he was trying to rewrite the script at his home in Surrey, the sickening word came of the enemy invasion of Finland, news both frightening and stirring.

His sense of outrage flared up in defense of the helpless Finns. He was in a turmoil—he, Bob Sherwood, the hater of war, the ardent pacifist, who had written "that every sacrifice in the name of war is wasted"; who had issued the powerful plea against war and the weapons of war in his postscript to *Idiot's Delight*—he was ready to rush into battle! So deeply stirred he could think of nothing else, he was galvanized into action after hearing W. L. White's dramatic broadcast from the Karelian front on Christmas Day. He sat down and began to write furiously, and inside of a few weeks had created *There Shall Be No Night,* including only a single speech from *Acropolis* in the new work. For the published version of the play, he wrote not a postscript this time, but a Foreword, offering a direct and fearless explanation of his complete "about-face," not so much to defend his position as to promote it. He wanted the world to feel the same urgency he felt to resist the forces of evil, if necessary with force itself. Not because war was morally any more right than it had been before, but because it was necessary to give mankind the chance to mature enough to know how to live at peace with his fellow men.

Elmer Rice

Susan Glaspell in about 1926

Eugene O'Neill, taken at Tao, O'Neill's home in Northern California about 1949

Philip Barry as a beginning playwright, 1924

Robert Sherwood at his desk in New York, 1953

Maxwell Anderson

Sam and Bella Spewack in the Twenties

Howard Lindsay and Russel Crouse, two long-time collaborators, in 1950

Elliott Nugent

One of the last photos of James Thurber before his death

The Kaufman-Hart combine at the peak of their partnership, just after winning the Pulitzer prize for *You Can't Take It With You*

Lillian Hellman discusses drama (with gestures) during her seminar course at Yale University, 1966

Clifford Odets scanning a movie script of his play, *None but the Lonel*
Heart, with Ethel Barrymore, in 1944 (The film marked his debut a
director)

Thornton Wilder in his library about 1959

Tennessee Williams

A recent photo, following Arthur Miller's marriage to Inge Morath

William Inge (between actress Lee Remick and master of ceremonies Jack Lemmon) at Academy Awards presentation for *Picnic,* 1962

United Press International Photo

United Press International Photo

Edward Albee (in 1963) standing in front of the Provincetown Playhouse, where his first successful one-act play, *The Zoo Story,* was produced in 1960, over forty years after the one-act plays of the sea, which launched O'Neill's career, were produced here by the Provincetown Players

The play itself concerned the plight of Dr. Valkonen, a psychiatrist, an intellectual of the highest order—friend of Freud, Jung, Pavlov, the Mayos; and a Nobel prize winner—who chooses to remain in his country fighting with the resistance forces against the army of invasion rather than flee. As the curtain rises, the doctor is to make a radio address; and as he speaks, his voice is Sherwood's voice, crying in the wilderness perhaps, but revealing his philosophy in earnest, moving tones. In going to London after the Nazis invaded Austria, the doctor says, "Freud was technically free—but he was silenced. What did he then have to live for? Nothing. . . . So he died. . . . No—I will not leave." And at the close of the play, although his son is dead, and the doctor himself is doomed, his daughter-in-law has gone to the United States, where she will bear his son's child. From the schoolroom converted into an ambulance station, Dr. Valkonen acknowledges that war is evil, but a necessary evil to stop the tyrant so that in some future generation the light will dawn and "there shall be no night." His final speech contains challenge as well as hope: "We have within ourselves the power to conquer bestiality, not with our muscles and our swords, but with the power of the light that is in our minds. . . . The true defenses of man are *in* man, himself."

As soon as the script was completed, it went into production by the Playwrights Company, with the Lunts once more in the leading roles. Opening night was March 29, 1940, and proved to be more effective than any of them had dared to hope. The audience was deeply touched by the moving drama. The critics praised Sherwood's fearless protest against imperialism, and the public responded by attending all performances. *There Shall Be No Night* played to full houses, and the playwright, pleased and gratified, gave most of his royalties to the Red Cross for aid to Finland and Britain. He was so committed to his cause that he could not be content until his message rang out across the country. Beginning in November, 1940, the play went on a twenty-eight weeks' tour, covering forty-five cities in nineteen states and two Canadian provinces. As usual, Bob's great height—or length—was a detriment to him in traveling on trains: he never could fold his long legs into a berth and suffered all sorts of torture trying to get comfortable enough to catch a little sleep. He would have begged off, but he felt it was important for him to be on hand with this play, at least until the itinerary was well along. Later, a second tour, made up mostly of one-night stands in little towns through the South and Middle West, took on the air of a crusade, but they all stuck it out till the end.

In between, Sherwood actively supported Roosevelt's crucial campaign for a third term, and, directly after Pearl Harbor, was asked to join the White House staff of writers. He accepted, and at that time turned over his house in Surrey to the British government as a refuge for London children during the blitz. For a while he served as a special assistant to the U.S. Secretaries of War and Navy. He was in charge of the Committee on Education, Recreation, and Community Service of the U.S. Army, and was First Assistant to Colonel W. J. Donovan, Coordinator of Information, sending short-wave broadcasts to Europe. He wrote in a heavily guarded building in New York and under pressure of time, but he was so imbued with the spirit of the battle for freedom that he hardly noticed. He became head of the Overseas Branch of the OWI, a heavy responsibility, but he took it on without considering the loss of his personal career or his physical strength.

During the 1944 election campaign, he of course supported Roosevelt, this time writing some of F.D.R.'s finest speeches, in collaboration with the President and Judge Sam Rosenman. And after the war, when both Roosevelt and Hopkins had died, Sherwood undertook the gigantic task of going through the forty filing cases of papers that Harry Hopkins had left—a massive but helter-skelter record of the brilliant but ambivalent association of these two colorful personalities who so often clashed. Fascinated by the hidden facets of both men revealed in the wealth of material, Sherwood was impelled to create an orderly document of the papers, unconsciously including his own impressions. He spent thirty months in steady work on a perceptive, detailed study, *Roosevelt and Hopkins,* nearly a thousand pages long, intended and published (on his part) solely as a serious work, without a thought of the popular market.

To his surprise, the book, subtitled, *An Intimate History,* had enormous dramatic appeal for the general public. It became a best-seller, and won for Bob Sherwood his fourth Pulitzer award, this time in history. He found himself famous in alien fields: he was in great demand as a screenplay writer, and accepted an offer to write the script for *The Best Years of Our Lives,* including an interest in the production, which was highly successful, and won an Oscar award. He also was offered a contract for a television series at "unheard-of terms," and he did write a few scripts, but after a short time he annulled the contract. He was exhausted from his long and arduous labor during and just after the war years. His attacks of the douloureux were at times so severe that he had to take morphine to dull the pain enough to go on working. His family and the doctors suggested neurosurgery with the hope that he would be permanently free of pain, and frequently he would consider going into the hospital; but he was afraid of facial paralysis, which occasionally resulted from the operation, and his fear was stronger than the agony of pain, once an attack subsided. (With the next seizure, he might again consider surgery, but he never went through with it.)

His condition was aggravated also by financial worries, in spite of the huge sums of money he had made, not because of donating his royalties to various causes during the war, but because the man in charge of his investments embezzled most of the fortune he had made on *The Road to Rome* and the other early plays. It was a shocking blow, because he had trusted the man completely, both as a friend and business associate, and the fact that the guilty party went to prison did not help the Sherwoods, who were used to living on a lavish scale. They had to give up the house in Surrey, which would have been ideal for the playwright just at this time.

His true interest was the theater, and although he admitted cheerfully at one period, "To be a successful playwright you have to cheat a little," he now wanted and needed desperately to write without cheating, even a little. Directly after VE Day, he had given vent to his feelings of relief, mingled with his continued belief in the fight for freedom over tyranny, in a play called *The Rugged Path.* His title was taken from an early Keats poem, quoted by Lincoln in the closing speech of the first scene of *Abe Lincoln in Illinois.* The plot again depicted the inner struggle of the sensitive man vacillating in his ideals, but finally choosing the rugged path of battle unto death to insure a better world in the future. Powerful in some of its scenes and lines, the drama lacked his sure touch, his sense of theater, and perhaps showed too strongly the traces of Sherwood's political dialectics. At any rate, in spite of the fact that the Playwrights Company produced it immediately, and also were able to secure Spencer Tracy for the leading role, the play failed. (The movie actor was nervous about appearing on the stage again after so many years in films, and, although the tryout in Providence played to full houses, it was obvious that the crowds came out of curiosity to see a movie actor. There was hardly more than polite interest in the play, and it required all the persuasive power that Bob Sherwood and Elmer Rice could summon through a whole night's confab to convince Spencer Tracy that he should open with the play in New York. When it was forced to close after a brief run, something in Bob Sherwood failed also.)

Heartsick, the playwright turned historian, and it struck him as ironic that John Mason Brown commented that Sherwood's *Roosevelt and Hopkins* was "his finest drama, and the most titanic in scale he has so far written." (In addition to the Pulitzer prize, the book received the Bancroft award for distinguished writing in American history, the Gutenberg Award of the Book Manufacturers' Institute, and was named the Book of the Year by the *Saturday Review*.)

No matter how much honor he might gain from other works, it could not compare with the soul-satisfying reward of good playmaking. To create a fine serious drama, to hear its lines strike a responsive chord in the audience, to regain the height he had reached in *Abe Lincoln in Illinois*—that was his goal. But it was too late, and he had been too long away. After he had done the "carpentry work" on Phil Barry's last play, he sought his own second threshold, but he could not find it. He tried various means. With fine bravado, he collaborated with Moss Hart and Irving Berlin on a musical, *Miss Liberty*. He started a long narrative play about the Mormons and their pursuit of freedom to worship as they chose, only to turn to bigotry themselves as soon as they won. He wrote another shorter historical drama, *Small War on Murray Hill*, but it lacked the spirit and the artistry that once had shone so brilliantly. He was plagued by his peculiar ailment, hounded by pain. He wrote doggedly, trying to override it. Then suddenly his long lanky body succumbed, and he died on November 14, 1955.

Whether Robert Sherwood ever realized that becoming a public citizen meant sacrificing his art as playwright, he could not have done otherwise. He could not have isolated himself, like O'Neill, in some remote castle, there to write about man's inner struggle for fulfillment while war raged in the outside world. It was not in his nature to sit writing in an ivory tower while persecution prevailed and freedom failed in country after country. Just as he had been against the senseless butchery of World War I, so he had to denounce the more devastating massacre and the denial of freedom before and during World War II. And up to a certain point, he was successful in blending his "big message," at first with good entertainment, and later with true artistry in playwriting. He reached the high point with *Abe Lincoln in Illinois*. And although in 1942 a critic summarized Sherwood's career by commenting, ". . . the consensus is that he is among the few American masters of high comedy, and that his desperate earnestness in recent years has added both depth and stature to his work," it is also true that, beginning with *There Shall Be No Night*, his plays were weighted down by his message.

His friend and close colleague, Elmer Rice, returning from a P.E.N. conference in Europe shortly after Sherwood's death, observed that the failure of *The Rugged Path* was a severe blow to Bob, following which his playwriting ability, like his health, steadily declined. Rice wrote a memoir for *The New York Times*, in which he tried to show how Sherwood's work reflected his character and psychological conflicts. (Saddened and depressed, Elmer had no heart to find another dramatist to take Bob Sherwood's place in the Playwrights Company, which broke up shortly afterward.) But whatever his conflicts, Robert Sherwood's contributions to dramatic literature are large, and his position as playwright-citizen is close to the top.

CHAPTER VI

———◆———

MAXWELL ANDERSON

Of all the playwrights to come into prominence in the late twenties and thirties, Maxwell Anderson, born two months after O'Neill, on December 15, 1888, rose from a background farther removed from the theatrical scene than any. His childhood was spent among the religious nomads of the Protestant church: his father, the Reverend William Lincoln Anderson, was a Baptist minister, who had just accepted a pastorate at Atlantic, Pennsylvania, when Maxwell arrived. But soon the Call came from other Pennsylvania towns, and as the Reverend moved around, he took his family with him. Maxwell's mother, the former Premely Stevenson, closely allied with her husband in church work, was accustomed to being "on the march" for Christianity. They made a slow but steady trek westward, through Ohio, Illinois, Iowa, and on to the Dakotas.

They led the typical itinerant ministerial life, which meant they had to accept whatever accommodations and living conditions the congregation could afford, and usually these were hardly adequate, bare of comfort, but often in pleasantly rural surroundings. The trouble was that as soon as one place became familiar, just when Maxwell began to feel at home in the neighborhood and school, his father would accept another Call, and the family moved on. However, the boy managed to glean a little learning from each village or township school he attended, which, supplemented by poetry readings and Shakespeare, amounted to a better-than-average education. He was nineteen when the family finally settled in North Dakota, where, somewhat to his surprise, he was eligible for the University of North Dakota. He graduated four years later, in 1911, and the same year married Margaret Haskett, one of the early "co-eds" at the university. He taught in Dakota township schools for a couple of years, but the salary was hardly enough to keep newlyweds. He and Margaret both wanted to live in California, so he applied to Leland Stanford, and received a teaching Fellowship while he studied for a Master's degree in English literature.

Armed with the added title, he went to join the faculty of Whittier College in Southern California in the fall of 1914, just as the First World War was shaping up in Europe. From his father's sermons, backed up by his mother's vehement approval, Maxwell had imbibed the doctrine of peace-on-earth to the point of blind credo, and he made no secret of it now. Rather, he promoted his views on campus when the subject of the war came up. He was violently against the United States' entry into the European struggle and he lost no opportunity to say so. He attended, and urged his students to attend, pacifist rallies.

His colleagues and superiors on the college faculty viewed his attitude with shocked amazement. To them it was downright unpatriotic if not treason, and Max Anderson seemed the last person to be a revolutionary. Mild-mannered and soft-spoken, he appeared retiring and tractable in spite of his great bulk. Over six feet tall, he was heavily built, with a full-moon face and massive head covered by a mane of dark wavy hair (which might have been called leonine, but was more like a big fuzzy brown bear). His large brown eyes were more earnest than fiery; and the fact that he should be vigorous, not to say militant, about any issue, let alone pacifism in time of imminent war, seemed doubly impudent. He was sent first a Memorandum, and then a warning from faculty supervisors to desist, but he kept on going to pacifist meetings, airing his views with calm, firm insistence. The upshot was that he was fired from Whittier College; but neither he nor Margaret were sorry to leave. Aside from his disagreement with its narrow chauvinism, Max felt that the school—and teaching in general—did not pay enough to support a family. The Andersons had two sons, Quentin and Alan, and were expecting another baby soon. They returned to San Francisco, where Maxwell got a job on the San Francisco *Bulletin*. All might have gone well, except that he was an editorial writer, which gave him excellent opportunity for spouting his theories on the international scene, reaffirming his belief in pacifism as the wisest course. His employers soon decided he was "too outspoken," as he said later, asked him to "look around for another job." He went over to the *Chronicle* in San Francisco for a while, but here, too, he was considered a "radical" because he advocated peace, or non-intervention, as the surest means of peace.

Hardly knowing where to turn next, he tried his hand at free-lance writing. One of the recent, progressive magazines, *The New Republic,* accepted his anti-war articles and asked for more. It was an outlet also for the occasional poetry he wrote, the kind of writing that brought him the deepest reward. Steeped in Shakespeare and other Elizabethan dramatists, Maxwell Anderson composed long dramatic verses in his spare time, a pastime that soon led him to writing plays in blank verse. He was, he declared, "weary of plays that never lifted from the ground." (Maybe his would never soar like Shakespeare, but at least they would not sink in sodden prose like so many of the melodramas and sentimental offerings that came on tour to San Francisco.) He sometimes had a piece published in *Poetry* or one of the "little magazines," and he established contact with some of the poets in the circle surrounding Harriet Monroe.

In 1918, the Andersons decided to move to New York. Maxwell had had a few feature stories accepted by the New York *Globe,* which led to a job on the staff of the paper. Since New York was the center of the writing world—newspaper, theater, and book publishing—there should be plenty of opportunity for a thoughtful scholar with practical experience and a bent for poetry. They were hardly settled in a cramped apartment when Maxwell started writing his first play, a tragic tale of the bleak Dakota prairie in winter, a work he had been harboring for a long time. The lines he set down were in meter, in the elevated language of blank verse. He did not know who could—and would—produce such a play, but he had to write it, and in the form that had the most meaning for him. One of his aims was to broaden the horizons of poetry, and to that end he founded a new magazine of verse, called *Measure,* along with Genevieve Taggard and Padraic Colum. The three had brave ideas for their tender publication, one of them being to print verse plays that could not secure production. The first copies came off the press in 1920, but the venture failed for lack of "circulation" even before Max had completed his play.

He was offered a job on the *World* after the *Globe* folded, and took it because he would have a chance to review some plays. One of the first he saw was Pirandello's *Six Characters in Search of an Author,* which had been given a fine sensitive production by Brock Pemberton. Here was the producer, Max Anderson decided, who could do his play—if he would. Taking the script, which he had entitled *White Desert,* he went for an interview with Pemberton, and before he came away, he had secured the producer's promise to consider his play for the next season. And so, wonder of wonders, it came to pass that *White Desert* went into rehearsal in the early fall of 1923. The playwright was thirty-five years old and had three growing sons by now, but he felt like a youngster taking his first fling.

He could not keep the incredible, all-important news to himself. Before long, the entire office staff at the *World* knew that Max Anderson was going to have a play produced by Brock Pemberton. One of the most interested was Laurence Stallings, a fellow reporter and war veteran with whom Max had become friends. Late one night while they were waiting for copy, they had discovered that they shared the same loathing for the war—Stallings out of bitter experience in the trenches rather than principle alone, but their common antipathy was a bond between them, besides the fact that both were writers. They would spend hours discussing the brutality of war—Maxwell asking questions, and Laurence in his answers giving a detailed, gory picture. As rehearsals drew to a close, the discussions had fallen off, because the hopeful playwright grew more and more involved with the all-important production of his play.

White Desert tried out in Stamford, and the theater in the little Connecticut town was packed for the occasion. George Abbott, then an actor, was playing the lead—the part of a mean and jealous man, guilt-ridden in regard to sex, who goads his young wife (half-crazed with loneliness on the Dakota prairie) into infidelity with a neighboring farmer, and then kills her when she confesses her unfaithfulness. The opening scenes were in a sense comic, though by no means broad, but the small-town audience laughed uproariously. And they continued to laugh when the action suddenly turned tragic in the second act. Maxwell, sitting in the back of the theater beside Margaret and the producer, "died a thousand deaths" as his beloved play was mocked by giggles and guffaws of misunderstanding spectators. He was so chagrined he could hardly look Brock Pemberton in the face; but the producer calmly suggested that he rewrite the first act before they took the show into New York.

He got busy as soon as the ill-fated performance was over, and when the play opened on Broadway, the first scenes were serious, in keeping with the dramatic theme. *White Desert* was praised by the critics, one of whom pointed out that it was ". . . the kind of thing for which the way has been made at once easier and harder by the work of the theatre of Eugene O'Neill. . . ." Others had a good word for the author's use of blank verse and poetic prose; but the audiences found it weighty and "wordy."

One of those who was deeply impressed by the play, however, was Laurence Stallings, who not only offered his congratulations to the playwright, but suggested that Maxwell and he pool their talents to collaborate on an anti-war play. He was burning to do a realistic drama of war as it actually was—army life as he had known it in camp and in the miserable, airless, filthy trenches. He was sick of the phony patriotism and false political, heroic language of the soldier on the stage. They would strip away the glamour and reveal the terrible cost of the legendary glory of battle.

Maxwell needed little persuasion. Night after night the two newspapermen huddled in the back office at the *World,* pounding out a "blood-and-guts" play, as Laurence termed it, about the characters and situations, the rough cynical gallows-humor of men facing possible death. He furnished most of the first-hand material, and Maxwell, with his imagination and affinity for words, built up the dramatic structure. The result was the tense, powerful, exciting script of *What Price Glory?* which proved to be a milestone in the development of the modern theater toward pure naturalism in dialogue.

Produced by Arthur Hopkins in September, 1924, almost a year to the day after *White Desert, What Price Glory?* sent an electric shock through New York audiences accustomed to stage dialogue devoid of profanity. Even the naturalistic sea plays of O'Neill had not dared to include, in the salty lines of the sailors, any sentence to compare with the initial oath of the soldier in the trenches: "God damn every son-of-a-bitch in the world who isn't here!" Low phrases indeed from the pen of the man who wanted to elevate the language of the theater! But Max Anderson and Laurence Stallings had set out deliberately to protest against the outmoded limitations of the old puritan barriers still existent in the twentieth-century theater, just as they were protesting against the barbaric custom of war to settle international disputes.

What Price Glory? took New York and later the whole country by storm. People flocked to see the ungilded portraits of Sergeant Quirt and Captain Flagg, the "heroes" created by the playwrights, as brought to life by William Boyd and Louis Wolheim. The scene of the two soldiers drinking and playing blackjack to decide which one will get the girl, Charmaine, epitomized the cynical, callous attitude toward love, the animal need for sex produced by the harshness of war. If it was "shocking" or "sensational," the picture was nonetheless true, and showed up the veneer of stereotyped patriotic plays.

After their overwhelming success, the team of Anderson and Stallings tried to continue their collaboration in two historical plays—*First Flight,* episodes in the life of Andrew Jackson, and *The Buccaneer,* a swashbuckling tale, but neither one was appealing in the eyes of the public, and the writing partnership dissolved. Stallings' career as a dramatist dwindled away, but for Maxwell Anderson the theater was the "Phoenix of the arts," always rising anew with each fresh idea. He considered it "the cathedral of the spirit," also, a place of worship he would never desert.

He attempted a number of realistic plays on his own, the most successful, *Saturday's Children,* a study of the struggle of a young married couple to cope with the strictures of poverty and still keep their love intact. It was forthright and honest, and in its humanity might be called a preview of the depression plays that were to follow in a few years. There were those who said that if Maxwell Anderson would only continue with his plain-spoken prose he could become another O'Neill.

But the poet-playwright was more interested in being Maxwell Anderson. He had no intention of abandoning, more than temporarily, his dream of bringing the "exalted speech" of Shakespeare back to the stage. In between the writing of realistic prose, he reread the classic poets of tragedy; and, in his own words, "discovered that poetic tragedy had never been successful written about in its own place and time. There is not one tragedy by Sophocles, Euripides, Shakespeare, Corneille or Racine that did not have the advantage of a setting either far away or long ago." He realized that this was the reason *White Desert* had failed.

Reaching back into the history of the Southwest, he chose the legend of Don Pablo Montoya, the Spanish grandee who ruled the colony of Taos in New Mexico, and depicted the ousting of the old order of aristocracy for the modern one of democracy. The play was to be entirely in verse, written for production by the newly formed Group Theatre, the outgrowth of the experimental wing of the Theatre Guild. With the success of *What Price Glory?* the Andersons had bought a farm in Rockland County, about thirty miles from New York, and here the dramatist did most of his writing, in a little shack in the woods back of the house. Winter months were spent in New York, but from early spring until late fall, they were at the farm as often as possible. Max preferred a pencil to a typewriter, and his first drafts in longhand needed little revising as a rule. After working for several hours, he relaxed by going for a walk or a drive. (He made no secret of the fact that he was no sportsman, played no games, and did not even care to go fishing in the stream close by.)

Night over Taos was hardly more than an artistic success, and not a marked one at that; but it was important as a stepping stone toward the goal Maxwell Anderson had set for himself. Personal tragedy befell him in 1931, when his wife Margaret died, leaving him and their three sons at the moment he had reached the turning point in his career. Not daring to dwell on his loss, he pushed himself harder than ever, and his next historical verse drama, *Elizabeth the Queen,* was an unqualified success as a vigorous heroic tragedy in the Shakespearean tradition. It was a distinct change from the fare of the preceding ten years, and theatergoers responded favorably.

Before continuing his course, however, he took a flyer at a political satire called *Both Your Houses,* which was a tremendous box office success and, ironically enough, won the Pulitzer prize for 1933. It was hard to believe, but he felt almost annoyed at receiving the award for a piece of clever but superficial writing, while *Elizabeth the Queen,* in his eyes of far greater merit, had been overlooked. With a feeling of defiance, he began work on another historical tragedy in verse, *Mary of Scotland,* a logical choice after *Elizabeth.* He wrote with concentration, taking time out, however, to get married again. His wife was the former Gertrude Maynard, familiarly known as "Mab," who had been a friend of the Andersons for some time. He had been lonely since Margaret's death in spite of the solace it gave him to write poetry, and he was glad to share his life again. A quiet, meditative man, he was not one to wail, but the ache of loneliness had been nonetheless deep.

Mary of Scotland, moving backwards in history from *Elizabeth,* highlighted the struggle between the daughter of Henry VIII and Mary Stuart for the throne of England. Although Anderson's play had by no means the power and depth of Schiller's *Mary Stuart,* it was moving and dramatic, with a feeling of heroic tragedy in Mary's decision to remain in prison rather than yield to Elizabeth's will. The scenes between Mary and Elizabeth, like those between Elizabeth and Essex in the earlier play, rang with the steel of suppressed fury as the opponents crossed swords. The critics for the most part praised the poetry of Anderson's lines, but there were some who found it pretentious and self-conscious. The poet-playwright kept on composing verse dramas, more engrossed with his creative endeavor than disturbed by criticism of it. As he was to admit, in the Preface to the publication of four of his works, he had discovered long ago "that the imagining, the word-finding, and the setting down of a poem were more intense delights than the reading of even the greatest poems by other men." In the early years, when a poem resulted, he "had a taste of what, for want of a better figure, men call 'heaven' ' "; and now, with the completion of each verse drama, he experienced a deep gratification and sense of achievement that deafened the sound of dissenting voices.

Turning to American history, he followed *Mary of Scotland* with *Valley Forge,* a stirring epic of Washington's indomitable courage and leadership during the long, bitter cold and deprivation of that crucial winter campaign. Some thought the play was too much of a patriotic hymn, others thought it was worthy of the Pulitzer prize that year (1934), but Max Anderson paid little heed to any of them. (He was to receive other awards, but he never won a Pulitzer prize after the one for *Both Your Houses,* a fact that, if he allowed himself to think about it, was both irritating and depressing.) He was too involved in a work of a different theme, a different era—the contemporary scene. Like most of the artistic intellectuals he knew, he had been greatly disturbed and outraged by the Sacco-Vanzetti case and the tragic outcome of the trial. He had written, with details furnished by Harold Hickerson, one of the defense lawyers, a strong dramatization of the controversy called *Gods of Lightning.* The direction was poor, however, and the production had failed in tryout. He had no intention of abandoning the theme or the form, and, after *Valley Forge,* had begun a new version based on the aftermath of the case.

The play, which he called *Winterset,* was at once the most significant and the most controversial of any he had created. Hailed by some as a real accomplishment in poetic drama, it was condemned by others for its use of exalted speech and metered line in a present-day problem play. Still others objected to the "radical" and even "socialistic" viewpoint implied. Realizing that he had reversed his theory that the verse form should be used only when dealing with the past, Max was urged to defend his work by his friends and associates, some of whom were connected with the production. Most of the time he was not one to speak up. At rehearsals he spoke with quiet dignity, "in a banker's voice," and he rarely raised it during the run of a play. In this instance, however, he decided to defend himself. *"Winterset,"* he explained, "is largely in verse and treats a contemporary tragic theme, which makes it more of an experiment than I could wish, for the great masters themselves never tried to make tragic poetry out of the stuff of their own times. To do so is to attempt to establish a new convention, one that may prove impossible of acceptance, but to which I was driven by the lively historical sense of our day." After a discussion of the basic issue, he concluded: "Whether or not I have solved the problem in *Winterset* is probably of little moment. But it must be solved if we are to have a great theatre in America."

For the most part, the play was not only accepted but praised by the public and critics alike. Burgess Meredith created the role of Mio, the Hamlet-like hero who has a compulsion to avenge his father's death at the cost of love, with poetic realism and restraint; the entire cast caught the spirit of the play early in rehearsal, which insured an inspired production. That year, 1935, the drama critics themselves, by and large disappointed with the awards of the Pulitzer committee, banded together to form their own judgments and present a medal to their own choices. That the first Drama Critics Circle Award in the American theater went to *Winterset* brought Maxwell Anderson a feeling of fulfillment far greater than his only Pulitzer award. To him it was a recognition of his artistic aims "to produce verse drama and to attain tragic elevation in the theatre"; and it sustained his faith in the ability of man to rise above darkness and the chaos of an unjust society. It was a faith he stated in the pulsating lines spoken by old Esdras at the close of *Winterset:*

> ". . . yet is my mind my own,
> yet is my heart a cry toward something dim
> in distance, which is higher than I am
> and makes me emperor of the endless dark
> even in seeking!"

Swinging back into the past again, he chose to retell the legend of Medea, giving it a nineteenth-century setting in New England; but the result, *Wingless Victory,* was more of a vehicle for poetic expression than analytical probing in depth, such as O'Neill had put into *Mourning Becomes Electra.* But if he was not as profound, Anderson was as prolific as O'Neill. The following year, 1937, he wrote three fantasies in verse and poetic prose: *High Tor, The Masque of Kings,* and *The Star Wagon.* The first of these, fashioned from the folklore surrounding Hendrik Hudson and the

Dutch sailors who roamed the hills above the river, was the most outstanding of the three. Using the theme of return to a forgotten era by present-day man, the play tells the story of a youth who refuses to sell High Tor, the mountain that has been in his family for generations, and who in a dream goes back to the days of Hendrik Hudson. Present and past are fused into one as the lad's sweetheart and the commercial interests who want him to sell are all the spectators in his dream, the events of which bring him a more mature point of view when he awakens with a new outlook on life. In its exploration of the fourth dimension the drama was experimental in concept as well as form, and evoked ambivalent reactions from the reviewers. Some praised the production extravagantly, others objected again to the verse lines and also to the mingling of "phantom" characters with "live" ones. But most agreed that this was the stuff of poetry, wrought with drama and imagination. *High Tor* won for its author a second Drama Critics Award, and there were those who thought it deserved the Pulitzer prize as well.

One of these was Burns Mantle, perhaps the playwright's greatest admirer (who had felt that *Valley Forge* and *Winterset* should also have received the Pulitzer award); as the contradictory opinions of Anderson's work continued, Mantle's voice was among the strongest in proclaiming its merits. In 1939 he wrote: "Maxwell Anderson took giant strides from 1930 on, to equal O'Neill as a figure in the American theatre. The combination of his gift for poetry and dramatic situation has produced plays of high artistic quality. . . . The standard of Anderson's plays from 1930 on has sustained a consistency of quality unlike any other American dramatist of the period." His high regard was given in full view of the fact that O'Neill had been off the scene for several years because of ill health; but even so, Mantle asserted, Anderson probably would have matched O'Neill in importance. Whether his estimate was an overstatement or not, he had support from other quarters. One of Max Anderson's colleagues in poetry circles, Stephen Vincent Benét, in a tribute entitled "New Grandeur," wrote in *Stage* Magazine: "He has brought verse and the form of verse back to the American stage—not as an experiment, not as an oddity, but as an essential of the later plays he has written. And because of it, he has opened a shut door."

The poets naturally were overjoyed to have a champion of their art in the modern theater, and there were several who tried to join "the poet in show business," as Anderson was called. His friend Padraic Colum wrote a number of plays (fantasies full of Irish whimsy and charm), but his form was too nebulous for production. With the formation of the Playwrights Company, Max was besieged with playscripts from poets, and he always had to explain that the five who banded together had done so expressly to produce their own plays, and there was no provision for the plays of outsiders. (The company swerved from policy to produce the musical *Knickerbocker Holiday*, which he wrote with Kurt Weill. Later Weill became a member.)

As the war grew closer to a horrible reality in the late thirties, Max Anderson, like Bob Sherwood, concentrated on writing plays that were against fascism, or dictatorship of any stripe. *Key Largo*, in 1939, drew a parallel between the Civil War in Spain and gangsterism in Florida to show that eventually some action must be taken against the forces of evil. *Candle in the Wind*, the following year, depicted the gallantry of the French underground movement during the German occupation. After December 7, 1941, he wrote of American soldiers' entry into World War II on *The Eve of St. Mark*, with lyric odes to their courage and vision that were a far cry indeed from the harsh, naturalistic prose of *What Price Glory?* But it was a time for encouragement, not exposure, and although there was some reference to the sexual needs of the men in service—and certainly no pussyfooting of facts—there was little profanity in the lines or grossness in the language. The play was chosen for a White House performance and opened in Washington. A distinguished production under the fine, sensitive direction of Lem Ward, well known for his little theater work, it was hit by tragedy eight days after opening: the young director, only thirty-seven years old, worn out with strain and overwork from extra long hours of rehearsal, died of a heart attack. His sudden death was a shock to the entire company. The playwright, who had been congratulating himself on having found a director at last who knew how to bring out the full feeling of his verse drama form, was stricken as if Fate had dealt him a personal blow. The tension, the pressure of war took its toll on all fronts: Lem Ward was as much a casualty as the soldiers who died in battle. *Storm Operation,* written toward the end of the war, was a worthy attempt to deal with the heat of combat in heroic language, but was a complete failure. The contrast of these plays with *What Price Glory?* with his whole outlook after the First World War, seems not to have troubled Anderson as it did Sherwood. To him the fact that the circumstances were vastly different—so severe that the United States was compelled to enter the war—spoke for itself in his mind. He felt no need to offer explanations.

Undaunted as well in the matter of the form he had chosen, he continued to write in verse and poetic prose. For most of his life he served with devotion the cause of poetry in drama to which he had committed himself. Let Edmund Wilson say, "Maxwell Anderson is at his worst in verse"—no matter! As long as there were occasional "passages of great beauty and poignancy" (as someone else had written), he would pursue the path he had chosen—"the road less traveled by," as his fellow-poet Frost had called it. And like Robert Frost, Maxwell Anderson felt that there was no equal gratification in all of life to the achievement of poetry. He had to go on writing as he did, no matter what the cost professionally.

When the war was over, disillusionment set in; but again, it was of a different shade than the pall following the first world controversy. Now there was not so much bitterness as confusion and maladjustment. In *Truckline Cafe* the playwright depicted the plight of a young wife who at first thought her husband had been killed in battle. When she learns he is alive, she seeks to rebuild their life together out of the emotional rubble left by the war.

His play was not particularly successful, but it led him to go back into history again, this time to the story of the Maid of battle—Joan of Arc. He called her Joan of Lorraine, and sought to parallel her struggle with the modern problems of the actress (Mary) playing the role. His *tour de force* caused a wide flurry in the stream of Broadway commentary. At first considered brilliant and compared by some to Shaw's *St. Joan,* it was later attacked from other points. Eric Bentley, the most biting of Anderson's assailants, observed that the switching back and forth between Joan of Arc and Mary, the actress, was not so clever as it seemed on first thought. The "use of the frame" was a "reach-me-down" to the audience, he thought. He denounced the poet-playwright's "moral and aesthetic pretensions" with vehemence and scorn. "Anderson is not abashed by anything," he declared.

So much was true. Unabashed by Bentley's remarks as well as by the magnitude of any subject he chose to examine, Max Anderson went on serenely writing as he pleased. His three sons were grown and on their own. (Alan worked closely with his father, in publication of the plays, as well as in versions of them for other media.) Mab and he had had one child, Hesper, now entering her teens, who, as the only daughter in his family of sons, received more than her share of attention. The tremendous box office success of *Knickerbocker Holiday,* with its customary tour, brought him enough income to live comfortably and still experiment and keep on trying new ventures where others might be more timid. (The Playwrights Company, too, enabled him—and the others—to produce the kind of play he wanted to do. They had an agreement that any one member could insist on production of his work if he was convinced of its merit, even though the others had voted it down as unfeasible for one reason or another.)

In *Anne of the Thousand Days,* he completed his trilogy (in reverse chronology) of British queens. The Anne Boleyn created by Maxwell Anderson possessed both vitality and spirit to insist on legalizing her relationship with the lusty king, and later to make the choice of death in order to insure the throne for her daughter Elizabeth. The inner workings that bring about her decisions, however, are not revealed, and the weakness in motivation was perhaps responsible for the meager success of the production.

By nature a scholar, from the days of his introduction to the classics at the University, Max made a habit of returning periodically to the study of the works included in the course given by Professor Hult, "a learned and lovable man" at North Dakota, who thought that Plato was as honest as he was great. But, as he said, "I was somewhat chilled, on first reading *The Republic,* to discover that the rulers of Plato's ideal state took stern charge of the arts, allowing only certain martial modes of music and throwing out the poets and romancers altogether. . . . More and more, as I grew older, I was troubled in reading Plato by discovering that I did not like the Socrates who continued to discourse so charmingly and so bewilderingly in the later dialogues. I didn't like him because I didn't trust him. . . . I distrusted my mistrust at first, for I had grown up reverencing the founder of the first academy and went to him in search of wisdom, not to criticize. But after the second world-wide war, when communism and military aggression became obvious partners, I went back to Plato to unearth what he had been getting at in his *Republic*, and what relation his utopia might have to modern times." He discovered to his dismay that, "When you examine Plato's *Republic*, you find that he is not describing a republic at all, but a dictatorship. . . . No doubt Plato set out to define a happy society in his republic, but what we find in his pages, if we boil it down, is something very much like Russia under the Politburo. Marx, too, intended a happy society when he planned his utopia. But to put such doctrines in the mouth of Socrates is a betrayal as deliberate as Alcibiades' betrayal of Athens."

So the poet playwright turned to Xenophon's *Memorabilia* and found an entirely different Socrates. Here the philosopher was "a wise old fellow, but nobody's pillar of fire." He concluded that as Plato grew older, he had substituted his own ideas for those of Socrates; and he added: "For myself I shall always thank Plato for writing truly, movingly, and gloriously about Socrates in his youth, and shall thank Xenophon for proving to me that what Plato put into Socrates' mouth in his middle and old age was largely lies." He decided to write his own version of the final days and death of Socrates, to portray the wise old philosopher as he defied the stupid men of Sparta with his concept of democracy—the freedom to speak, to question—and who preferred the cup of hemlock to dictatorship. The outcome was *Barefoot in Athens*, Maxwell Anderson's final offering in verse tragedy. It was produced in 1951, the summation of nearly six years' study and subconscious creation while he was writing the other postwar plays.

He had envisioned the work as the culmination of his art, representing both the philosophy and form he had championed over a lifetime. As realistic as experience had taught him to be, he could not help hoping that this would be hailed as his finest play, if not his masterpiece. Certainly it was the most scholarly. He was doomed to disappointment, for both the critics and the audience were apathetic about *Barefoot in Athens*. Only a few found it poetic and moving. Although there were passages of truth and brilliance in some of Socrates' long speeches (as, for example, "The air of a democracy is only healthy when inquiry bites constantly at the heels of every proposal and every project, even at the foundations of our way of life." Or, "Men of Athens, I am a man of doubt, as my accusers have said. All my wisdom is in knowing how little I know. . . ." Or his last words to his wife, Xantippe, and his prayer: "Give me beauty in the inward soul, For outward beauty I'm not likely to have./ May I reckon the wise to be wealthy, And those who need least to be most like the gods."), it was pointed out that the verse form alone could not insure a masterpiece in the theater. Erudition and meter could not be substituted for fire and passion— nor even great talent for the indefinable quality of genius. The lines of poetry were studied rather than spontaneous; and unless they flowed as from a fountain they could not be effective. (Of all Anderson's verse dramas, *Winterset* was perhaps the most successful because the most impassioned.)

To assuage his sense of failure, Maxwell wrote a detailed account of his research, entitled *Socrates and His Gospel,* for the published version of the play, which was brought out in the fall of 1951. The flyleaf bore the inscription, "For Mab," as a tribute to his wife's patience and understanding in putting up with his hermit-like existence when he was gathering material for the play. She had not been well for some time, but she did not complain or let her illness intrude on his working hours. She died less than two years later, in 1953, and in 1954, he married Gilda Oakleaf—his third wife.

The same year saw the production of his last play, if such it could be called, *The Bad Seed*. It was not an original work, but a dramatization of the novel of the same title. The theme—inheritance of homicidal tendencies—although questionable from a scientific standpoint, was considered good theater, and had quite a successful run. Yet Max Anderson was done with playwriting, in verse or prose. He had set down his credo in a book of essays, *Off Broadway*, in which he stated that he believed with Goethe "that dramatic poetry is man's greatest achievement on earth so far," and further that "the theater is essentially a cathedral of the spirit, devoted to the apostolic succession of inspired high priests which extend further into the past than the Christian line founded by St. Peter." In the main, he had been faithful to his religion of the theater, but he had denied it in *The Bad Seed* because of his bitterness over the indifference toward *Barefoot in Athens*. He had no more heart to continue fighting for a lost art.

His health began to fail at about this time, and he did little writing of any kind. He lived in Stamford, Connecticut, now, no longer on a farm with a shack in the woods to give him seclusion and inspiration. He had published a volume of poems, *You Who Have Dreams*, some years before, and continued to write poetry purely for his own satisfaction. He died in 1960, following an operation. In dealing with Anderson's work, critics had run a course of extremes, all the way from rating him second to O'Neill down to berating him for pretentious and overwritten drama; from praising him as an experimentalist to denouncing him as a regressor. The fact that his accomplishments did not measure up to his aims is perhaps best stated in George Jean Nathan's estimate of Maxwell Anderson: "No man writing for the theatre has a higher sincerity [than Anderson] and no man a higher goal. But none, also, has a mind more critically incapable of meeting the demands it imposes upon itself." Gentle, mild, and peace-loving, he was hardly cut out to be a warrior for his art. Yet he did not hesitate to state his convictions, and he did achieve, if not the pinnacle, then a high plateau of elevated language and verse drama in the theater.

CHAPTER VII

——◆■◆——

SOME CLEVER COLLABORATORS

Sam and Bella Spewack

IN THE twenties and thirties, the tendency to pool their talents flourished among the writers of comedy to bring forth a number of notable collaborators. Two of these whose intellectual merriment did much to lift the gloom of the depression were a pair of witty young newspaper people who collaborated in life before they began to add to the comedic literature of the theater. At the time of their meeting they were Bella Cohen, pert petite columnist of the New York *Daily Call*, and Samuel Spewack, cub reporter on the New York *World*. It was the crucial period just after the United States' entry into the First World War, and the *Call* was being threatened with a shutdown on charges of sedition by the U.S. Post Office Department because of its pacifist policy. Bella, whose column, "Pippa Passes," was one of the most intelligent ever to grace a women's page, could hardly depend on the paper for a living in normal times, and now it seemed she would have to turn to one of her other sources of income—acting or publicity writing. (She was to be national publicity director for the Campfire Girls at one point!) The small brunette, with her bright brown eyes and brisk manner of speaking, was a bundle of energy, and could handle three jobs at once if necessary.

Around the corner at the *World* office, Sam wondered how long it would be before he was drafted, and whether he should try to serve as a war correspondent or enlist in the Army.

The two used to get together after work in the wee hours of the morning. When the publisher-editor of the *Call*, Charles Ervin, came down from the office at around 2 A.M. after putting the paper to bed, he would find Bella and Sam sitting on the lower steps, talking earnestly about the immediate future as well as the more remote past. More than once Charlie, known for his lion's roar, his heartiness and warmth, had to assure them that the *Call* would find some way to publish in spite of Postmaster Burleson's edict; and he would chuckle to himself as he carefully stepped over their held hands in the aisle they made for him. (In later years he was fond of saying that he had seen the prologue of *Boy Meets Girl* on those rickety office steps.)

Soon after they met, Bella and Sam discovered they had been born in the same year—1899—she in Hungary, and he in Russia. The Cohen family emigrated to America when Bella was three years old; and a year later, at the tender age of four, she had made her debut in the theater by singing in Victoria Music Hall. She was "a born entertainer," her talent quickly recognized by her teachers. She played comedy characters in school plays, and at fourteen, while editing the Washington Irving High School magazine, she directed a play at Madison House. When the Provincetown Players brought their efforts to Macdougal Street, Bella was among the first to join the group, working at any and all jobs for the experience. Once she was the offstage voice for George Cram Cook himself. Watching "Jig" direct, and working on the production of *Suppressed Desires*, the high school editor-actress-director was probably inspired to try her hand at playwriting as well. As soon as she graduated from high school, she started working part-time on the *Call*, in addition to publicity jobs and free lance writing on the side. It was then she had met Sam Spewack, and both felt an immediate bond, deeper and far beyond the fact that they were both in the newspaper writing profession. At the moment neither of them knew what the future would hold—or indeed, whether there would be a future for them, with the threat of war practically at the door.

Sam had come to the United States a few years later than Bella. Like her, he was brought up in New York, attended public schools and worked on school papers. He also attended Columbia University, where his greatest aptitude was in writing. He wrote everything from short stories to one-act plays.

Both the *Call* and the young writers survived the war, and the paper lasted until 1922, when it folded for lack of funds. That same year Bella and Sam were married in Brooklyn, deciding suddenly when Sam was assigned to Berlin and Moscow as foreign correspondent for the *World*. They left right after the wedding and stayed overseas for four years, first in Berlin and then in Moscow. Bella assisted her husband as correspondent, a training which led naturally into collaboration in more creative fields. They worked easily and well together, a rarity to begin with; and both possessed the same sort of quick bright wit that was essential for fast-moving dialogue.

The year of their return, 1926, Broadway was a blaze of lights representing every sort of theatrical fare from musical revues and variety shows to the complex mask-drama of O'Neill, *The Great God Brown*. Drama was cherished as an "exalted art," and all the theater was bathed in reflected glory. New York was a veritable rialto, seething with the activity of show business. Bella Spewack had no trouble finding press agent jobs—for the music studio of the Moscow Art Theatre, for the revue *The Chauve Souris,* and for *The Miracle.* Caught by the general fever (or, "seduced by the theater," as Sam said), the Spewacks wrote their first play in collaboration, *The Solitaire Man.* It was followed by *Poppa,* and, in 1928, a satire called *The War Song*. Although none was an outstanding success, the comedic quality was high, and won for the Spewacks a reputation for clever dialogue, which soon led to offers from Hollywood for scenario writing jobs. Louis Weitzenkorn, who had been on the staff of the *Call,* had become an immensely successful producer, and a number of noted playwrights, including Elmer Rice, had yielded to the lure of Hollywood contracts, so the Spewacks decided to accept some of the bids they received. Like most playwrights, they found the mechanics of movie-making, the set formula for film-writing, incredibly synthetic, to the point of being ridiculous. Out of their experiences in several movies (and two more plays in between) came the brilliant and hilarious satire, *Boy Meets Girl.*

Produced and staged by George Abbott at the Cort Theatre, the satiric comedy, which opened in November, 1935, took Broadway by storm, and enjoyed continued popularity till the close of the 1936–37 season, a record run of 699 performances. Their apprenticeship over, Sam and Bella Spewack took their place among the foremost collaborators in the theater. They had bought a farm in New Hope, Pennsylvania, a few years before, where they spent the spring and summer months writing the sort of thing they wanted to write, not according to the dictates of some movie magnate. The two worked so closely together that it was impossible, even for them, to tell which part of a play was contributed by one or the other. Bella, noted for her sharp wit, was always quick on the uptake in conversation, which may have resulted in the fast-paced dialogue; and Sam continued to contribute short stories to the top "slick" magazines (*Collier's, Redbook,* and *Saturday Evening Post*) of the time, which may have meant that he was responsible for plot and action to a greater extent than she. In the main, however, their collaborations have always represented a skillful merging of their talents. (Earlier Bella had also written short stories, one of which was included in the O'Brien collection of best short stories for 1925.)

With the success of *Boy Meets Girl* ringing in their ears, the Spewacks made capital of their experience in Moscow to concoct a satiric musical, *Leave It to Me,* which Bella described as, "The study of a Kansan who is made ambassador to Soviet Russia against his will, and who devotes himself to the business of getting recalled." In this project they lined up with a third collaborator, Cole Porter, who "provided wonderful music and lyrics" for their play, and, in the course of conferences, became their good friend. The musical, with Victor Moore as the bumbling ambassador, was produced in 1938, and had a successful run on Broadway.

With the advent of the Second World War, the Spewacks left their play-making for action in the service of their country. In 1942, Mr. Spewack was appointed Chief of the Bureau of Motion Pictures for the Office of War Information. In this capacity, he wrote and directed the first full-length film on war to be produced by the United States government, entitled *The World at War*. A year later he was appointed Press Attaché in Moscow for the Moscow Conference, after which he produced the documentary film *This Is Russia*. He was also head of the Russian division for the overseas office of OWI. Mrs. Spewack wrote a series of programs for the American Broadcasting Company on the work of UNRRA, and reported on conditions abroad from London, Paris, Berlin, Prague, and Geneva.

As soon as the war was over, they collaborated on one of the first —and finest—original "screen plays" for the entertaining and unusually perceptive movie, *Week-end at the Waldorf*. Then, almost immediately, the Spewacks went to work on an idea that had been taking shape for a long time—writing a musical version of a Shakespeare comedy. They chose *The Taming of the Shrew,* and gave it a modern framework, a backstage story of the marital battles between the actor and actress playing the leading roles. When the Spewacks relayed their idea to their friend Cole Porter, he was tremendously enthusiastic. The three had many a merry session combining the "book" with his inspired music and lyrics. The title was as fetching as the tunes: *Kiss Me, Kate,* from one of Petruchio's speeches, it was the final touch in composing a high-comedy musical. It received universal praise from the critics as a superior production from every point of view, and ran for two or three seasons in New York, from 1948 to the end of 1950, followed by a London production, which Sam Spewack directed, in 1951.

In between, he made two solo ventures as a playwright—the first in 1949, with *Two Blind Mice,* a spoof on Washington and its bureaucrats. Although clever in parts, it lacked the spontaneity of the collaborations. His second try, a play called *Golden State,* which Bella produced, was a dismal failure, professionally and financially. After directing the London production of *Kiss Me, Kate,* Sam Spewack made a last attempt on his own with *Under the Sycamore Tree,* starring Alec Guinness, presented in London in 1952. Perhaps because of the star's performance, the last fared much better than the other plays; but it was obvious to both Sam and Bella Spewack that they did their best work together—and that they were writers, not directors or producers.

As if to prove the point, the Spewacks' next play, *My Three Angels,* which opened on Broadway in the spring of 1953, was a decided hit. Based on Albert Husson's *La Cuisine des Anges,* it was written in close collaboration, and caught the fanciful spirit of the French comedy to perfection. In the matter of short stories and a novel or two, the Spewacks have been independently successful; but when it comes to plays, they have proved that two heads are better than one.

Howard Lindsay and Russel Crouse

In 1959, a special "Tony" award, never before offered, was created to honor "long, successful collaboration in playwriting." The two authors who received this unique medal were Howard Lindsay and Russel Crouse,* then celebrating their twenty-fifth anniversary. A significant fact regarding their relationship is that each had carved out his own career before they began to collaborate.

The senior member (by four years), Howard Lindsay claims to have been a "confirmed wincer" all his life, which began on March 29, 1889. His father was a German immigrant with charm and imagination but little practicality, and his mother an upstanding "down-easter" from Maine. More mismated parents he could hardly have found, and since he inherited his mother's New England conscience along with his father's fertile imagination, he was inclined to flinch at difficult situations from the time he was a youngster. (He never could enter into boyhood pranks or prevarications without a twinge or two of conscience; not that this kept him from participating, but it prevented him from thoroughly enjoying the mischief.)

When Howard, the youngest of four children, was about four years old, his mother, who decided she could not tolerate his father's "inveterate lying" any longer, packed up her brood and took them to live in Atlantic City, where her mother and brother had been living for some time. The latter gave her a job on his struggling newspaper, *The Daily Union;* and "Grandma Lindsay," from whom Howard took his stage name, presided over the household.

* Russel Crouse died on April 3, 1966, just as this book was going to press.

They were barely able to make ends meet. As soon as he was old enough, Howard, like the other children, was expected to help out with any odd jobs to be found.

He early showed both ingenuity and theatrical ability when, at the age of eight or nine, he started selling his uncle's newspaper on the Atlantic City boardwalk. He would holler at the strollers:

"The Daily Union—one cent,
To help my mother pay the rent!"

The day of the sinking of the *Maine* (February 15, 1898), he ran up and down the length of the boardwalk shouting, "Extra, extra!" in great excitement. He kept selling and selling without stopping for hours, and when he finally got back to the printing office, he found he had wet his pants. He soon invented easier ways to augment his income.

His uncle's paper had a number of small advertising accounts that were always lagging behind in their payment, and frequently the family took it out in trade. For one such bill, long past due, Howard was given free elocution lessons. After he had memorized—with gestures—a number of stirring pieces, he would go up in front of the big hotels on the boardwalk and recite them before the guests sitting on the verandas. He would take off his cap, make a low bow, and launch into a ballad or lengthy ode. At the end he would pass his cap, and pennies, nickels and dimes would plink into it. On a fine day, when the rocking chairs were filled with patrons, he might come home with a capful of coins.

On another such deal, he was supplied with free coaching by a mathematical wizard to write the correct answer to very difficult problems on a blackboard in front of an audience. Howard never did find out how his tutor arrived at these answers, nor did he care. He loved to perform, and used to recite poetry at family gatherings in the parlor, at meetings he attended with his grandmother— for sheer pleasure as well as profit. It was only logical that this experience should lead him into the theater; or, as he himself has put it, he "became an actor on a due bill."

He also enjoyed being a spectator, again through his uncle's newspaper. There were usually a few extra passes for shows lying around the office, and Howard was always ready to make use of them. The first play he saw was *Richard III*, with Creston Clarke, a nephew of Edwin Booth, in the lead, a performance which held the future actor-playwright enthralled. He also frequented the Wilbur Opera Company, which put on light operas on Young's Pier. These musicals filled him with such delight that he not only attended performances, but he used to sneak into the balcony and watch rehearsals. He seemed to be drawn instinctively to show business. A rather stocky boy, with traces of his German ancestry showing in his muddy blond hair and strong square jaw, he was hardly the type for a matinée idol, but he realized even at that early age that he was happiest when he was watching others perform or exhibiting his own talents.

A third influence, also theatrical from a slightly esoteric standpoint, was the number of Spiritualist meetings Howard Lindsay used to attend with his grandmother. (His mother and Grandma were "freethinkers": they believed in God, but had no formal religion; and the séances filled his grandmother's need for communion with heavenly powers.) It was from these sessions that young Howard first observed the art of sleight-of-hand. His natural curiosity prompted him to find out how the medium "divined" the name written on a slip of paper pulled from a bowl, a device he used to good effect nearly fifty years later, when he and Russel Crouse were writing *The Great Sebastians* for Alfred Lunt and Lynn Fontanne.

Both Howard and his sister, the next above him in age, felt that the freethinkers were sadly lacking in prestige among their schoolmates, and so began to shop around for a Sunday school. They chose the one that had the highest social standing—and the best pot-luck suppers—the Episcopal. Howard joined the choir, and thoroughly enjoyed the pageantry of dressing up, marching down the aisle, and "performing" for the "audience" of worshipers. His freethinker background and native curiosity combined to make him a doubting Thomas in Sunday-school class, and he argued with the teacher on various points, an unheard-of effrontery which led to the question of his baptism. When the Sunday-school teacher learned that he had never been baptized, she was shocked. He was given the cold shoulder by everyone until he finally, of his own volition, chose to be baptized at the age of eleven. This chapter in his life rose up before him in *Life with Father*, where the business of getting Father baptized (against his will) forms most of the action.

The following year, his mother took her family to live in Dorchester, a suburb of Boston, where Howard attended the Edward Everett grammar school and the Boston Latin School. Away from the entertainment center of Atlantic City and the lure of the theater, Howard drew closer to the church, and began to consider becoming a minister. He won a scholarship from the Boston Latin School to Harvard, but he was most unhappy there. He hated the class distinctions, the snobbery of the clubs, and left after one semester.

He had been going with a girl in Dorchester whose sisters were chorus girls. One weekend they brought back from New York a catalogue of the American Academy of Dramatic Arts, which caught Howard's eye immediately, and in so doing changed his destiny. The catalogue stated that the course consisted of two semesters, six months each, covering every phase of dramatic art. He decided to become an actor then and there.

His mother opposed the idea, but Grandma spoke up promptly: "I think Howard will make a good actor," she said. "He's so fond of staying up late nights." Her reasoning was logical enough for Howard, and moreover, she offered to help him pay for the course, so the matter was settled. He had no trouble graduating from the Academy, and went on tour at once. He played the vaudeville circuits as well as in road companies of Broadway shows. In 1913, he joined the company of Margaret Anglin as a "super," glad of the chance to be anything at all in the organization of the great actress-manager. She and her husband both served as managers of the actors who were associated with them. Although she could see that Howard Lindsay had amazing talent for writing as well as acting, and raised his position in the company to "sub-director," a post which gave him the opportunity of rewriting plays with her and broadened his knowledge of the theater considerably, she and her husband were not very generous with their pay raises. When the time came around for a raise in salary, no mention was made of it.

At the time of the First World War, Howard was due for a second raise, but again there was no sign from Miss Anglin or her husband. Mr. Lindsay held his peace. After the war, he returned to find the actors on strike, prior to forming Equity. Like many actor-managers, Miss Anglin was anti-Equity; Howard Lindsay was definitely "pro." It was a bitter strike, with much hard feeling on both sides. Howard could not stay with a company unwilling to get rid of the many abuses that had gone on for years in the theater. He parted from Miss Anglin without tears, in spite of his deep respect for her ability. He went with the George Tyler Agency, and started on a career as a director. (George Tyler had staged one of the Anglin shows a few years before, and had told Howard then that he would be glad to have him in the agency at any time.)

He had done everything in the theater from acting to stage managing and directing, but the first play to carry his name as "director" was *Dulcy*. One of the prominent actors in the cast was Elliott Nugent, who had been writing plays with his father, who was J. C. Nugent. The two became friends, and before long Howard received an offer to stage *The Poor Nut*, a comedy the Nugents had just completed. After its success, he collaborated with them in writing *Kempy*, this time on a percentage basis, as a bona fide author. (He received 24 per cent; Elliott, 25; and the elder Mr. Nugent, 51 per cent.)

It was not till a few years later, however, that he became "coauthor" of a play he called *Tommy*, written with Bertrand Robinson. The plot was based on his own experience with a girl in Dorchester, whose parents had liked him so much and tried so hard to promote him that their daughter would have none of him. It was lucky for him that she refused him, Howard decided, or he probably would not have gone into the theater. In the play, he added a kindly uncle who advised the boy, Tommy, to act in such a way that his girl's parents would dislike him, which would probably make her rush to get the marriage license. It was produced in 1926, and the following summer he was directing a stock company in Skowhegan, Maine, when he met a girl who knew her own mind. This was Dorothy Stickney, who was the ingénue in the company. They were married on Friday the thirteenth (ever since his lucky number), in August, 1927.

Now a playwright as well as actor-director, he began to concentrate on the first. He had visited his father one summer, and had discovered that the parent who had always been described as a liar and ne'er-do-well was something of an artist when it came to exercising his imagination. He had married a woman who enjoyed and encouraged his tall tales, so they got along famously. Howard, although only thirteen at the time, realized that his father was an amiable fellow, and that he—Howard—must have inherited his father's gift for fabrication. He would put it to good use, however, especially since he had his mother's conscience to keep him from being an outright liar. He had begun writing stories for the Boston Latin School *Register*. From the day he began studying to join the theater, he continued to create everything from dialogue (with Margaret Anglin) and vaudeville skits, to plays.

His first comedy that could be called a hit was *Your Uncle Dudley*, which ran for three months in spite of the depression. The title became a familiar phrase to denote a kindly and wise old fellow, universally used, even by people who never saw the play. *She Loves Me Not*, a dramatization of Edward Hope's novel, had been well accepted in New York, but a failure in London in 1934, and he was feeling rather low, weak from an attack of the flu, when Vinton Freedley, the producer, called. He needed a rewrite of the book for the Cole Porter musical, *Anything Goes*, and needed it fast—within ten days, to be exact. The playwright's spirit was willing, but his flesh was still weak from the flu; he could not do a rush job like this without some help.

In recalling the incident for a reporter thirty years later, he said, "I agreed, provided he got me a collaborator. He went down the available list and I said 'No' to this one and 'No' to that one until he came to Russel Crouse and I said 'Yes!' "

At that particular point in his life, Mr. Crouse was writing a column for the New York *Evening Post* in addition to having four plays to his credit, all of which had been written within three years. (The first, a period piece, *Mr. Currier and Mr. Ives*, had been one of the hits of 1930.) Before then, Russel Crouse had been principally a newspaperman. He was an Ohioan, born in Findlay, in 1893. His parents, both of German extraction, had moved north from the densely populated German colony around Cincinnati, but had found Findlay too small a village. A few years after Russel's birth, they moved to Toledo, a middle-sized city at the top of a middle-sized state. He and his sister attended Monroe grade school and the "Old Central" high school. He was not a brilliant student by any means, but he took great interest in sports, and became sports editor of the high school paper. He had an easy way with words and with people; and right after graduation, in 1910, he went to Cincinnati, where he became a cub reporter on the *Commercial Tribune*. After a year of various assignments, including sports events, he received an offer from the Kansas City *Star* to join the staff as a sports columnist in addition to reporting. He grabbed it, mostly for the chance to write his own column, and stayed for four years, until 1917, when he returned to Cincinnati as a political reporter for the *Post*.

He served as an enlisted man in the Navy during World War I, and, like the other writers who survived the war, was disillusioned by the false patriotism, and the shambles that followed the so-called victory. On his return to civilian life, he decided to stay in New York, which was much more to his liking than the Midwestern cities. With the experience behind him, he had no trouble landing a reporting job on the *Globe*, where he found other writers, notably Maxwell Anderson and Laurence Stallings. It was a common saying around the office that every newspaperman had at least one play in him, and Russel Crouse meant to find out if it was true. His anti-war feelings were serious enough, but he knew his expression would be in the form of comedy. He was a frightful punster, who could not refrain from a play on words, no matter how many copy-pencils came flying at him. A middle-sized man, with a large nose and a broad smile that highlighted his friendly brown eyes, he was well-known in newspaper circles for his bright quips and outrageous puns.

He went from the *Globe* to the New York *Mail*, and by 1923 had his own column in the New York *Evening Post*. On St. Patrick's Day of that year he married Alison Smith, whom he had known for some time. He began experimenting with playwriting, but had nothing produced until 1930. *Mr. Currier and Mr. Ives* was so successful that he followed with *It Seems Like Yesterday*, in 1931, and two offerings the following year.

Howard Lindsay, who had admired Russel Crouse's work and felt akin to his wit, decided he could not have made a better choice for the rewrite of *Anything Goes*. The job was done in ten days, and the show was a hit. The two men worked well and easily together. Both were in their forties, and had seen enough, worked enough, and experienced enough to have the same outlook on life. They rejoiced together over the smoothness of the completed script for *Anything Goes,* and immediately started on a new effort, a musical called *Red, Hot and Blue,* which brought Bob Hope to stardom.

Both Lindsay and Crouse preferred to write comedy that had "some comment to it," as Russel put it. He had not forgotten his idea for an anti-war vehicle, and their next attempt was *Hurray for What?* The idea was sound enough, and the satire on the glory of battle was keen; but Ed Wynn, who starred, was "not a book comedian," as Lindsay said. He was used to acting in revues, and was not able to put over a satirical idea-play like *Hurray for What?*

At about this time, Dorothy Stickney began having trouble with her eyes. When it became difficult for her to read, Howard began the practice of reading the paper aloud to her in the evening. Clarence Day was writing his famous *Life with Father* columns, a favorite with the Lindsays. They laughed over Day's reminiscences every evening, remembering incidents in their own family past that brought out the flavor of the nineties; and when the columns included Mrs. Day's maneuvers to get Father baptized, Howard, recalling his voluntary, and, indeed, calculated entry into religion, felt moved to turn Mr. Day's column into a play. He and Dorothy could play Father and Mother Day out of their own backgrounds, their own empathy with a bygone era. (Both Lindsays liked to collect antiques, and in their house in the country, had a good deal of period furniture.) The more they thought of the idea, the better it appeared, and when Howard suggested it to Russel Crouse, the script was started.

They had no trouble in securing permission from Clarence Day, but when the production began, certain problems arose. They had trouble finding four boys of the right size and age—and coloring. (It was said that all the young boy or juvenile actors in New York were dying their hair red during initial tryouts, and at times during the next eight years when one had to be replaced. During the war years, the older boys were drafted; the younger ones got too old for the parts after a year or two.) The play was an instant success; Howard Lindsay and Dorothy Stickney were universally hailed for their delightful performances. They usually took a cab home from the theater at night; and on the way they would often discuss the performance, catching each other up on various slips they made. One evening, after *Life with Father* had been on the boards about two years, Dorothy said thoughtfully on the way home, "You know, Howard, 'Father' was a hot-tempered man; he wasn't mean-tempered." It was a nice distinction, and her husband realized that he had let his performance slide until it was all in one key. There were advantages, he decided, in a husband and wife acting together.

For about six months, Russel played the bit part of the doctor in the matinee performance—"just to see," he quipped to a reporter, "if there's a doctor in the Crouse." It was this kind of joke that made Howard Lindsay shudder, yet he was ready to acknowledge that his collaborator was never at a loss for a "gag" line when one was needed. From then on, the two have had some production on Broadway nearly every year. (In 1941, they turned co-producers to stage *Arsenic and Old Lace;* and subsequently two more hits, *The Hasty Heart* and *Detective Story.*) Always they worked on some play of their own.

The method they worked out for the script of *Anything Goes* suited the situation so well that they have continued to follow it to the present day. They talk out an idea thoroughly before starting to write, as a rule. When both have had their say, they make a few notes. Crouse, accustomed to turning out newspaper copy on a typewriter, starts pounding the keys, while Lindsay paces up and down the study where they work. "After that we outline all the scenes in the play—all before we put down a single line of dialogue," Mr. Lindsay told an interviewer in 1964. "Finally, we dialogue it, and that work goes very quickly. But we know just how the play is going to end before we start writing. Generally when a play has failed it's because the author didn't know where he was going. The conception is all-important."

The Lindsays and the Crouses were close friends, congenial in recreation as well as work, who often made a foursome at Sardi's or some other haunt of theater people. They spent weekends together in the country, working and relaxing at the same time. When Mrs. Crouse died early in January of 1943, the Lindsays shared Russel Crouse's sorrow, and did what they could to help him over a difficult period. Two years later, he was married to Anna Erskine (on June 28, 1945). When their second child, a daughter, was born, they called her Lindsay Ann, a gesture of affection in which the Lindsays took great pride.

Shortly before her birth, the two collaborators received the Pulitzer prize for one of their most brilliant and entertaining satiric comedies, *State of the Union,* which held up to ridicule the machinations and foibles of the democratic process, the snarls of political campaigns, and the bumblings of bureaucracy. The script was checked by Thomas Stokes in Washington beforehand to make sure the details were correct. Tom, whose syndicated political column was one of the clearest and most objective, had been a friend of Crouse since his newspaper days, and had known Lindsay from the first year of the collaboration. Following the opening night success, the play had to be rewritten and rechecked frequently as events occurred or situations altered. One night they had to rewrite eleven pages and the actors had to memorize the new lines before the next performance. Another time, in reading the headlines of a newspaper onstage, the actor gave the actual results of a close gubernatorial election that had been held that day. (Some of the audience heard it in the theater before they read the voting results in a real newspaper.) When the show went on tour, the authors consulted with politicians in various cities to make sure their facts and details were correct. (In Pittsburgh a seasoned politician gave them a tip on the business of tipping that took place in one scene: no politician, he said, would give a dollar bill to a bellboy unless there were other people in the room. Otherwise, he would hand out a coin, preferably a dime.)

There were other hits. *Call Me Madam,* starring Ethel Merman in 1950, and most recently, *The Sound of Music,* the story of the famous Trapp family of singers, which, in spite of its rather cloying "book," was enormously popular, responsible for the biggest of their box office receipts.

In addition to writing, producing, and acting in plays and musicals, these two remarkable collaborators started the New Dramatists Committee to help budding playwrights get the all-important initial break; Paddy Chayefsky and Robert Anderson were among those who benefited from the Committee's work. Perhaps even more significant was the establishment of the Dramatists' Play Service, which put an end to the monopoly of Samuel French in printing bound copies of plays for rehearsal use. Both Lindsay and Crouse have been active in the Dramatists Guild of the Authors League (Russel Crouse was president for several years) and both have belonged to the Players' Club—of which Mr. Lindsay has been the fifth president for ten years. Both served on the War Writers' Board in the Second World War. The Antoinette Perry (Tony) special citation they received on their twenty-fifth anniversary read: "For distinguished achievement in the theater in collaborating with" (here each document bore the other's name) "over a period of twenty-five years."

In 1964, the two celebrated their thirtieth anniversary in typical fashion: the Lindsays and the Crouses attended a performance of a current comedy hit, *Luv,* by a somewhat younger colleague, Murray Shisgall; afterwards they went to Sardi's, where a festive candlelit cake was sent around. "We're the longest collaboration since Sodom and Gomorrah," Russel Crouse told Stuart Little of the *Herald Tribune* at that time, "but for different reasons." Inside of those thirty years they had presented fifteen shows. They still work every afternoon in the study of Lindsay's home on E. 94th Street. (The foyer of the house has two seats from the Empire Theatre screwed into the floor, mementos of their longest-run hit, *Life with Father;* "E, 101," and "E, 102," fifth row, center aisle, "the best seats on the floor," Mr. Lindsay explained. Across the room are two straight chairs from Daniel Frohman's box at the Empire.) Sometimes, if the playwrights "strike a big vein," they are likely to push ahead right straight through the evening, and, on the road, keep at it until dawn, if necessary.

Theirs has been the longest, most profitable, and most pleasant writing partnership in theatrical history.

Elliott Nugent and James Thurber

If Howard Lindsay and Russel Crouse represent the longest collaboration, then Elliott Nugent and James Thurber exemplify the briefest. Yet they were lifelong friends, both born in the same state —like Mr. Crouse, both came from Ohio, not far from Columbus— and both attended Ohio State University at the same time. And their play was an achievement in modern American comedy, one which has placed it alongside Aristophanes in a recent anthology of great comedies through the ages.

The reason for the brevity of their playwriting relationship of course is that James Thurber did not consider himself primarily a playwright, and he was not interested in pursuing the career beyond helping out his friend, Elliott, and proving that he *could* write plays if he chose. If *The Male Animal* had not been so outstanding, the collaboration would not be sufficiently significant to mention.

Elliott Nugent, on the other hand, was a collaborator of longstanding experience, literally a product of the theater from birth. His mother and father, starting on the lowest rung of the theatrical ladder, were "hoofers" and vaudeville actors in the years when the "two-a-day" circuits made Keith and Orpheum common names in country theaters.

Elliott was born in Dover, Ohio, on September 20, 1899. He and his sister, Ruth, were as much children of the theater as the Barrymores, whose father, Maurice, was a good friend of J. C. Nugent. As a boy, Elliott played child roles in plays like *Robinson Crusoe* and he and Ruth often appeared in vaudeville with their parents. His mother, the former Grace Fertig, was a seasoned trouper who could put over a song and dance number with ease and probably would have been content to stay in the acting end of show business; but his father had playwriting ambitions, and began to try his hand while the children were still in grade school. When Elliott started in at Ohio State, he saw all the plays that came to the college, and took a course in playwriting as part of his English major. It was at this time that he met James Thurber, and the two became best friends on the campus; even then the cartoonist-writer showed a zany streak that appealed to Elliott; between them, they could always think up some form of novel entertainment. Thurber, who was five years older than Elliott, had attended the University earlier, but "took a year off to read," as he said.

Thurber had lost one eye in a boyhood accident and could not be in the armed forces during the war but, like Philip Barry, served as a code clerk in Washington and as attaché at the American embassy in Paris. Elliott Nugent joined the Navy, serving in the Reserves for a year. Both came back to Columbus and took their A.B. degrees in 1919. Thurber, who was born in Columbus, began his writing career as a reporter on the Columbus *Dispatch*. His strong sense of the ridiculous enabled him to see home town and family life in the clear, broad light of humor and bring them to fame in his book, *My Life and Hard Times*. Although he and Elliott followed different roads, they kept up the friendship through the years, by letters during periods when they did not see each other.

Elliott wrote his first play at Ohio State, a script which so impressed the professor of the playwriting course that he suggested selling it to a producer. Unfortunately, it was sold outright so the youthful playwright received no royalty. His father saw the possibilities of Elliott's talent, and before long they were co-authors of a number of comedies, the first of which was *Kempy*. Howard Lindsay, whom Elliott met when he came to New York right after graduation in 1919, became a third member of the collaboration after they became friends in the cast of *Dulcy*, which Howard had staged. That remarkable cast included, besides the two young playwrights, Lynn Fontanne, and a pretty actress by the name of Norma Lee. Elliott promptly fell in love with her, and they were married in 1921.

One of the most successful comedies co-authored by J. C. Nugent and Elliott Nugent was *The Poor Nut,* showing a broad satire of psychoanalysis in its story of the college bookworm with the inferiority complex, who wins a track race and overcomes his emotional handicap, winning his girl as well as the race. It was claimed by the movies, and in 1929, Elliott and Norma Nugent went to Hollywood. They stayed for ten years, and Elliott wrote, directed, and acted in any number of movies. In that time they had three children—Lee, Barbara and Nancy. By the time they returned to New York with their family, in 1939, James Thurber had become a well-known writer, first on the staff of the *New Yorker* magazine, then as cartoonist and free-lance writer, a humorist-commentator on life and literature. He and his second wife, the former Helen Wismer, whom he had married in 1924—in a typical Thurber turnabout fashion—spent the winters in Connecticut and the summers in New York (or anywhere he happened to feel like going).

In Connecticut, Thurber raised dogs, but not the kind he drew. He was fond of animals, and took care of the kennels himself. He had begun to have eye trouble at that time and had already had the first of several operations. Oddly enough, in spite of his great difficulty, he wrote at night. He was "a nocturnal animal," he said, and could think best after midnight. He was inclined to be absent-minded and forgetful of the details in daily living, especially when he was at work on something new, so if he did his writing late at night, he could concentrate on it with a free mind. He wrote slowly, in an agony of perfectionism. Sometimes he would make ten drafts of a piece before one suited him. A tall man, very thin, and very shy, Thurber could stay hunched over his desk until daybreak, but he did not enjoy public appearances or crowded parties.

Elliott Nugent, who was also tall and slender, with thinning blond hair and an amiable, open face, looked more like a "juvenile" than a leading man, for all his forty years. He was often in demand for various plays written by his colleagues, and decided to write a vehicle for himself. In 1939, freedom of speech and democracy were being threatened by the totalitarian governments and the possibility of war. Taking the basic idea of *The Poor Nut*—the worm who turns—Mr. Nugent looked up his old friend, James Thurber. Between them, they hatched a plot about a mild, intellectual professor in a "Midwestern" university (obviously Ohio State), who is forced to assert himself when his right to read Vanzetti's last speech to his class is at stake and his marriage is jeopardized by the return of a hulking All-American football player once in love with his wife.

Drawing on their recollections of a professor at Ohio State (who looked like "a puzzled spaniel"), the two old friends proceeded to write a comedy that was timely, hilariously funny with serious overtones, and universally true. They used "the balloon system" developed by Elliott and his father in writing plays: after making an outline of the play, they wrote the scenes separately, not in sequence, and later fitted them in according to the outline. Since each could stand independently, the order was flexible to a certain extent, and permitted greater elasticity in plot development.

The Male Animal, produced by Herman Shumlin, opened on January 9, 1940, at the Cort Theatre, with Elliott Nugent in the role of the professor. It was universally praised for its dialogue, acting, and content—its message regarding academic freedom of speech clearly defined, but without preachment. The Thurberian touches of terror-charged humor, evident throughout, were hailed by the critics for the high comedy level of the play. (The published version was illustrated with his inimitable drawings.) Elliott Nugent's skilled delineation of Professor Turner assured a long run that year. In 1952, when the House un-American activities hearings were at their height, and all sense of proportion seemed to have vanished, *The Male Animal* was revived in a production by John Golden, and ran even longer than the original.

James Thurber never collaborated with anyone else, and the closest he came to further playwriting was to put together *The Thurber Carnival* of his own writings, in 1960. In spite of the operations, his eyesight deteriorated steadily. He was almost totally blind at the time of his death after a long illness in the fall of 1963.

Elliott Nugent followed his success in *The Male Animal* with the starring role in *The Voice of the Turtle,* opposite Margaret Sullavan (and later Betty Field). He was the co-producer and temporary star of *The Seven-Year Itch.* Until the past few years he has spent much time in Hollywood, where he wrote, directed, and acted in no less than thirty movies. He has recently published his autobiography, which contains reminiscences of his friendship-collaboration with Thurber.

George S. Kaufman and Moss Hart

For exactly a decade, from 1930, with *Once in a Lifetime,* to 1940, with *George Washington Slept Here,* two masters of comedic playwriting, George S. Kaufman and Moss Hart, contributed their combined wit and humor to the American theater in the form of six plays and two musicals. Three of the plays were outstanding works, one of which captured the Pulitzer prize. Their initial effort was an achievement in high comedy that ran for two years and won the Roi Cooper McGrue prize.

George S. Kaufman, the older of the two by some fifteen years, was born in 1889, the son of Joseph and Nettie Kaufman, in Pittsburgh. There seems to have been little out of the ordinary in his background or upbringing. He went through high school and studied law for two years, but decided the intricacy of legal lore was "too hard" for his particular mind. He drifted from one job to another for a couple of years, discovering that he was an indifferent traveling salesman, but a rather good stenographer. Wherever he worked, he had a knack for entertaining his colleagues with an unexpected wisecrack, a dry wit, delivered in a laconic tone, which completely surprised them. He was tall, taciturn in appearance, even gloomy. He rarely smiled, and then but briefly. His black hair stood up in a broad bushy pompadour; his tortoise-shell glasses were apt to slip down on his large nose, allowing his piercing black eyes to peer out over the rims with startling penetration. His full lips were twisted in a wry expression which was at best a sardonic grin that occasionally emerged when his listeners burst out laughing at some off-hand, side-splitting remark.

His hum-drum jobs, however, had little to offer young Kaufman in return, either spiritually or financially. He found that he had a flair for comedy in the written as well as spoken word, and at about twenty, he left Pittsburgh for New York, where the lights of the theater blazed, and the newspapers offered an outlet for his native wit. He had admired F.P.A.'s (Franklin P. Adams) column in the *Evening Mail* for some time, and now became one of its regular contributors. Before long, George S. Kaufman began to acquire a following—readers who looked for his tidbits, and requested more. By this route, he came into a column of his own on Munsey's *Washington Times*. While many readers thought it was riotously funny, Mr. Munsey did not appreciate its quality of broad exaggeration, of brash unadulterated attack on stupidity and narrowmindedness. After a "slight disagreement" with the publisher over one of his satiric verbal assaults, the future playwright walked out of the Washington office never to return.

He came back to New York, and for a while took FPA's place

on the *Evening Mail* when that gentleman took his column else-where. From there, Kaufman went on to become theater news reporter on *The New York Times*. Because his interest in the theater was immense, he was soon promoted to the post of drama editor on the paper—a job he continued to handle with great effi-ciency long after he had succeeded as a playwright. Brooks Atkin-son, who came to work for the *Times* in 1926, has described him as "even-tempered, amusingly sardonic, pleasant and obliging, though never exactly cordial; . . . he came in and out of the office several times by day and night to keep his work moving. His habits were his own; his work was authoritative and final. . . . Everything went like lightning when Mr. Kaufman stood on the south side of the makeup table. Although he was one of the most envied men on Broadway, you would never have suspected it from his informal and preoccupied appearance and his quiet concentration upon what he was doing." The playwright himself said that having a job "kept him out of such mischief as idle hours might suggest, espe-cially with bridge and poker pals." It also prevented his wife, the former Beatrice Bakrow, whom he married shortly after joining the *Times* staff, from scheduling too many social engagements for him.

Kaufman's collaborations began as early as 1917. In spite of his extraordinary talent for the quick, devastating jest, the acid quip, the incisive criticism, he preferred to work with other writers from the start. *Someone in the House,* which he wrote with Larry Evans and Walter Percival, was produced in 1918; and, while it was not an outstanding success, the lines contributed by the young theater news reporter showed promise of a brilliant future to follow. The first big hit came in 1921, when he wrote *Dulcy* with Marc Con-nelly. It preceded a long and dazzling array of successes: two hits, *Merton of the Movies* and *Beggar on Horseback,* with Mr. Con-nelly and half a dozen others with a variety of authors, including such notables as Edna Ferber (*The Royal Family,* 1927), Ring Lardner (*June Moon,* 1929), and Alexander Woollcott (*The Chan-nel Road,* 1929). Moreover, in 1925, he wrote two of Broadway's most hilarious offerings as the sole author of *The Butter and Egg Man* and the book of *The Cocoanuts* for the Marx Brothers in

1925. All of this was accomplished before Mr. Kaufman teamed up with Moss Hart in 1930.

That dynamic young aspirant to Broadway (later called "forked lightning" by his playwriting partner) was then emerging from the thorny path of a long, arduous period of training. He gazed upon Mr. Kaufman (already known as "the great collaborator of his time") with worshipful eyes, "very much as a boy of ten would come upon Dick Merriwell, or the captain of the winning eleven." George S. Kaufman had been Moss Hart's hero for almost ten years by the time the younger man met his idol face to face. It was, in fact, while sitting entranced in "the gallery of the Broadhurst Theatre, drinking in a performance of *June Moon,* that the idea" for their first collaboration came to him like a bolt out of the blue, demanding to be set down on paper that very night. It was typical of the way he had streaked through most of his life up to that point: not without reason did Kaufman compare him to "forked lightning."

Moss Hart was born under the heel of poverty in a crowded section of the Bronx toward the end of 1904, to the harsh strains of family discord, mainly over finances. Theirs was not abject, but "unrelieved," mean, niggling poverty, unmitigated by any harmony there might have been in the home if his parents, Barnett and Lillian Hart, had not been at silent swords' point most of the time. His father's unspoken complaint was against the in-laws who lived with the Harts but did not contribute to the family budget, particularly his wife's old-maid sister, who lived with them most of her adult life. But if she was a thorn in his father's side, Moss Hart's "Aunt Kate" provided the ointment in the otherwise prickly existence of his poverty-stricken boyhood. For Aunt Kate was in love with the theater, and she imbued her nephew with the same passion from the time he was a small boy. The tiny legacy left to her by relatives went for a Broadway show every week, and when she came home, she would regale Moss and his mother with an account of the performance she had seen. And every Thursday afternoon she took her nephew to the plays at the Alhambra Theater in the Bronx, so that by the time he was twelve years old, Moss Hart was stagestruck. His feet might be in the upper Bronx, but his eye was on Broadway, though he had never seen it. In his words, he had "the goad and the goal. The goad was poverty, the goal—Broadway and the theatre."

He took his first step in the desired direction at the age of twelve, when he went to work at a music store near his home, an after-school job paying four dollars a week. Here he pored over the pages of *Theatre Magazine* every chance he got, dreaming of Broadway, the street he had never seen. His first glimpse of it came one day when the manager of the store sent him down to Schirmer's for some sheets of music. As he came up from the subway at Times Square, bands were playing, flags were flying and the carnival spirit of a parade pervaded the scene. He shortly learned it was an election parade, but he could never disassociate Broadway from the blare of trumpets and the beat of drums; the heady excitement of it never left him.

During his high school years, Moss Hart wrote festival sketches and one-acts, always bearing in mind his objective, to become a playwright; or perhaps, an actor, or a director, something connected with the theater. He managed to work his way through high school, and a year or so at Columbia, but at that point his formal education ceased for lack of funds. He took a job in the garment district, which lasted just long enough for him to write the annual employees' show. Determined to work in the theater, he discovered that Augustus Pitou needed a secretary and typist—not exactly creative work, but an office-door entrance to the theater was better than none. Pitou was Manager for Fiske O'Hara, the Irish tenor and hero of melodramas produced by Mr. Pitou. He set his new secretary to play-reading, a dangerous assignment, for Moss Hart immediately got the notion to turn out a script himself, confident that he could match any he had read by the prolific Anne Nichols, playwright for O'Hara. Some imp of fancy made him give a fictitious name instead of his own when he handed the first act of his play, *The Beloved Bandit,* to Mr. Pitou. Surprisingly, the producer was taken with the work of such a promising new playwright as "Robert Arnold Conrad" seemed to be; before Moss Hart could complete the plot, his boss wanted to meet the author—and the cat was out of the bag! Nevertheless, Pitou produced the play, which unfortunately failed in its initial tryout in Rochester, and did no better under a change of title in Chicago. As Hart wrote long afterward, *"The Holdup Man* or *The Beloved Bandit* was a composite of all the plays Anne Nichols had written for Fiske O'Hara. The Rochester audience recognized it as a fake and a dishonest facsimile . . ." After the second fiasco in Chicago, the show folded, never to see the light of Broadway. Moss Hart was fired from his job, but by no means defeated. The year was 1923; he was only nineteen; he had time.

He turned to directing little theater groups in New York and New Jersey during "the season." In the summer, he became social director at adult resort camps in the Catskills; one year he staged the plays in the Labor Temple at Camp Utopia. His was a rough apprenticeship in the theater, one that required "constant invention and sheer physical endurance to provide vacationers with entertainment." He was lucky if he worked as little as sixteen hours a day, and he rarely found time to enjoy resort pleasures himself, as the supervisor who hired him had promised. Once or twice a summer, following a late rehearsal, he and his assistants took a dip at three o'clock in the morning, but otherwise they scarcely saw the out-of-doors. However, Moss Hart was well-suited to the demands of such a job, both physically and emotionally.

He was tall, and almost theatrically attractive, with black hair and snapping black eyes, full of fun and mischievous curiosity. Above them, the twin peaks of his eyebrows pointed toward his early, "humorously receding" hairline, which, as Atkinson noted, broadened in twin bays over the years, leaving "a satyric peninsula of hair in the middle of his scalp." More than one writer of the time remarked on his resemblance to a satyr, and he seems to have had much of the mercurial spirit, the love of riotous fun and merriment that marked the attendants of Bacchus in Greek mythology. The improvisations, the inventive stage business so necessary to Chatauqua and camp shows seemed to come naturally to him; his tremendous drive and firecracker enthusiasm sparked those who worked with him into meeting the stringent deadlines of resort entertainment. He soon gained a well-earned reputation in the field, and by 1929, on that fateful night when he sat in the gallery watching *June Moon,* he was known as "King of the Borsht Circuit," a title of dubious honor artistically, but of great significance as practical training in the theater.

As he related, he began writing his play the same night—the only occasion on which the title came to him first: he wrote on a big yellow paper pad, *Once in a Lifetime,* and proceeded from there. Three weeks later, he completed the script, and submitted it to six managers all of whom were interested; he chose to sell it to Sam Harris, principally because the producer promised to get George S. Kaufman to read it with an eye for possible collaboration. Shortly afterward, he received the magic message that the Great Collaborator had not only read his play but wanted to start working with him at once. They met in Harris' office—an historic meeting in theater annals, marked by Mr. Kaufman's extreme lassitude (wearily lifting one finger in greeting and uttering a barely audible, "Hi") and Mr. Hart's dewy-eyed hero worship.

Earlier in the same year, Moss Hart had written a musical with Dorothy Heyward, *Jonica,* which had been produced in the spring to fairly good notices. They had worked hard, but he was used to that. However, neither that experience, nor all his rigorous training in the borsht circuit had prepared him for the gruelling sessions that began the next day on the top floor of Mr. Kaufman's brownstone in the East Sixties. Here the two playwrights, congenial intellectually, but entirely opposite emotionally, temperamentally, slaved for several months, rewriting the script. They started at ten in the morning and worked straight through until two or three the next morning—or until they were about to drop from exhaustion. Moreover, Mr. Kaufman seemed oblivious to bodily needs for food, while young Mr. Hart had a lusty appetite, and found the fifteen-minute break for tiny tea sandwiches (and perhaps a piece of chocolate cake) in the middle of the afternoon so insufficient that he would leave for home weak from hunger as well as work.

Kaufman was methodical, even in his eccentricities. He would always scrub his hands in the little washroom off the study before starting the day's stint. (He liked to do four pages a session, but would sometimes spend a whole morning on a single line or a proper exit.) When concentrating, he stared hard at the floor, as if searching for the right words, and if he bent to pick up small pieces of lint, he would usually come up with a good line for the play as well. If he stretched out on the floor or paced the room, it meant trouble—or, as Hart later learned, he was trying to avoid the smoke from the younger man's cigar (which he could hardly bear, but never complained about). He liked to proceed according to plan, and usually did so; but if there were delays, writing "humps" that took time, he was patient, good-natured, reassuring.

Moss Hart, on the other hand, was buoyant, enthusiastic, bursting out with rapid-fire ideas as he puffed away on the long black cigars he had taken to smoking during his directorship days. While *Once in a Lifetime* was in process of revision, the cigar-smoking was his sole outlet, for he was too terrified of the Great Collaborator to move from the overstuffed chair that Mr. Kaufman indicated the first day. Hart fondly recalled the whole period as "The Days of the Terror." Later on, when he felt at ease with Kaufman, and they had a roomy work place in the country, he would roam around while thinking out a situation, and seemed to click more rapidly if he had a few distractions. He was fond of hot dogs and other indigestibles that set Mr. Kaufman's pompadour even further on end (possibly the taste for Indian nuts that George indulges all during *Once in a Lifetime* could be traced to Mr. Hart); and he would wax wildly enthusiastic over a gourmet dinner, while Kaufman regarded meals as an interruption.

Eventually the first draft was finished, followed by a slight respite until rehearsals began, and then the treadmill pace resumed. The lines did not "play" as intended when they were typed; most of the scenes required some rewriting, and as rehearsals progressed, it became routine for the two playwrights to sit up half the night revising, and "to appear at rehearsals fresh and bright at ten o'clock the next morning." Kaufman himself took on the role of Lawrence Vail, the forlorn, forgotten playwright of the comedy—the only time he attempted to act in one of his plays. The initial performance of the tryout in Atlantic City elicited a terse message from the producer: "It needs work, boys"—as if they had been idling before!

But by the end of the second tryout at Brighton Beach, both of them knew Sam Harris was right. Drastic cutting and revision was necessary if their brainchild was to survive the final tryout in Philadelphia. Their working sessions (which had always been rugged) now seemed to Moss Hart like the confines of a concentration camp, "and an eraser took on all the semblance of a rubber truncheon." In contrast, Mr. Kaufman came to life as never before, and now seemed able to exist entirely without food. In spite of all their efforts, however, the script still ran way too long on opening night in Philadelphia. The collaborators went into hiding in their hotel room (except for the hours that Kaufman had to be onstage) and for six solid days worked around the clock to perform the herculean task of final revision before the New York opening. During one of their sessions toward the end, Moss Hart insisted on a break for fresh air. As they strolled by a little public park, they spotted a children's carrousel, and, to Hart's surprise, Kaufman made for it as eagerly as he. For half an hour they 'swung madly around' like a pair of truant schoolboys. Then they returned calmly to work, with an added feeling of comradeship. From the moment of that pre-dawn spree they were friends as well as collaborators.

Once in a Lifetime proved to be a hilarious satire on the movie industry, shown in the throes of adjustment to the "talkies." On opening night, September 24, 1930, at the Music Box Theater, the play and its authors received a standing ovation, which George S. Kaufman acknowledged with the briefest, most generous of curtain speeches. "I just want to say," he confided to the audience, "that this play is eighty per cent Moss Hart." The night before, as the final dress rehearsal was about to begin, he had smiled reassuringly at Hart, who for three days had a nervous stomach (and in fact usually spent opening night in the men's room). "Don't worry too much," he had comforted the younger playwright. "It 's been swell anyway. And let's do another one."

Although they "married and had several beautiful children," as Mr. Hart put it, an interval of four years elapsed before the second one came along. During those years, the no longer impoverished Mr. Hart spent money as fast as it poured into his pockets. He transferred his whole family from their house in Sheepshead Bay (where they had moved some years before) to a hotel suite in Manhattan, leaving all their household possessions behind them, like unhappy memories. He bought a farm in Bucks County (on which he planted thirty-five hundred trees) as a retreat for both work and relaxation. Kaufman purchased an adjoining farm; and, when not writing, the two became "Broadway agriculturalists." The plot of their next play, *Merrily We Roll Along*, concerned a young playwright who leaps into fame with his first offering, and, while it is principally a character study in relation to moral values, there are certain surface resemblances to Hart's life: the sudden, stunning success after years of struggle; the thrill and glamor of moving in celebrity circles, hobnobbing with people in the theater who had been mere names before; the new sensation of having plenty of money, and plush surroundings in place of pinched pennies and patchy apartments. The title is ironic, for there is nothing "merrily" done except some of the bright chatter in the play, which is more of a melodrama than anything the two collaborators ever wrote together. Its experimental structure, with the scenes moving backward chronologically, in rapid succession (not to be confused with the backflash narrative) is diffusive and highly unsatisfying, because it never makes the connection between past and present. Nevertheless, the subject matter lent itself to clever Kaufman commentary on the theater, and there were enough admirers to give the play a fair-sized run.

Getting back into character, Kaufman and Hart followed the venture into serious drama with their most successful, laugh-evoking, and most human comedy, *You Can't Take It With You*. Produced in December of 1936, this delicious, captivating piece of playwriting depicted a family whose delightful idiosyncrasies and wise sense of values quickly won the hearts of American audiences. Awarded the Pulitzer prize for 1936–1937, the play, after a long Broadway engagement, became a classic of its kind, produced over and over again in theaters throughout the country; and its timeless quality was irrevocably proven when it was revived nearly thirty years later, in December of 1965, to the equal delight and unrestrained laughter of jaded audiences. The family of Grandpa Martin Vanderhof, who, with him have been doing just what they like to do ever since he decided not to go to his office one morning, plus an odd assortment of people who came to the household and stayed, mark a high point in character creation for the Kaufman-Hart combine. Grandpa's married daughter, Penny Sycamore, for example, at rise of curtain, "is doing what she likes more than anything else in the world. She is writing a play—her eleventh." In Penny (whose flightiness is reminiscent of Kaufman's earlier Dulcy, minus the latter's irritating qualities, and with a charm all her own) the authors evidently enjoyed themselves immensely. She is a gentle spoof at playwriting, and a joyous one. The primary fact that she began writing plays—and left off painting—because a typewriter was delivered to the house by mistake, is hilarious enough; but when the audience is witness to her professional dilemma, as she switches her heroine from El Morocco to a monastery, asks everyone's advice on how to get her out after six years, and gets the following reaction from Rheba, the family factotum, "Six years? My, I bet she busts that monastery wide open.", the effect is side-splitting.

Penny's husband, Paul, makes firecrackers with Mr. DePinna, a former milkman, who came one delivery day and just stayed on. Her older daughter, Essie, loves to take ballet and make candy; her husband loves to play the xylophone, and operate a hand-press. Grandpa himself enjoys going to commencement exercises and the zoo—with equal pleasure. All, like Grandpa, do not believe in taxes, or in making more money than needed to live on (hence, the title). Even the younger daughter, Alice, although she does not share the philosophy of the others,—she has a job and seems to prefer a greater degree of social conformity—can appreciate their attitude, and regards them tenderly. It is undoubtedly Penny, however, who represents the authors' objective point of view and perhaps wishful thinking in regard to their profession. As she goes through her stack of manuscripts, murmuring the subject matter—"labor play . . . religious play . . . sex play . . ." (a riotous pun)—one has the feeling that both Kaufman and Hart might have longed to write plays for the sheer pleasure of it.

In reality, however, the outlook was more like Kaufman than Hart, who made the most of the monetary rewards of the theater; he took great delight in spending money—buying presents for friends, traveling, and entertaining. Kaufman was reserved, retiring, almost provincial in his preference for Manhattan; he rarely took trips. Yet both men hated the harassment of opening nights, and the petty quarrels of their world. Both were active in the Dramatists' Guild, which Kaufman had helped to build into an effective organization to combat contract abuses beginning in 1925, when a handful of playwrights had bound themselves to make the Guild more than a mere name.

It is interesting to note that, with the possible exception of *The*

American Way (1939), all of the Kaufman-Hart plays brought in some aspect of the theater, in varying degrees. Yet they never resorted to the "backstage story" so popular in the thirties; and fondness for the theater outweighs their criticism of it. As a matter of fact, the hero of *The Fabulous Invalid,* their next offering, was the theater itself—always dying, always being revived.

By this time the two had evolved a comfortable course of collaboration. If one or the other conceived an idea for a possible play, they would toss it around at random, sometimes for months, until it had enough substance to warrant a daily work schedule, free from interruption. With the exception of *Once in a Lifetime,* most of their playwriting was done in the country, where there was room enough for both to stretch out—or pace—as they chose. They continued to talk over an idea for several weeks before the typewriting stage began. (When it came to the actual typing, Moss Hart, now on an easy, first-name basis with his collaborator, was willing to "let George do it," while he roamed around, giving vent to pent-up energy, and making sure his cigar smoke did not offend his writing partner. They usually tried to produce four pages a day and often did; but just as often they fell short of the mark, trying to perfect a single speech or line. As much attention was given to stage directions and character descriptions as to dialogue. One of the things that makes *You Can't Take It With You* delightful reading is the ironic commentary running through it. For example, following the description of Penny as, "A round little woman in her early fifties, comfortable, gentle, homey," comes the authors' aside: "One would not suspect that under that placid exterior there surges the Divine Urge—but it does, it does."

The first draft of a script was usually overwritten, on the theory that it was easier to cut than to pad, a premise on which most writers agree. The time it took to complete a script varied from as brief a period as five weeks, for *You Can't Take It With You,* all the way up to six months for *The Man Who Came to Dinner,* their third big hit. (In between two of their plays, these prolific collaborators turned out the book for the musical *I'd Rather Be Right,* and they worked separately on other projects—George S. Kaufman with Edna Ferber, in writing *Dinner at Eight,* and *Stage Door;* and Moss Hart in furnishing the book for musicals with Irving Berlin,

Face the Music, and *As Thousands Cheer;* and with Cole Porter on *Jubilee,* after they had journeyed around the world together.) George worked better under a deadline, a hangover from his journalism days, and liked to set his own by having the theater rented, and the opening date set for the première before he started to write. Moss preferred more leeway, so they usually compromised by setting the dates when the primary "blocking out" of the acts was completed. *The Man Who Came to Dinner* written with the whirlwind personality of Alexander Woollcott, their colleague and crony, in mind, mushroomed as they went along, inventing scenes and surprises that were only a mild exaggeration of some they had witnessed in real life in which the fabulous Mr. Woollcott figured as the rascally, obstreperous protagonist. The dedication of the published work read, "To Alexander Woollcott, *For reasons that are nobody's business.* The Authors."

In this spirit, the portrait of Sheridan ("Sherry") Whiteside was drawn, and superbly enacted by Monty Woolly. It was shown before thousands of appreciative playgoers (and, later, movie fans) from its opening night, October 16, 1939, for an extended run. Like *You Can't Take It With You,* this play has also been popular with little theater groups and repertory companies, although it is not as much of a perennial, does not withstand the changes of the times as well.

A year later, in 1940, Kaufman and Hart wrote their final comedy in collaboration, *George Washington Slept Here,* a rather obvious and contrived satire on city dwellers becoming country squires, set, naturally, in Bucks County. The redeeming feature of the play is the glimpse one gets of the inevitable summer theater, including the classic line from the actress, who, when asked what she expects of a summer theater, replies: "Not a great deal . . . I would just like them to take the pigs out before they put the hams *in,* that's all."

After 1940, the team of Kaufman and Hart separated professionally, though it remained steadfast in friendship, and through various business ventures in the theater and out. For one thing, Kaufman found a new collaborator in life as well as playwriting: he was divorced from Beatrice around this time, and married the actress, Leueen McGrath, with whom he subsequently wrote a number of plays, mostly comedy. Moss Hart, reaching out for more profound expression, underwent psychotherapy, and wrote *Lady in the Dark,* a play with co-ordinated music by Cole Porter, dealing with the effects of psychoanalytic treatment. As played by Gertrude Lawrence, the subject was distinctively, artistically handled, and made Moss Hart a name in his own right. In 1946, he was married to Kitty Carlisle, a happy combination; the ceremony was performed August tenth, in New Hope, Pennsylvania, close to the Kaufman-Hart farms. Two children—a son, Chris, and a daughter, Cathy Carlisle—were born in the next few years. Mr. Hart was notably happy in his matrimonial venture, yet his next play, *Christopher Blake,* dealt with the effect of divorce on a small boy. He seems to have had the desire to develop the serious side of his effervescent nature, but his reach exceeded his grasp. He was more successful in the lively and diverting first volume of his autobiography, *Act One,* of which he said that George S. Kaufman was the hero. (Kaufman, for his part, when asked how the collaboration started, replied, "I very quickly knew, when I met Moss, on which side my bread was buttered.")

Both men were interested in directing and producing in later years, although Kaufman wrote plays well into the fifties, with his wife, and others. Both died of heart attacks in the same year, 1961, six months apart. (The second and third "Acts" of Moss Hart's memoirs were never written.) But the Kaufman-Hart canon of comedy lives on, a laughing, sunny presentation of the American scene.

CHAPTER VIII

---◆●◆---

LILLIAN HELLMAN

Few women writers in the theater have shown the strength and determination of Lillian Hellman. In both her life and work she has demonstrated extraordinary power and integrity of ideas.

As the setting of most of her plays indicates, Miss Hellman is a Southerner, more by birth and background than actual living in the South. Her mother's family was from Alabama, and her father's from Louisiana. She was born in New Orleans in 1905, just as her father had acquired a large shoe store in that city. Five years later (when she was five), he decided to move his family to New York City to expand his business, and from then on, they spent six months of every year in New York and six in New Orleans. Lillian was shuttled from one school to another as they traveled back and forth; and each time she had to adjust her outlook and scholastic standards from Northern to Southern, and vice versa. She used to wish her parents would make up their minds to stay in one place or the other.

They finally "came to rest" in New York, when Lillian was about sixteen. She went to high school there, and after graduation, continued her education at New York University and Columbia. Without a college degree in hand, she was trying to decide what sort of career to follow, when, "by a pleasant accident," she went to work for the publisher, Horace Liveright. Finding herself with enough time on her hands to experiment, she began writing short stories, sending them out hopefully here, there and everywhere. (All but one came back with discouraging regularity; and the exception was published in a Paris magazine that folded soon afterwards.) She began to doubt her ability to write, but she found the publishing world more interesting than business so she stayed on at the Horace Liveright office, making the most of the opportunities her job afforded. One of these was book reviewing for the *Herald Tribune,* which was then starting its Book Section.

At about this time, she met a young writer, newspaperman, and press agent, Arthur Kober, who was then working for the Schuberts, doing publicity for musical revues, and anything else that fell to his lot. Of Austro-Hungarian parents, he had grown up in the Bronx, where he had absorbed the particular brand of American-Jewish culture that was to characterize his own comedies in later years. Starting to work at fourteen, he had been everything from clerk to bellboy on a ship bound for San Francisco through the Panama Canal, to Social Director for a vacation camp in the foothills of the Catskills. Lillian, a striking girl with straightforward serious dark eyes in contrast to her light reddish-blond hair, slim and sleek of figure, was attracted to the mercurial young man with the dark curly hair and dancing eyes, whose amiable humor had helped him to win his way in the world. His connection with the theater made him much more interesting than book salesmen. (Soon she was also doing publicity work in the theater, and one summer was the promotion and subscription manager for a stock company in Rochester, New York.) As for Kober, he was fascinated with her forthright philosophy of life, her bold yet subtly feminine ways.

They were married on December 25, 1925, and went to Paris to plunge into the intellectual stream of the embryonic artists who overflowed the Left Bank in the twenties. Both wanted to be freelance writers eventually, to give full expression to their individual talents, but they had to earn a living. Arthur landed a job on the Paris *Comet,* the magazine which finally published a couple of Lillian's short stories—"lady-writer stories," she labeled them many years afterward. When the magazine went out of print, they returned to New York. In 1930, as the depression was setting in, they had an offer from the Metro-Goldwyn-Mayer studios in Hollywood —Lillian was a manuscript reader, and Arthur in the publicity department. A year later they were divorced. Mr. Kober stayed on in Hollywood, subsequently writing screen plays for prominent movie stars of the thirties, among them Carole Lombard and Kay Francis.

Although M-G-M had offered to promote Lillian Hellman to a "junior writer" at fifty dollars a week, she chose to return to New York. Dashiell Hammett, one of the first writers she and Arthur had met when they came to Hollywood, an extraordinary man who had an immediate and lasting influence on her life, was going back to write a novel. He had been invited by Nathaniel ("Pep") West to stay at the Sutton Hotel, which Pep was managing for a kind-hearted uncle who had given him the job for the duration of the depression. The Sutton had been built as a luxury hotel, complete with swimming pool, and was now standing half-empty, in deserted splendor. West was taking in all the struggling writers he knew, and "Dash" Hammett was sure there would be a place for "Lilly."

There was. Dash had the Royal Suite—three very small rooms— where he settled down to write his novel. Lillian had been his inspiration for his new book, and the model for one of the main characters. He was just then gaining some recognition for his detective stories—a thorough artist who took his work seriously. He thought Lillian might do well at fiction, too, but she was more interested in writing for the theater. Among the other guests who lived half-free—and sometimes all-free—at the Sutton, was Louis Kronenberger, who also wanted to write plays. The two began collaborating on a comedy which they called *The Dear Queen*. It was about a royal family who wanted to be bourgeois. They had a good time laughing at their own lines, but Dash said the play was no good because they didn't laugh at each other's lines. Lillian realized she could not collaborate with anyone, and the play was never produced, but the project started her on the career that was to win her the title of "America's Number-One Woman Playwright."

New York was swarming with unemployed actors and starving

playwrights in 1932. There was nothing to do, so the parcel of playwrights at the Sutton spent a good deal of time in the swimming pool. (They had to eat at the hotel most of the time because they "didn't have enough money to eat any place else. It was awful food, almost spoiled. . . . Pep bought it extra cheap," she recalled for an interviewer in 1964.)

Jobs in the theater were scarce, but she finally managed to get part-time work as a play reader in the office of the producer, Herman Shumlin. One of her "discoveries" was Vicki Baum's *Grand Hotel,* which was a great success; but most of the manuscripts that came into the office could hardly be called plays. Reading them only made her more eager to write her own. She needed a good theme; she didn't want to write about herself at the age of twenty-six. One night when they were sitting around the hotel talking, Dash told her she would do better if she chose a situation that had foundation in fact, at least for her first play. He had been reading a book written by Britisher William Roughhead in 1931, which dealt with little-known lawsuits in history. (Dash, who was self-educated, was an omnivorous reader on a wide variety of subjects.) He selected one for her to read with an eye toward dramatization. Under the title of *Closed Doors, or The Great Drumsheugh Case,* it contained the records of a suit for scandal fought through the Scottish courts in the early nineteenth century. They told the story of two teachers in a girls' school, accused of lesbianism. Impressed with the drama in the case, and as a kind of exercise in playwriting, Lillian Hellman was moved to adapt it for the theater.

In the book, the case was described as that of "a malicious child who said that the two headmistresses at her school had 'an inordinate affection' for each other." Bringing the story up to the twentieth century, and with unerring instinct, Miss Hellman created the neurotic adolescent girl, Mary Tilford, one of the unforgettable characters in the drama of the thirties. The playwright herself later wrote of Mary: "On the stage a person is twice as villainous as, say, in a novel. When I read that story I thought of the child as neurotic, sly, but not the utterly malignant creature which playgoers see in her." In order to motivate the accusation, she had to make the girl paranoic and maladjusted, but not the epitome of evil. She also invented a fiancé for one of the headmistresses, so that if lesbianism were present, it was on the unconscious level, and the child's accusation would be false. "It's the result of her lie that makes her so dreadful," Miss Hellman continued in her discussion of Mary. "This is really not a play about lesbianism, but about a lie."

When the first draft was finished, she wanted Dash Hammett to read it before she went any further; he was always "tough and generous" in his criticism and she appreciated his comments. She entitled the final draft *The Children's Hour* and submitted it to Herman Shumlin. Much to her surprise, he decided to produce it almost at once. Several prominent actresses refused the role of either schoolteacher because they were leery about public reaction to lesbianism—no matter that it was only implied. But the play was cast finally and rehearsals began. It opened in 1934, an instant and complete success. Everyone knew the run would be a long one, but no one suspected it would reach the figure of 691 performances that carried it over until the end of 1935. Perhaps the fact that *The Children's Hour* was banned in Boston had something to do with the stir and excitement it caused on Broadway and in the cities it toured. William Lyon Phelps, one of the judges on the Pulitzer Committee, refused to go to see it, and the prize that year ironically went to *The Old Maid,* a tepid study by Zoë Akins.

Now there was money to pay the back hotel bill and other debts, to rebuild the bank account that was down to fifty-five dollars when the play opened. There was more than enough to help friends who were struggling or had been struck down by the depression. Dashiell Hammett completed the novel he had been working on—*The Thin Man*—as it turned out, perhaps his most famous mystery, pivoting around the adventures of a debonair detective and his (equally debonair) wife—Nick and Nora Charles. Nora Charles, with her captious wit and spunky loyalty, had been inspired by Lillian Hellman. (The character, although charming, had little of Miss Hellman's intellectuality or insight into the duplicity of human nature. Privately the playwright thought Nora was "often a foolish lady," who went around getting her husband into trouble.) The fun-loving spirit, the give-and-take between Nick and Nora Charles expressed the essence of the good time that Dash Hammett and Lillian Hellman usually enjoyed together. They were amused by each other, as Nick and Nora were; and they both felt a deep gratification in the admirable portrayals of the two characters by William Powell and Myrna Loy when *The Thin Man* was made into one of the few high comedies of motion pictures in the thirties.

The movie made a great deal of money, which Dash gave away almost as fast as it came in—"always he gave it away—to the end of his life, when there wasn't much anymore." They both lived well, and ate no more of the Sutton's questionable food. Nathaniel West (who was soon to give up the managership of the hotel) completed the manuscript of *Balso Snell,* which he let Lillian read as he went along. (Manuscripts made the rounds regularly at the Sutton.) Then S. J. Perelman, who was "Pep's" brother-in-law, and his wife bought an old house in Bucks County, and all the writers went trouping down for weekends in the country. William Faulkner, an old friend of Dash, came up to New York periodically, sometimes for long visits. Faulkner, a gallant Southerner, used to call the playwright "Miss Lillian." On one visit they met him every night at a different place. The three would have lengthy literary discussions, and a running argument about Thomas Mann went on for weeks.

Both Miss Hellman and Hammett were interested in the Federal Theater Project, and the general welfare of working people (unemployed actors included). "Roosevelt gave you a feeling that you had something to do with your government, something to do with better conditions for yourself and for other people. With all its foolishness the thirties were a good time and I often have regrets for it," she said recently. The endless queues of people—artists and factory workers alike, who formed the lines of those on relief—had aroused Miss Hellman's sense of justice; and the various welfare plans increased her respect for Roosevelt. At one point she stated, "Politically, I am a liberal; I choose to think that means that I believe more in the rights of the working man than I believe in any other rights." She was not enough of a "political person," however, to ally herself with any political group, or to allow politics to creep into her plays—except perhaps in *The Searching Wind* (1944), one of her least rewarding efforts.

In 1936 and 1937, Miss Hellman made an extended tour of Europe and Soviet Russia. She was curious about Russian ideology, whether in practice it had benefited the working classes, or was weighted down by bureaucracy. (Before she left New York, she had written a play dealing with labor strife, *Days to Come,* more from the industrialists' point of view than the unions'. She realized too late the play was too complex and poorly structured. In her own words: "The whole production was botched, and I helped to do the botching. It was an absolute horror of a failure . . . the curtain wasn't up ten minutes and catastrophe set in." She could hardly bear to think of that night. The lines fell like lead from the lips of the actors and were received in dull silence by the audience. William Randolph Hearst caused a little excitement by getting up in the middle of the first act and leaving with his party of ten. Lillian, watching from the back aisle, actually vomited. She had to go home and change clothes. The fiasco had sent her sailing to Europe to forget.)

From Russia she went down into Spain, where she was caught up in the meshes of the Loyalist cause, under bombardment by French forces. She had had enough of other countries, and came home determined to write a play that was at least as good as *The Children's Hour;* she ended by creating her masterpiece in the study of evil, *The Little Foxes.* Going back to the locale of her childhood, she chose to portray a degenerate family of Southern Reconstruction businessmen, the Hubbards, who made a fortune after the Civil War by exploiting the Negroes and the poor white trash. Two brothers, Oscar and Ben, are matched in their sly cunning by their sister, Regina, who has married a banker. The story of their greed, their monstrous cupidity as each schemes to grab the family fortune, was fascinating, gripping drama in its final form. There were many problems in writing such a play, however.

Miss Hellman used less of an outline than she had in her first plays, but she wrote more drafts of this one. She conceived her characters one way to begin with, but they kept changing before she had gone very far. They didn't always go her way and she would have to alter the action. She had reached the sixth version and, once going, she worked all night long to complete it. At five o'clock in the morning, weary, but pleased with her efforts, she felt she had finally "got it right." She wanted Dash Hammett to read it, and put the manuscript near his door with a note, "I hope *this* satisfies you." When she got up around noon, the manuscript was outside her door with a note saying, "Things are going pretty well if you will just cut out the liberal blackamoor chitchat."

"No other praise, just that," she commented in relating the incident. She knew Dash well enough, knew how dedicated he was about writing—"tough and generous"—to realize that he meant her play was still far from right. She sat down and wrote it all over again. More than once she turned to him for help with a speech or scene before the script pleased both of them. Then, taking her title from the biblical quotation, "Beware the little foxes that steal the grapes," she went about the business of getting the play produced.

The Little Foxes opened in 1939, with a superb cast (particularly Tallulah Bankhead, whose remarkable portrayal of Regina won her an unrivaled reputation for that kind of role), and was hailed as a dramatic achievement in the theater. Miss Hellman was praised for her craftsmanship as well as her content—her use of suspense in building up a climax, her clear handling of plot and sub-plot—and pronounced an artist and champion of "the well-made play." (She recently objected strenuously to her reputation for the latter. "Survival won't have anything to do with well-made or not well-made, or words like melodrama," she said. "I don't like labels and isms. You write as you write, in your time, as you see your world. One form is as good as another . . . if you are any good.")

The play was both an artistic and financial success. When the movie rights were bought by Hollywood, the playwright wrote the adaptation herself, for the most part. (By an odd coincidence, Arthur Kober's first comedy, *Having Wonderful Time*, won the Roi Cooper McGrue prize in 1939, after being a Broadway hit for two years; and he was one of the screen writers who assisted in the adaptation of *The Little Foxes*.)

The rise of Hitler and the sadism of the Nazi regime, the brutality of Fascism she had witnessed in Spain, seemed to Lillian Hellman a manifestation on a monstrous scale of the same evil in human nature that motivated the Hubbards. She felt on her return that the people in the United States were but dimly aware of the danger of Nazism to the entire world. She summed up her attitude in a few sentences: "I am a writer. I am also a Jew. I want to be quite sure that I can continue to be a writer, and that if I want to say that greed is bad or persecution is worse, I can do so without being branded by the malice of people making a living by that malice."

In a powerful, chilling drama, *Watch on the Rhine,* she gave voice to her feeling, and, through artistic expression, uttered a ringing indictment of Nazi dictatorship. Taking a typical, lesser American diplomat's household, secure and isolationist, the playwright brings about a gradual change among its members when a Nazi refugee, Kurt Muller and his family, come to stay with them. Also stopping there is a penniless Rumanian count, Teck de Brancovis, a Machiavellian character who tries to blackmail Kurt when he discovers that the refugee is an active anti-Nazi working with the underground. Kurt quietly plans to kill Teck rather than give up the fight against the Nazis, and when he does so onstage, the action is tense and entirely justified. (In writing the scene, the playwright consulted Dash Hammett on the best fake murder technique to employ, but he objected to visible violence and said if she was going to include the actual killing, she was wasting time to worry about details of the best method. But for once, she did not listen to him—he wasn't writing for the theater—and as it turned out, her instincts were right.) The feeling of loyalty and love between Kurt Muller and his family evoked a sympathy in American audiences and made the Count's death a triumph over evil, a feeling that was increased by Muller's return to Europe to fight the Nazis. In this respect, *Watch on the Rhine* differed from Miss Hellman's previous plays, in which the force of evil was unrelenting. One of the most effective dramas to come out of the war years, it won the Drama Critics Circle Award in 1941, and placed Miss Hellman among America's leading playwrights.

After Pearl Harbor, both Miss Hellman and Hammett were involved with the war effort. Though he had contracted tuberculosis while serving in World War I, Dash was determined to enter as an enlisted man, and joined the Army Service Forces in the rank of corporal. By no means tall, Hammett gave the impression of being a bigger, stronger man than he was. His aristocratic face, set off by his prematurely white hair, and the proud bearing of his finely built figure made him seem taller and more muscular. In a snapshot he sent to the playwright, he was wearing his overseas cap tilted at a jaunty angle on his white hair, a picture of soldierly defiance.

Miss Hellman spent considerable time in Hollywood during the war years, working on the adaptation of *Watch on the Rhine* for the screen, and writing the screen play for *The North Star,* a wartime film revealing the heroism of the Russian people in the face of the German invasion. Summers she spent at Hardscrabble Farm, a place she had bought near Pleasantville, New York. She hoped to follow *Watch on the Rhine* with a play that would be even more scathing in its denunciation of American indifference to the evils of Hitlerism. The passive complacency of the generation that could sit idly by and witness the persecution of an entire group of people without active protest was perplexing, to say the least. It was at this time that she wrote the nearest thing to a political play that she ever attempted, *The Searching Wind,* which again dealt with an American diplomat, an attaché in Rome who follows an isolationist policy during the rise of Mussolini and Hitler in order to escape from the ugly truth. His political philosophy is a carry-over from his unresolved emotional life, which he also avoids facing. "But even there," Miss Hellman said, "I meant only to write about nice, well-born people who, with good intentions, helped to sell out a world." The play, produced in 1944, came as an anticlimax, when the Allies were on the point of annihilating the offenders. Its "message" seemed pointless, and the run was short.

Directly afterward, late in 1944, Miss Hellman was invited to visit the Soviet Union as an honored guest, on "a kind of cultural mission—maybe because they were producing *Watch on the Rhine* and *The Little Foxes* in Moscow"—and, in the interest of cultural exchange, she accepted the invitation. In Moscow, she met Serge Eisenstein, who was pleasant and easy-going; in attending rehearsals and state affairs, she saw a great deal of him, and in the short time she was there, grew very fond of him. The production of *The Little Foxes* was excellent, but *Watch on the Rhine* was very bad, to her surprise; she had expected it to be the other way around. She and Eisenstein would be sitting at rehearsals of *Watch on the Rhine,* and when she "made faces or noises," he would placate her by saying, "Never mind, never mind. It's a good play. Don't pay any attention to what they are doing. They can't ruin it."

On her return from Russia, she plunged into work on a new play, which was to be the second in the trilogy she originally planned to write about the Hubbard family of "little foxes," and might well be called the prologue to the first play. The action takes place twenty years before, in 1880. Regina had been about thirty-eight in *The Little Foxes*, and the year was 1900. Now the play-wright delved into the imaginary past to unearth the psychological factors that made Regina and her brothers the predatory creatures they became as a result of their father's sadistic, driving ambition for wealth and power. The motivation of the children became evident in the sins of their father, Marcus Hubbard, a ruthless carpet-bagger who had piled up a huge profit in black market salt during the Civil War (the original fortune) and keeps increasing it by foreclosing loans. He ignores his wife, and treats his two sons, Ben and Oscar, like hired help. Once again, Miss Hellman used the inadvertent discovery of a piece of information (in this case, the accidental knowledge of the older son, Ben, concerning his father's betrayal of Confederate forces to the Union army) as the pivotal point for the machinations of her wily characters. By the end of the last scene, the later action of the plundering "little foxes" appears inevitable, illuminated by the lightning flash into their past. It was fitting that the title for such action should be Shakespeare's stage direction, *Another Part of the Forest*.

Produced in 1946, the play was well received, although it did not evoke as much enthusiasm from the critics as *The Little Foxes*, perhaps because it was more analytic and less concentrated in its picture of evil. Some of the critics, however (notably Eric Bentley, who is perhaps overly severe in his attitude toward American play-wrights), felt that *Another Part of the Forest* was equally good the-ater. Mr. Bentley condemned both plays by concluding his remarks (which had begun with the observation that Miss Hellman's latest play was "nothing if not well-made"): ". . . Like *The Little Foxes*, *Another Part of the Forest* is Grand Guignol in the guise of real-ism. Despite the outward trappings of seriousness, the spirit of Broadway carries the day." These were harsh words, but they were more than balanced by words of commendation from other critics. John Gassner called the play "a picaresque account of the Hub-bards' predatory beginnings in an almost self-contained world of comedy and melodrama." Miss Hellman's audiences renewed their speculation as to the origin of the avaricious Hubbards; many people thought it must be her mother's family history.

The playwright herself paid little heed to anything that was said, one way or the other. She was writing as she had to write, as she saw the world, past or present. She was getting tired of the people in *The Little Foxes* and had begun to conceive a new set of characters closer to her own time. Moreover, she was preoccupied with concern for Dash Hammett, who had contracted emphysema during the war, and was a sick man, although he kept going, and few knew of his suffering. Miss Hellman and he were both deeply interested in civil rights and freedom of speech, both believing that if World War II was not fought in vain there must be a broadening of human rights. The playwright, never really "political," was not as active as Hammett, who headed an organization labeled "left-wing." (He once said he thought it was "impossible to write anything without taking some sort of stand on social issues.") Neither one of them could be undermined in their convictions by the hysteria of McCarthyism following the war. Indeed, it was quite by accident that the playwright learned she had been blacklisted.

She and William Wyler had planned to make a movie of Dreiser's *Sister Carrie*. But an executive of one of the large companies told Wyler that Lillian Hellman could not be hired. And the "unwritten, unofficial, powerful blacklist" stayed in effect nearly twelve years. Shortly after the first blacklisting, she was offered a contract by Columbia Pictures, the kind she had always wanted: to direct, produce, and write, in any combination, including an enormous amount of money. But it came at the time the producers were facing attacks from "Red-baiters. Trying to appease them the contract contained one clause that was a lulu." Miss Hellman did not sign.

She concentrated on her latest cast of characters, a group of people in a shabby-genteel summer boarding house in the South. All of the ten gathered together had so mismanaged their lives that they were moral failures searching to fill up the emptiness of their existence, but their personal unhappiness had no basis in the social problems of the time. (One exception was an old grandmother who holds the depression responsible for all the "touchers" and "leaners" of society.) This play seemed to come easier to the playwright than any she had attempted in several years. She had translated, and produced, Emanuel Robles's "Monseurrat," a grim melodrama of nineteenth-century rebellion in Venezuela, only a year earlier (1949). It was an interesting if not profitable venture, but gave her none of the satisfaction of creating her own characters and then thrusting a probing pitchfork into them. Toward the end of the script, however, she worked on one speech over and over again, a philosophic paragraph spoken by the retired general, Griggs; but the words would not come right. One night Dash said to her, "Go to bed and let me try." It was a passage defining the general's attitude toward the turning point in life, and because of Dash Hammett's enormous courage, his quietness in bearing the sickness and trouble that had come to him, he was able to grasp and set down the idea she had wanted to convey.

Autumn Garden was produced in 1951, bringing its author a wide variety of commendation and cautious criticism. The work was called "a poignant, reflective drama," as well as an "ineffectual, baffling, and most psychoanalytic play." John Mason Brown pronounced it "in many ways the most mature and probing play to come from her gifted pen"; and went on to speak of "the same muscularity of mind, the same command of authentic dialogue, the same willingness to face unpleasant people as they are, and the same instinctive awareness of the theater's needs that have always animated her writing." Harold Clurman, who directed the production, found *Autumn Garden* the "most deftly constructed, the most scrupulously written play produced here in a long time," and "lucid, witty, incisive drama," but felt that the playwright failed, despite her probing, to reveal the quality in her characters' weaknesses which still makes them great—love, the love of the author for the characters, the affection always present in Chekhov's plays. "Miss Hellman is a fine artist; she will be a finer one when she melts," he concluded.

Just at this time the House Un-American Activities Committee subpoenaed Dashiell Hammett for questioning in regard to four alleged Communists who had been convicted, and jumped bail, disappearing before they could be tracked down. Hammett, as trustee of the Civil Rights Congress, which had supplied bail for a number of writers on trial for "conspiracy against the U.S. government," was asked to name the sources of the bail fund and to produce the books of the organization. He flatly refused. He was convicted of contempt of court, with a six months' jail sentence. Lillian Hellman, who had been appalled at the proceedings of the McCarthy Committee from the time she discovered her name among those blacklisted, was now seething with angry outrage and anxiety. The fact that Hammett had served his country voluntarily in two wars, and as a result was a very sick man, seemed to count for nothing. If Dash had named a few names, he would have been praised for his unscrupulousness and released, in all probability. It was perplexing, maddening. The playwright used all the influence she could to get the case into a higher court, but the appeal failed, and Hammett went to jail for six months, from July until December, 1951.

He kept up a fine show of bravado, acted as if he was amused, and joked about the "college" he was in, but he could not get the proper medicines in prison, and the playwright was worried about him. It was a time of anxiety, frustration, and sheer puzzlement. What bothered her the most was that so few people fought, so few people spoke out against McCarthy—or spoke up to him as Dash Hammett had done. Writers abroad thought it was a "disgrace" that he was in jail, and that "nobody had lifted a finger" to save him. Miss Hellman excepted, writers as a whole made no effort to protest or "raise a row" about the entire proceedings. Many who were investigated, in the theater especially, decided to "inform," and called their friends beforehand to tell them what they were going to do. (One man said, "I'm going to rat.") In several cases those to be injured actually gave permission. All were supposed to understand the motives. "The fraternity of the betrayers and the betrayed," the playwright called it; to her it was worse than the testifying. There was a great deal of telephoning around, of hypocritical reassurances, followed by bitterness on both sides. A kind of grim clownishness pervaded the whole period, like a nightmare.

Joke as he might about jail, Dash was so ill when he was released that he was virtually an invalid. And two years later, the same Committee subpoenaed him again, and then Lillian Hellman to appear before its insatiable hearings. A subcommittee, consisting of Roy

Cohn and David Shine, were investigating charges that "pro-Communist" books, including three hundred copies of Hammett's books, were on the shelves of USIS libraries. His famous mystery, *The Maltese Falcon*, had already been removed when the hearing took place on television. Miss Hellman, who was terribly afraid that Hammett would talk himself back to prison and get sicker again, watched the screen tensely. When McCarthy asked, "Mr. Hammett, if you were in our position, would you allow your books in USIS libraries?" Dash, who was "a remarkably handsome man and looked nice," answered with a gleam of amusement, "If I were you, Senator, I would not allow any libraries." It was a good remark, and luckily McCarthy laughed. ("Nobody else did, but McCarthy did," Miss Hellman said in telling the story. She noticed that after every answer, Dash would shrug his shoulders, an annoying habit she used to nag him about. After the hearing, he called her from the airport. "Hey, how did you like it? I was shrugging my shoulders just for you," he said.)

In May, 1952, it was the playwright's turn to appear before the Committee. At a preliminary, which she attended with her lawyer, Joseph Rauh, it developed that the investigators were more interested in the names that an important person in the theater like Miss Hellman could furnish than they were in her own past, which was obviously nonpolitical. Answering their questions calmly and collectedly, she said that she was willing to testify about herself as long as she wasn't questioned about other people or asked to give names. When someone tried to persuade her that it was a pattern everyone was following at the time, she snapped, "I can't cut my conscience to fit this year's fashions." She might have been cited for contempt, but she didn't care. However, no charges were brought at the end of that day, and her lawyer was proud and pleased at her brilliant retort.

She repeated her remark with emphasis in a letter drafted by the lawyer and Miss Hellman two days before the actual hearing. It said in part: "I am most willing to answer all questions about myself. I have nothing to hide from your Committee and there is nothing in my life of which I am ashamed. . . . But I am advised by counsel that if I answer the Committee's questions about myself, I must also answer questions about other people and that if I refuse to do so, I can be cited for contempt. My counsel tells me that if I answer questions about myself, I will have waived my rights under the Fifth Amendment and could be forced legally to answer questions about others. This is very difficult for a layman to understand. But there is one principle that I do understand: I am not willing, now or in the future, to bring bad trouble to people who, in my past association with them, were completely innocent of any talk or any action that was disloyal or subversive. . . .

"But to hurt innocent people whom I knew many years ago in order to save myself is, to me, inhuman and indecent and dishonorable. I cannot and will not cut my conscience to fit this year's fashions, even though I long ago came to the conclusion that I was not a political person and could have no comfortable place in any political group."

The Committee no doubt knew that Miss Hellman was innocent, and they apparently were not interested in hearing about her past unless she gave them a few names. The charges against her were dropped, and directly afterward she went to England to make a movie. The whole affair of the hearings had been so sordid that for a while she was tempted to stay there, and she wanted Hammett to come over to save himself from further attack, but he would not. Since she really preferred her country to any other, she returned to join him in his fight to prolong his life—or to make it as comfortable as possible—in the face of the cruel disease that was causing him to waste away. They had bought an old yellow farmhouse on Martha's Vineyard, and here, in the tower room of an abandoned windmill on the east wing, Dashiell Hammett spent the few years left to him, an invalid and almost a recluse. He started a novel, but could not work on it long because of his illness. The playwright saw to it that he was not disturbed by the guests who often overflowed the network of small square rooms in the house; she explained his sudden exit if someone happened in unexpectedly when he was offguard, perhaps reading in an easy chair. She relayed messages and questions from friends, and, through her, he would answer. (Shortly before his death, when he frequently felt too weak to sit at the table for meals, the *Paris Review* writer, John Phillips, sent a request for an interview. The answer read: "Sorry. Don't think it would work. Lilly will explain.")

During those years, Miss Hellman worked on the adaptation of Voltaire's *Candide* for the brilliant musical which was produced in 1955. She "had a good time" doing it as long as she was alone—writing by herself, but the collaboration was "stormy" and she got nothing but pain out of the production. She let herself be persuaded to do things she didn't believe in, she admitted later, and she was "no good at all at that game." Although a box office failure, *Candide* was a *succès d'estime,* and eventually became a "cult show," with a huge following of music lovers who insured the popularity of the recording of Leonard Bernstein's score. For the first time, the playwright was worried about the cost of the production, and felt guilty when it closed because the loss was so tremendous. It was bad for her morale and she realized that failure, like success, could come faster in the theater than in any other art; but it was "necessary" not to allow herself to become frightened of failure.

She thought of writing the last of the trilogy about the Hubbard family. In 1949, Marc Blitzstein had composed an opera, *Regina,* based on *The Little Foxes,* emphasizing the evil of the central character above the others. Miss Hellman, although a close friend of Blitzstein, had not collaborated with him on the book for the opera. She did not see *Regina* in that light, and in a new play had meant to show her twenty years after *The Little Foxes,* in Europe. Her daughter, Alexandra, was to have become a spinsterish social worker—"a rather angry woman." But so much had been written or conjectured about the "badness" of Regina and the Hubbard family that the playwright was tired of hearing about them. (She never thought of her characters as "good" or "bad," and felt that moral judgments did not apply to the characters an author created.)

She chose for her next play a contemporary Southern family—the remnants of a once proud dynasty—two sisters and their wayward brother, a wastrel who has just returned to the old home with his bride, after having run away many years before. Once again the playwright sought to expose the weaknesses of her characters in picturing their neurotic behavior—the jealousy of the sisters, the sadistic trickery of the brother, and the deranged helplessness of his bride. But the action of the play, which she called *Toys in the Attic,* was somehow confused and contrived. It did not have the authentic ring of *The Little Foxes, Another Part of the Forest,* or

Autumn Garden. Produced in 1960 and performed by an admirable cast, including Jason Robards, Jr. (fresh from his triumphs in *The Iceman Cometh* and *Long Day's Journey into Night),* as the brother, the play did not last on Broadway, but neither could it be considered a failure.

Whether she experienced success or failure, however, Miss Hellman has always kept on writing. Her latest play, *My Mother, My Father and Me,* was a departure in setting and subject matter from her other works, and perhaps for that reason did not appeal to an audience that came expecting to see another degenerate, predatory family in the South and found a middle-class family in the Bronx occupying the stage. Miss Hellman had wanted to see it produced off-Broadway, and felt that the presentation was "botched" because it was not the type of play for Broadway.

After Dash Hammett died, in 1959, Miss Hellman sold the yellow frame farmhouse on Martha's Vineyard and, at the bottom of the sandbank that hid it from view, built a new white house of modern design, with a wooden deck looking out to sea. Here, in full view of the busy harbor, she spends her summers, working on a new play or literary project of some sort. She edited the letters of Chekhov, published in 1955, and since Hammett's death has been compiling and editing an anthology of his short stories. When she is not writing, she likes to read melodrama and poetry, as well as the writings of such authors as Chekhov, Henry James, Dreiser, Dostoievsky, Mark Twain. (In 1961, she received an honorary doctorate in Literature from Wheaton College.) Whatever she writes, it is predictable that Lillian Hellman will not stray from the theater for long. It is her world, and she feels strongly that "to do a play, no matter how much one wishes to stay away from it, one has to *know* the theater. Playwrights have tried to stay away, including Shaw and Chekhov, but in the end, they were involved. . . . A play is not only on paper. It is there to be shared with actors, directors, scene designers, electricians." So speaks "America's number-one woman playwright!"

CHAPTER IX

CLIFFORD ODETS

From the time he was thirteen years old, Clifford Odets was ardently attached to the theater. Starting as an adolescent performer in vaudeville, he was an actor for twelve years before he wrote his first play. The son of Louis and Pearl Odets, he was born in Philadelphia in 1906, but he was brought up in the Bronx, New York, in a neighborhood that grew too fast for comfort. He was an integral part of the second-generation American community that furnished the setting and dialect for his moving folk-drama of typical American-Jewish family life, *Awake and Sing*.

As a child in a crowded, pinched, if not impoverished district, he knew the struggle and deprivations endured by the naturalized citizens of the Bronx. The battle to make their mark in a new land without sacrificing the customs of the culture they had cherished from "the old country" was a never-ending source of strength and aggravation. He knew the penny-pinching, the street fights, the name-calling that all the Bronx boys went through. He listened to the impassioned arguments of his parents and relatives over religion and politics, the eternal squabbles over money. At an early age he sought escape by haunting stage doors.

Like Elmer Rice, young Clifford Odets had to "help out" the

family income, earning whatever he could after school, during vacations or any free time he had. Since he loved the theater, he did not consider it a hardship to go to work as a vaudeville performer while he was still in the eighth grade. When he left high school, he continued his education in the theater. At nineteen, when the radio was just finding an audience, he began reading dramatic poems over the air—romantic pieces by Rudyard Kipling and Robert Service. He had a rich, resonant voice, which brought him a following among the "dial-twisters" of the twenties and led to a job as a juvenile in a stock company in Camden, New Jersey. Here he learned the tricks of the trade, the magic art of make-up, and the endless possibilities of the stage in spite of its apparent limitations. In short, he mastered the rudiments of the theater, an apprenticeship that brought him a coveted spot in New York as understudy to Spencer Tracy in *Conflict*.

Two of the actors in the cast were Edward Arnold and Albert Dekker, both of whom befriended the young actor from the Bronx with the stormy yet poetic face. Because of his smoldering, dreamy dark eyes, his full red lips and fair hair waving softly above a high forehead—"his Byronic countenance," one of the ingénues called it —he might have made a career as a performer, superb in romantic leading roles. But he harbored secret ambitions to be a writer, and had already written a melodramatic novel and part of a play; if he could have summoned the courage, he would have told his friends about them, but he was too unsure of his talent, too fearful of being ridiculed. The next year Dekker introduced him to the Theatre Guild, and he went on tour in several Guild productions. When the company came back into New York, *Roar China* was going into rehearsal, and Odets had no trouble in getting a part in it.

At about this time, the young people of the Guild were beginning to rebel against what they considered the conservative policies of the old-timers (the former Washington Square Players) who had formed the Guild. The new generation in the theater was seething with ideas and wanted to form its own organization—a "junior Guild"—with the backing and cooperation of the senior members. The instigators held meetings in a bare studio room in Steinway Hall, and among the first to join the group was Clifford Odets, who was brimming with enthusiasm for a theater that would take into account the social problems surrounding them on all sides in 1932. He had always possessed a passionate awareness of soul-suffocating conditions, but now it was time to speak out against a system that had given birth to the rows of bleak tenements in the Bronx and allowed depression to settle over the land every seven years until it had reached rock bottom. Exciting discussions went on at those meetings in Steinway Hall, out of which grew the communal structure of the new organization, and Clifford Odets was one of the charter members. They decided to call themselves the Group Theatre, so their philosophy would be unmistakable. The Theatre Guild sanctioned the insurgents as an experiment, but they would have to prove worthy of the backing by their choice of plays and excellence of production before they could be independent.

As a future playwright, hopeful but penniless, Odets, during his experimental days, continued his acting career, but with less and less enthusiasm. He was a creative rather than a performing artist, but he was not given an opportunity to express himself. He resented having to earn his living by acting when he wanted to write, and he used to let off steam, complaining to the "Groupers" whose apartment he shared. They let him fume as much as he liked, but this did not lead him any nearer production of the play he had been hammering at in his spare moments—a dramatization of the dreary wrangling and constant worry of the family life he had found so stifling in his boyhood. The other Groupers understood his feeling of frustration but had no immediate solution to the problem of earning a living. So he put the manuscript in the trunk that took up half of his tiny room, which held little else besides the army cot he slept on.

In the summer, the Group went to the country in a body to select and rehearse plays for the coming season. With a mixture of hope and fear, Clifford Odets took along his playscript and, much to his surprise, the second act was tried out. The scenes "played" quite well, he thought, and little adverse criticism was offered; but nothing was said to indicate that production would follow. In fact, the committee seemed to forget all about it in their excitement over *Men in White,* a realistic drama of hospital life by Sidney Kingsley, which the Group Theatre produced in the fall as its initial offering. A huge success, it set the Group up as an independent theater and won the Pulitzer prize in 1933. Flushed with victory, the new organization went about the task of winning public support for its basic philosophy.

Kingsley seems to have been a "natural" to launch a little theater of large and unorthodox ideas. A native New Yorker, born on October 22nd, 1906, of a middle income background, he attended Townsend Harris Hall and won a state scholarship to Cornell University. Here his first, and principal, interest was the Dramatic Club, which asked new members for plays. Sidney did not have any, but he wrote some—quite a few in fact—and began winning prizes before his graduation in 1928. He continued his play-writing while acting with the Tremont Stock Company in the Bronx, and in 1930 completed a script he called *Crisis*. A startling drama about doctors, it was optioned three different times to three different producers (who, like him, bore the first name of Sidney, by an odd coincidence), and was finally produced by the third, Sidney Harmon, in conjunction with the Group Theatre and James Ullman. They changed the name to *Men in White;* and so it was that Sidney Kingsley's first produced play, enacted by a strong cast, including Alexander Kirkland, J. Edward Bromberg, Morris Carnovsky, and the impatient Clifford Odets in a bit part, won the Pulitzer prize, and established Kingsley as a purveyor of realism in the drama.

His second play, *Dead End,* dealing with the effect of slum conditions on adolescents, produced by the Group in 1935 with tremendous sets by Norman Bel Geddes, has been called "the highwater mark of American naturalism." The daring use of profanity and the graphic phraseology of the gutter in boys' gangs, shocked the public into a realization of the danger of slums as the breeding place of crime. The melodramatic plot developed the crying need for slum clearance and had great box office appeal. A big financial success, *Dead End* won the Theater Club medal, and gave its author the impetus to try producing his plays on his own. Following his happy marriage to Madge Evans (who, as a child actress, had previously won wide fame), Kingsley's career as a dramatist, experimenter in artistic media, and producer, has been marked by theatrical ups and downs. The first of his notable works was *Ten Mil-*

lion Ghosts, in 1936, an antiwar play dealing with munitions makers; although a box-office failure, it is interesting as the forerunner of *All My Sons,* and as an attempt to fuse techniques of motion pictures and the legitimate theater. *The Patriots,* written during Kingsley's service in the signal corps (1940–1944), produced by the Playwrights Company in 1943, was a sensitive interpretation of post-Revolutionary history in America, and received three awards, including the Drama Critics Circle and the Theater Medal. *Detective Story,* a return to the naturalism of *Dead End,* was a popular success in 1949; and *Darkness at Noon,* based on a novel by Arthur Koestler, won several awards in 1950. Since then Mr. Kingsley has written for both stage and screen, keeping up his lively interest in the theater as director and producer in addition to playwriting. But perhaps his greatest contribution to the theater was the production of *Men in White* that catapulted the Group into recognition as a new force, a voice to be reckoned with in the reshaping of the drama that grew out of the depression.

In the rush of activity the possibilities of Odets's play were overlooked. He revised and completed the script in spite of the rebuff he felt at the indifference his work had met. He had to go on trying. A friend of his gave the script to the producer, Frank Merlin, who took an option on it, the first sign of recognition (which called for a celebration in the little furnished apartment); but unfortunately Merlin could not raise the capital to produce the play.

However, the hopeful playwright, with his option check in hand, zealously went to work on a second script, strong in his belief that he possessed the ability to be a voice in American theater, in the world of the future, a world where equality among human beings was more than a word written into the Constitution. Young, ardent, idealistic, he believed that equality as a principle practiced by a socialist government could, in curing the economic ills, heal the emotional wounds of mankind by giving him the freedom to enjoy the arts. From boyhood he had been passionately fond of music, and at one point longed to be a great pianist; but the Odets family had no piano, nor any money for lessons, so he listened to Caruso records on the wheezy second-hand phonograph with his grandfather. And he had written a sad novel about a great pianist who lost his left hand in an accident. It was a "poor novel," he said some years later, but served its purpose unexpectedly when he became a playwright. He made use of the general theme now, in creating a character—the hero's sister—Pearl, an overwrought pianist whose boy friend leaves town to find a job somewhere; she sits at the piano alone in her room, brooding: "The white keys banked up like lilies and she suckin' at her own breast."

He had not quite finished the script when the Group again moved to the country to prepare for the new season. He decided to give his first script another try for production. He felt that the revision, and the title, *Awake and Sing!*, which he took from the Old Testament verse: "Awake and sing, ye that dwell in the dust," might sway the committee in his favor. But again they pushed aside consideration of his script to begin rehearsals on a play called *Gold Eagle Guy*, by Melvin Levy. It had a flashy part for J. Edward Bromberg, who had scored a hit as the main doctor in *Men in White*, and the Group voted to produce a play which would further its reputation as a revolutionary force by promoting the popularity of one of its actor-members. As a Grouper, Clifford Odets could see the logic in this reasoning, and was even playing a part in the vehicle for Bromberg; but he was bitterly disappointed that his play had not received more attention, and vowed to continue working until it did.

When *Gold Eagle Guy* opened for tryouts in Boston, Odets, as a member of the cast, had little time to write. But one night after the performance, when some of the actors were having a bite of supper, he heard of a contest for one-act plays sponsored by the New Theatre League in New York.

The League was one of several organizations besides the Group which were born during the depression to bring the social problems into the American theater, with the idea of pointing up the evils of an economic system that could evoke such financial chaos. By producing plays of protest, the founding members sought to promote certain social reforms that would avert another depression. Among the leaders was John Howard Lawson, a graduate of Baker's 47 Workshop, who, as early as 1922, had written an expressionistic drama of social consciousness, *Roger Bloomer*. It was produced by the Actors' Theatre, an organization that grew out of the successful actor's strike of Equity in 1919. *Roger Bloomer*, which is still a subject for discussion by sociologists and psychologists as well as historians in the theater, was followed by *Processional,* called by John Gassner "a jazz symphony of American life and class tensions." Produced in 1925 by the Theatre Guild, its bold plot line included the effects of a labor strike, a scene in which a strike leader is beaten up. (Lawson also wrote *Loud Speaker,* and the stylized account of world revolution, *The International,* in the prosperous but restless period of the twenties.) Another cluster of playwrights for the proleteriat had banded together as Theatre Union, dedicating themselves to promoting the general welfare through the medium of the spoken word, the drama. Headed by able young experimentalists like Albert Maltz, Paul Peters, and George Sklar, Theatre Union struggled valiantly to stage plays that reflected the grim drama of starvation and unemployment being enacted all over the country. The New Theatre League served as co-ordinator among the various "left-wing" theater units of the thirties, and tried to stimulate the writing of new plays by arranging contests like the one Clifford Odets now heard his fellow-actors talking about.

Asking for particulars, he was told there were only a few days left to enter. He went back to his hotel room, told the desk clerk he did not want to be disturbed, locked himself in and went to work. In three days' time he had written his one-act play, *Waiting for Lefty,* a drama carved out of the actual circumstances of a cab strike then taking place in New York. He entered the script in the contest and tried to await the results calmly.

Gold Eagle Guy opened in New York as scheduled, but it fell far short of expectations. Although reviews were not bad, it failed to catch the interest of the subscribers or the public. During the time it lingered, the New Theatre League announced that it was staging the best of its contest plays on a Sunday night. One of these was *Waiting for Lefty.* Excited and overjoyed, young Clifford Odets could hardly be calm. He attended rehearsals with Betty Grayson, a warm, sympathetic and highly intelligent actress he had become friends with in the Group; he saw to it that all the Group officers and most of its members knew about the performance of his play and would be there.

That Sunday night in the old Civic Repertory Theatre on 14th

Street (where the New Theatre League was presenting the winning plays) proved to be an historic evening in the annals of modern playwriting in America. *Waiting for Lefty* was more than a sociological "protest" play. Its episodic form, as various union members act out their reasons for voting to strike; its use of the Greek chorus motif as the other taxi drivers hover listening in the shadows while they all wait for their leader, "Lefty," gave it the quality of classic drama. The audience on that evening merged with the players in the thrilling finale, the dramatic moment when the word comes that Lefty, who never appears, has been murdered on the way to the meeting. At the shouted question directed out front from Joe, one of the principal characters, as to what the vote shall be, the audience in one voice shouted back: "Strike!" And the curtain rang down to thunderous applause. Those who were there claimed immortality as part of an unforgettable moment in the theater for years afterward. The effect of the play was like an electric bolt; the furor it created was tremendous.

The Group Theatre members were wildly enthusiastic and voted to bring it to Broadway at once. Moreover, they were now eager to produce *Awake and Sing*. Odets, feeling rather stunned, sat in on the conferences with Harold Clurman, Director of the Group, Cheryl Crawford, Lee Strasberg, the Adlers (Stella and Luther) and others to decide whether to produce the two plays on one bill. They all agreed that *Waiting for Lefty* was too long and could not be cut; so the young playwright offered to write another one-act to go with it. The result was his powerful, skillfully written *Till the Day I Die,* a passionate arraignment of the Nazi purge in Germany. (Overshadowed by the theatricality of *Waiting for Lefty,* it has never been recognized for its true worth.)

Both one-acts and *Awake and Sing* were produced in the winter of 1935. The full-length play opened in February, with a brilliant cast headed by Stella Adler as Bessie Berger, the domineering mother; Morris Carnovsky as the philosophical old grandfather (who plays Caruso records and feels that "human life should have some dignity"); Luther Adler as the son, Ralph (who recalls painful incidents from his childhood that undoubtedly paralleled early experiences in the author's life); and J. Edward Bromberg as Uncle Morty, the most prosperous member of the family. In this, his first play, Clifford Odets created perhaps his most fully rounded characters, all of whom, he stated, "share a fundamental activity: a struggle for life amidst petty conditions." It was his handling of his people, however, in a well-motivated plot that reaches a moving climax, and dialogue sparked with humor, pungent in Jewish idiomatic expressions, that brought *Awake and Sing* the warm embrace of critics and audiences alike. In March, *Waiting for Lefty*, with the playwright in the cast, was presented as planned, along with *Till the Day I Die,* and again created a furor, because of its outspoken defense of labor unions and the hated weapon, strikes. Some said the play was pure propaganda, others that it was art created out of gross reality, but all agreed that Clifford Odets was the most original playwright the theater had produced since Eugene O'Neill. He had arrived, practically in one leap, and he still felt dazed by the suddenness of his success. (Asked later what he thought about it, he answered with disarming frankness, "I didn't *think;* I felt, and I felt sad, shocked, as if I'd been hit on the head and was lying in a dark room unconscious, while critics and others were talking about some impostor with the same name.")

Now he was one of the leading figures of the Group Theatre, foremost among its writers (who included, during the ten years of the Group's existence, Paul Green, Maxwell Anderson, William Saroyan, Sidney Kingsley, and Irwin Shaw), and frequently one of its most generous contributors in terms of funds. Ardor was the keynote of his emotional make-up, and he believed in the Group ardently. He had no deep attachments to Broadway, outside of organizations like the Group, because he felt that the commercial theater was concerned with "trifles." His concern was to find the causes of human unhappiness, which he thought lay largely in the economic ills of the world. He had enough faith in human nature to feel that, given the opportunity, those who dwelt in the dust would awake and sing. And to that end, he was ready to devote himself tirelessly to the success of the Group.

Like the Provincetown Players of the generation before, the Groupers hoped to prove the practical as well as the ideological worth of the communal system—to set an example for the rest of the world to follow. Their principles, however, were laid down on firmer lines than the Players, their dreams were less diffuse and more attainable than the lofty aims of the Provincetowners. Odets, more than any of the other playwrights, helped the Group to establish a permanent acting company—a company which worked together, studying and discussing the plays to be produced, and even having a voice in the management of the organization. Teamwork and continuity were the hallmark of the Group. A second identity was an almost religious dedication to the Stanislawski Method, a worshipful regard for the director of the Moscow Art Theatre. (In a moment of fiery adoration, Clifford Odets went so far as to join the Communist Party in 1934; but, as he testified nearly twenty years later before the House Un-American Affairs Committee, he left after six months because he would not agree to write along Party lines.)

Very often the voice of the newly recognized playwright could be heard among the chorus of socially conscious theater people that clamored for a welfare program for unemployed actors. He and half a dozen others might gather in the Adlers' big, comfortable living room, which served as a sort of informal headquarters for the officers of the Group, and sit up half the night harassing each other about the relative merits of communism and democracy, Chekhov, O'Neill and Shaw, Dostoievsky and Steinbeck (whose novel, *Of Mice and Men*, was soon to be dramatized). Odets could be argumentative and hotheaded; or discursive; or narrative in his talk; he told stories extremely well, with a flair for the dramatic. Or if he was in one of his frequent "moody" spells, he just wanted to listen to music, his greatest passion outside the theater. If Aaron Copland, who was a close friend of the Adlers', happened to be there, he might play part of his latest composition for them. (Still struggling for recognition at that time, Copland had the use of the piano in the Adlers' living room, and could often be found there during the day, plucking out some complicated phrase or bar of music, while his half-eaten lunch—usually a corned beef sandwich—lay forgotten at the edge of the piano lid.)

Occasionally Odets would invite everyone over to listen to records at his new rooftop apartment at Number One University Place. Here, where he had space at last, he built up a library of recordings, adding the latest equipment as it came along. (He became something of an authority on long-playing records, high-fidelity mechanisms and other later developments.) When he was not writing, he would play music for hours, looking out across the treetops and university spires of Washington Square. If friends were present, he would seemingly forget them all, lost in the music. There were those who considered him rude in removing himself so completely, and others who found it boring to sit in the absolute quiet he demanded, even when he adjusted some wire or mechanism. But the passion within him drove him to extremes in the things that had deep meaning for him.

Romantic as he was, he had no inclination to marry as yet, although he and Betty Grayson had been almost inseparable for a long time. As soon as *Awake and Sing* and *Waiting for Lefty* were well launched, he plunged into work on the play he had begun after his first summer with the Group. This also depicted a middle-class family trying to survive the dark flood-waters of economic depression; but, with the exception of his portrait of Pearl, the pianist, and neurotic sister of the weak hero, Julie, his characters lacked the humor and the individual traits that made the Berger family so outstanding. The new play, entitled *Paradise Lost*, was produced in 1935, but it did little to advance his stature as a dramatist in the public eye, since it was more of a political protest against conditions than a work of dramatic art.

However, one benefit he derived was a reawakening in the theme of a frustrated musician; the sub-plot of Pearl's unfulfilled longing to be a pianist sent him back to his "poor novel," the basis of which he had never really abandoned. Now he sought a motive for the injury to the musician's hand; and while he was mulling over the plot, he heard of a lightweight boxer from "little Italy" in the Village who was also a violinist, and had suffered a hand injury in the ring. Excited, the playwright made a point of meeting the fighter-musician and learning his story. The man, a genial Italian, friendly and talkative, often came to One University Place at Odets's invitation; the sole support of his parents and sister, he said he had gone into the ring because he could not earn a living as a violinist. He was an all-around athlete, and eventually became a recreation director, but at the time he was trying to adjust his life, hoping to play the violin again someday.

With all the background material he needed, and the germ of an idea for the true drama that was to grow from these talks, Clifford Odets began to outline a play built around the warring factors in the life of a boxer-violinist, expanding and deepening the causes and motives behind his pugilistic career. Before his characters and situations were fully created, however, the playwright received an offer from Hollywood, and he decided to take it, to the dismay of his colleagues in the Group. They felt he was deserting his ideals, betraying the Group, selling his soul. But he insisted he was going because funds were low after the failure of *Paradise Lost,* and that he was by no means deserting the cause of the theater as art, of the collective theater. And he proved the sincerity of his words a year or so later, when he returned to New York, bringing with him the script for perhaps his finest play, one that has been called "one of the few important tragedies in American drama"—*Golden Boy.* (His title grew out of the Golden Gloves boxing competition, which had been responsible for the initial success of his model for the play.)

Using the fabric of the true-life story, Odets fashioned a central figure fully as real but more complex, and a plot far more dramatic and profound than the tale he had been told. The play, which opened in 1937 and more than remade the fortune of the Group, deals with the fate of Joe Bonaparte, a violinist of Sicilian parentage, who is torn between the desire for material wealth, plus the accompanying fame of the boxing ring, and his passionate love for music. Because of poverty and an oversensitive nature, he suffers from a deep-set insecurity and diffidence, hidden behind an outward belligerence toward the world. "You can't get even with people by playing the fiddle," he says, when his feelings have been hurt. "If music shot bullets, I'd like it better." His attitude leads him to become a boxer, but he fights with the constant fear that he may damage his hands and be forced to give up playing the violin. Eventually he wins fame and fortune and his manager's girl, Lorna, with whom he falls madly in love. But in the process he does break his hand, an injury that prevents him from playing the violin, but does not hamper his boxing career; and he finally delivers a fatal knockout blow to his opponent in an important match. Aghast at his monstrous brutality, he cries out brokenly: "What will my father say when he hears I murdered a man? Lorna, I see what I did. I murdered myself, too. I've been running around in circles. Now I'm smashed!" In a last-ditch attempt to save the only element of beauty left to him, his love for Lorna, he runs away with her in the high-powered car his prize-fight money has bought. They are killed in a crash, news of which comes to the Bonaparte family in the final poignant scene.

A superb character study, *Golden Boy* has been interpreted as a realistic version of the *Faust* legend; as an indictment of the economic pressures of a society which demands too great a price for the integrity of the soul; and indirectly as an autobiographical outlet for Odets, who, in spite of his denial, must have suffered some guilt feelings in "selling out to Hollywood" after denouncing all commercialism in the theater. While he was writing the screen play for *The General Died at Dawn,* he sent back money to help the Group, and *Golden Boy* put the organization on a foundation firm enough to preserve it for at least another five years before dissolving.

Moreover, like his hero, Odets fell ecstatically in love six months after he accepted his role of fame in Hollywood; he was smitten by the glamorous charm of the Austrian actress, Luise Rainer, and could not rest until they were married, in January, 1937, shortly before the opening of *Golden Boy.* For a time his head was in the clouds, and the fact that this was literally so when his actress-wife had to fly back and forth between Hollywood and New York for film commitments did not bother him at first. He once remarked to a friend that when he met her at the airport, he "watched the plane coming in and thought of it as a great bird, bearing his beloved." However, the novelty of being married to a famous movie actress began to pall when the trips became more frequent, and their careers were at cross purposes with each other. Miss Rainer was temperamental, unreasonable, and showed little understanding of his art. By the end of 1938, they had quarreled bitterly and were separated. Although they came together briefly in 1939, the marriage would not work, and they were divorced in 1941.

Following the divorce he was not well, suffering from the nervous strain of writing several plays produced by the Group Theatre during his unhappiness. These were *Rocket to the Moon,* in 1938; *Night Music,* in 1940; and *Clash by Night,* in 1941. While none was as skillful as *Golden Boy,* all were marked by strong characterization, and the last two revealed a veering away from social problems as the predominant theme. The shift in emphasis toward individual emotional difficulties was to increase as the playwright delved more and more deeply into the psychological aspect of his characters' behavior. Although *Clash by Night* received mild interest in some opinions, the play was never evaluated as the powerful, probing, and original drama it was. Disappointed, disillusioned, Odets might not have come through his illness if it had not been for Betty Grayson, who had loved him long before and all during his miserable marriage. She had never condemned him, and now she was sympathetic and kind, taking care of him.

As he grew stronger, he realized that all the qualities he had found lacking in Luise Rainer he had taken for granted in Betty during the early years. All their friends and associates in the theater were as pleased as the couple themselves when Clifford Odets and Betty Grayson were finally married on May 14, 1943. In the next ten years they were never long apart. Miss Grayson starred with John Garfield in the film version of *Golden Boy,* which was tremendously successful, perhaps because of the strong casting. (On the stage, Luther Adler and Frances Farmer had created the roles of Joe and Lorna; and while both gave fine, sensitive performances, neither of their interpretations had the hard-core vigor, the impulsiveness and even lusty side of Odets's characters. Garfield seemed to be a "natural" for Bonaparte, his first starring and most famous role.)

The Odets had two children, Nora and Walt, and spent half their time in Hollywood during those ten years. In 1943, the playwright wrote and directed the motion picture, *None but the Lonely Heart,* which led to other film scripts. He did not get back to playwriting until 1949, with *The Big Knife,* the story of a neurotic movie actor who, like Joe Bonaparte, tries desperately but fails to keep his integrity, here against the filmland background instead of the prize-fight setting. John Garfield created the role of Charlie Castle on Broadway, and also in London, where the play was called *A Winter Journey.* There were a number of colorful portraits in *The Big Knife,* particularly of the men in the studio, types that Odets had come to know well during the decade. But it was not until the following year, with *The Country Girl* (1950), that Clifford Odets lived up to the reputation he had won in *Awake and Sing* and *Golden Boy*. The new play, perhaps his most mature and consistently constructed, dealt with people of the theater rather than Hollywood, and presented a probing analysis of individual problems—for the first time to the exclusion of sociological influences. And here, in *The Country Girl*, Georgie, young, warm and compassionate, married to a down-and-out actor, was Odets's most affectionate picture of a woman. The triangle plot, built around the "country girl," the actor (Frank Elgin, who is an alcoholic), and the director (Bernie Dodd, who is giving Frank a chance to make a comeback), mounts steadily in intensity and reveals a delicate interplay of the forces in each character influencing their behavior.

In contrast to most of his stage women, Georgie emerges as Odets's most definite heroine; and, in her loyalty to her husband, her understanding of his problems, her intelligence in dealing with him and the ambivalent feelings of the director, suggests the qualities of Betty Grayson, who may have served unconsciously as the model. *The Country Girl* came as a pleasant surprise to critics and audiences alike, for many had ceased to expect a play by Odets that measured up to his early work in characterization, strength and artistry, and yet was a distinct departure from his usual genre. Not long after the successful filming of the play, Betty Grayson became ill, and, although she put up a valiant struggle, she died in 1954.

Shortly before his wife's illness, Clifford Odets had begun another play of family life, this time of religious, philosophical significance, in a retelling of the story of Noah and the Ark in modern terms. Entitled *The Flowering Peach*, it opened between Christmas and New Year's in 1954, and was his last play. At first puzzling, *The Flowering Peach* seems to symbolize the need for living in peace and harmony in a world that has shrunk to Ark size through modern science; if we are to survive, the nations of the world must learn to get along with each other, just as Noah and his family did. It may well be that Odets felt he was issuing a subtle warning just before the fire and flood caused by the atomic age. Although he lived nearly ten years longer, he did not write another word for the theater.

Much of the time he was not well, and he died of a heart attack in 1963, a few months before Sammy Davis, Jr., opened on Broadway in a musical version of *Golden Boy*. The production was a far cry from the original play of 1937, but the basic appeal of the boxer with the sensitive soul (who fights this time with the added handicap of color) still retains its power to the point of attracting audiences for a long extended stay on Broadway in spite of lukewarm reviews.

Whatever his faults and inconsistencies as playwright and person, Clifford Odets possessed a vitality combined with a poetic spirit that enabled him to create, with insight and affection, strong characters who reflect the feeling of his times. He has been compared to Chekhov and to Sean O'Casey, but the Odetsian spontaneity, impulsiveness, and passions of his people represent an original American talent that remained intact despite the weakness of his later plays. Accused of writing "propaganda plays," Odets once countered by contending that "all plays, just like all literature, are essentially propaganda." He added, with his customary candor and considerable heat, "My problem and business in the world is to present truth dramatically, appealingly, and entertainingly." And in large measure, he conquered his "problem."

William Saroyan

William Saroyan might well be called the Robin Goodfellow among modern American playwrights. Although the locale of his plays is far removed from the woodland scene, his Puckish humor and abundant good nature in the face of economic depression and the impending doom of war provide the atmosphere of a summer idyll in a San Francisco honky-tonk setting. Like O'Neill, he knew the scene by heart, from firsthand experience. From Fresno, the "ugly little city containing the large comic world" where he was born on August 31, 1908, the son of Turkish-Armenian parents, he had migrated to the metropolis on the Pacific before coming to the one on the Atlantic, and was well acquainted with the honky-tonk way of life on San Francisco's waterfront when he came to dramatize it for the Broadway theater.

Half-orphaned at three, when his father (a former clergyman with a touch of the poet, who worked the vineyards in the company of the itinerant fruit pickers) died in 1911, Saroyan, with his brothers and sisters, had been stowed in a San Francisco orphanage for a time while their mother, Takoohi Saroyan, took a job as a domestic. When she was able to reunite her brood in Fresno, small William, the youngest, and the one most like his father, "endured" a few years of public schooling, and then decided to educate himself. His quick bright mind, ebullient spirit, and incorrigible imagination had been the despair of his teachers; but in the public library (which, like Elmer Rice, he regarded as his second home), he could cut loose and let his fancies soar with adventure writers, who "liked to live a life." He read rapturously, if indiscriminately. He devoured everything from Jack London and Mark Twain to Mencken, Gorki, and Chekhov, with a rich topping of poetry by Whitman and Sandburg; but of them all, it was Bernard Shaw who personified "health, wisdom, and comedy" for him and became his idol. At the age of eighteen, Saroyan knew he must write for the theater somehow.

Hitchhiking to New York in the depths of the depression, he was variously employed as Western Union messenger, postal clerk, and newspaper reporter, always busily writing on his own. His first attempts found publication in the Armenian little-magazine press; but in 1934, *Story* Magazine accepted his wholly original piece, *The Daring Young Man on the Flying Trapeze,* destined to make him famous before the end of the year, when he had a volume of short stories published under that title. Taking his authors' copies with him, he sailed off to Europe for a sampling of life on the continent before beginning his career as a playwright. His first endeavor, *The Subway Circus,* never reached Broadway. His second, *My Heart's in the Highlands,* a long one-acter which had the indefinable quality of a tone poem, was beautifully produced by the Group Theatre in the spring of 1939. Hailed as a minor masterpiece by most of the critics, the play (a lyrical presentation of Saroyan's basic philosophy, as seen from recollections of his childhood on San Bonito Avenue in Fresno, during a summer day in August, 1914) received the Circle award, and set Saroyan in rapid motion as a rising young playwright.

Before the end of the year, his first full length play, *The Time of Your Life,* which he wrote in record speed, was produced in October of 1939 by the Theatre Guild, and captured both public and critical fancy completely. The odd fantasy of bizarre characters in a San Francisco saloon, in which love and benevolence triumph over evil, and the delights of childhood are regained, served as a panacea to a troubled world, and was awarded the Critics Circle and the Pulitzer prizes by unanimous decision. (Typically, Saroyan turned down the Pulitzer award, because the committee had not been able to agree on his first produced play.) Then came in quick succession, *Love's Old Sweet Song* (1940), and *The Beautiful People,* a fragile, poetic piece, in 1942. By then, however, World War II had begun, and Saroyan's delicate theme was lost in the thunder of cannon fire and the serious tenor of the times. He has persisted in his outlook over the years, with diminishing success. His perceptive one-acter, *Hello, Out There!* was a notable exception; but for the most part, William Saroyan is too esoteric a writer—and perhaps too hasty in the execution of his ever-flowing ideas—to attract a permanent or wide audience today. An inveterate gambler, he takes risks with his writing as with the money it earned, plunging into various media and the public taste be damned.

In private life married and divorced, the playwright has lived abroad for several years, written several autobiographical volumes, screen plays (though he rebelled at Hollywood tactics) and television scripts in addition to short plays and a novel or two. He took delight in spending a summer in Paris with his son and daughter, and never seems to lose his *joie de vivre.*

CHAPTER X

———◆———

THORNTON WILDER

Perhaps the most scholarly among modern American playwrights, Thornton Wilder is also the most paradoxical. A brilliant student, he was widely educated in schools and colleges on two continents, yet he is known for the utter simplicity of his prose, the eloquent starkness of his dialogue. The friend of James Joyce, Gertrude Stein, and Sigmund Freud, Wilder has been called "eclectic," "cosmic," universal, yet typically American in his playwriting.

His beginnings were scarcely remarkable. His father, Amos Porter Wilder, was a New England newspaperman, who moved his family to Madison, Wisconsin, to take over the editorship of a paper shortly before Thornton was born, on April 17, 1897. His mother, who had been a New Englander, the former Isabella Niven, bestowed her maiden name on her infant son also, but he never used it in his professional career. His childhood years, up to the age of nine, were spent in Madison, where, like most Midwestern boys, he attended public school with the other Wilder children, two girls and another boy. Thornton was closest to his younger sister Isabel, the one next to him in age and nearest him in spirit. Both shared an interest in books from an early age, both were quick, bright pupils. Their father, who loomed over the family as its dominant head, demanded high marks of all his children, and pushed those who showed promise into doing even better. As editor of a small-town newspaper around the turn of the century, Mr. Wilder had an alert knowledge of any number of subjects, from details of the daily life in Madison to foreign policy. His wide range of interest made him restless, dissatisfied with life in a small Midwestern university town, and he took steps to change it.

When Thornton was nine years old, in 1906, the whole family sailed away to the Orient, for his father had been appointed American Consul General in Hong Kong, China. The strange sights, sounds, and smells of the teeming oriental city might have been more bewildering to the band of children from Wisconsin, except that they saw little of it. They were whisked from the American Consulate to the German day school they attended and back again every day, but rarely went outside the American quarter otherwise. At the end of six months, Thornton's mother decided that the children were not getting the proper education or upbringing in Hong Kong, so she took them back to Berkeley, California. Here she lived with her brood while Mr. Wilder stayed in the Far East. With his brother and sisters, Thornton attended Berkeley schools for the next five years, at the end of which time they all returned to the Orient. His father had been transferred to Shanghai, and felt that it was high time his family joined him.

Now nearly fourteen, Thornton would have enjoyed discovering China and Chinese culture for himself, but again he had little opportunity. After attending another German school for a few weeks, he was sent to the English China Inland Mission School at Chefoo, where he was a "boarding pupil" for a year and never got outside the school gates except to visit his parents on holidays.

After that he was sent back to California once more, where he spent the next year in the Thacher school in the mountains at Ojai. His last two years of high school were spent in Berkeley, where, for the first time in his life, he was allowed certain freedoms, and one of his greatest pleasures was to go to the matinees at Ye Liberty Theatre in Oakland. There the stock company put on a different play every week, and he followed them avidly. They were for the most part nineteenth-century plays, performed in nineteenth-cen tury staging, with elaborate sets and, very often, period plays in full costume. But he lapped up this first taste of theater, all in one gulp, from the melodramas of Bronson Howard and James A. Herne and the comedy-dramas of Clyde Fitch to the translated dramas of Ibsen, with a thirst he never knew he had. His imagination went beyond the world of make-believe he saw on the stage to his own world of fantasy—nebulous now, but a faint indication of the path he was to follow.

After graduating from Berkeley High, he chose to go to Oberlin College in Ohio for two years, and here began to express himself in literary terms, fragments of prose later to become works of fiction and drama, which were published in the *Oberlin Literary Magazine*. From there he transferred to Yale to complete his degree, as his father had resigned from the Consular Service and the Wilder family had been reunited in New Haven. Writing was essential to Thornton's well-being. He tried his hand at short plays and his initial attempts were successful enough to be published in the *Yale Literary Magazine,* much to his surprise. He had had a number of essays published, but he did not expect his playscripts to be so readily accepted. He was eager to continue, but the war intervened. During the summer of 1918, he worked as a clerk in the War Industries Board in Washington while trying to get into one of the Services. He was always turned down because of his eyesight, which had been weak from childhood. Otherwise, he was sound and muscular, and was finally accepted by the Coast Guard artillery. He served as Corporal at Fort Adams, Rhode Island, for eight months, and returned to Yale—and playwriting.

Almost immediately he started working on a full-length play. Called *The Trumpet Shall Sound,* it was published serially in three issues of the *Literary Magazine* during his senior year at Yale. With his B.A. degree in 1920, he also received an appointment to the American Academy in Rome for a year. Although not enrolled in archaeology, he followed the courses with deep interest, storing up the knowledge which he was to use twenty years later to great advantage in portraying the perilous survival of man through the ages in his plays.

Quiet, scholarly, retiring to the point of shyness, Thornton Wilder was most at home in schools or colleges, and with people who spoke his language. Usually silent, he could discourse brilliantly and spontaneously when moved or stimulated by an idea, a subject under discussion. He was good-looking, with neat, straight features and a high forehead. His eyes were meditative behind the glasses he had to wear from an early age; and when he smiled, there was an expression of kindness in his glance. During these years, he kept mostly to himself, but when he did come out of his shell and meet people, he gave the impression of liking them—of having known them always.

He spent the next four years teaching French at Lawrenceville School in Lawrenceville, New Jersey, and tutoring in a boys' camp in New Hampshire during the summer. He had begun writing a philosophical novel while at the American Academy, but had had little time to complete it after he returned from Rome. In New Hampshire, he discovered the MacDowell Colony one summer, and it seemed to him the ideal place to write. He took a year to study at Princeton University for a Master's degree in French, which he received in June, 1926. That summer was the first of many that he spent writing in the shelter of his studio at the MacDowell Colony just outside Peterborough, New Hampshire. The little hillside town, with its white clapboard houses, fronted by wide green lawns and shaded by urn-shaped elms, its tall church spires and red barns, set against the backdrop of Mt. Monadnock, gave him a sense of his own roots in New England soil. It was as if he had come back to his birthplace. He was a great walker, and he found himself walking down to the village in the valley, and up over hills to Hancock, getting acquainted with the townsfolk and farmers alike. He formed the habit of thinking creatively as he went along. And as the terrain became familiar, he could compose long passages without being distracted by some detail in the landscape that aroused his curiosity. (Much later he told an interviewer, "Sometimes whole pages are created during my walks. When I return, I put them down, and I seldom change a word. I rewrite very little.") Even on days when he did not hike, he and some of the other colonists would go down to the village drugstore in Peterborough, or stop in at the white-pillared town hall that housed the post office, the centers of neighborhood news and gossip. He came to know the common history and characteristics of New England villages and towns. He studied the tombstones in the cemeteries spread out behind the churches, learning the names and dates of early settlers.

He had not quite finished writing his novel, when his first summer at the MacDowell Colony ended, and he headed for Europe along with many other Americans seeking self-expression in the mid-twenties. He completed his manuscript, which he called *The Cabala,* and which was published that same year, 1926, and immediately began writing another novel.

He had submitted his play, *The Trumpet Shall Sound,* to the Laboratory Theatre before leaving for Europe, and on his return he received the amazing news that it was to be produced and directed by Richard Boleslawsky, the brilliant Russian-born director of the experimental group. It was exhilarating to see his work performed, but the play, although an artistic success, did not create much of a stir. He would have enjoyed writing more plays immediately, but the Boni brothers, who had published *The Cabala,* were waiting for his second novel, now nearing completion. Published in 1927, *The Bridge of San Luis Rey* astonished him, bringing him as it did a sudden leap into fame, his first Pulitzer prize, and a financial security greater than he had ever known! He was astonished because, although *The Bridge* had an interesting story base, skillfully built around a group of unrelated characters brought together by fate in accidental death, he considered *The Cabala* a much finer work, and always would.

He had gone back to his teaching post at Lawrenceville, but directly after receiving the Pulitzer prize, he resigned (in 1928). He and his sister Isabel went to Europe to spend several months touring and studying the techniques of stage productions in various countries. On his first visit, Thornton had become interested in Continental theater, and now his particular concern was to find a workable method of presentation for the "three-minute" plays he had been writing from his college days at Oberlin—brief poetic parables, dealing with moral and religious questions, drawn from his knowledge of the Bible, Plato, Greek and Roman myth, etc. He was searching for some practical means of nonrealistic presentation appropriate for his themes, his poetic, even fanciful style. He and Isabel, who was, like him, passionately fond of the theater, attended performances in France, Austria and Germany. If she could not go for some reason, her brother went alone. In one breathless interval of sixty-three days he attended fifty-two plays. He was steeped in a detailed, visual knowledge of sets, props, backdrops, incidental music and acting styles of the various countries they visited before they left. He and Isabel both kept a "Travel Diary," in which they wrote down their impressions, and when they returned to New Haven, they collaborated on an article entitled, "Play-going Nights: From a Travel Diary."

Before it appeared in the June issue of *Theatre Arts Monthly*, 1929, the first volume of Thornton Wilder's three-minute plays was published by Coward-McCann. Titled *The Angel That Troubled the Waters*, after the last one, the book contained sixteen plays which he had selected out of the forty he had written. (Many are more dramatic poems than plays, and, while beautifully structured and provocative, they are unsuited for the living stage.) He started working on a third novel, hoping to complete it within a few months.

He was also invited to make a cross-country lecture tour, the mere thought of which shook him at first, but he overcame his shyness, grew a clipped mustache for the sake of his appearance as a public figure, and found that he had less stage fright in front of an audience than he did in small gatherings of people in a drawing room or dinner party, unless they were close friends. (With his friends and colleagues, his conversation was lively and charming, or serious, as the mood or subject demanded.) He had a clear, resonant voice, and a calm, easy stage presence which captivated and held his listeners to the end of his lecture.

From this time on, for the next seven years, he followed two careers—one on the lecture platform as public speaker and professor; and the other in his writing studio as creative artist in fiction and drama. He gave two more cross-country tours, speaking to large audiences as the author of the best seller, *The Bridge of San Luis Rey*, and in the process spent stretches of five and six weeks in Hollywood, working on the script for the filming of his novel. Beginning in 1930, he accepted a post at the University of Chicago, at that time recently reorganized under the presidency of Robert Hutchins, who had been a classmate of his at Yale. Half of each year he taught, lecturing in Comparative Literature, and the other half he wrote. Summers he usually spent at the MacDowell Colony, working in the Mannex studio on the outlying edge of the premises, the one he had used during his first summer. In moments of relaxation, if he had had a "productive day" and felt like socializing, he would join the heated croquet games that went on after dinner; or he might indulge in the mystic art of "table-tipping," popular among a small circle of souls with a feeling for the occult. One night when a few of the select were holding a séance, somebody from the spiritual world "came in" with a strange kind of tapping. It puzzled most of the mystics present; but Thornton said calmly, "That's Chinese." And he translated the message.

Thornton Wilder's third novel, *The Woman of Andros,* was published in 1930. Considered by some his finest piece of writing, it was Wilder's favorite among his novels. It did not have the wide appeal of *The Bridge,* but its readers were selective and appreciative, the reward which meant most to its author. At the time, he was reading proof on the second volume of early plays, *The Long Christmas Dinner and Other Plays in One Act* (six altogether, four of which had been produced in New Haven by the joint Yale and Vassar Dramatic Clubs), which came out in 1931. *The Long Christmas Dinner,* a classic of its kind (which Gassner has called "the most beautiful one-act play in English prose), took place over a span of ninety years, foreshadowing the playwright's technique and style in maturity. It had been conceived and written in fragments twelve years earlier, at Yale.

He still read enormously, his special interests being Joyce, Proust, Kafka, Kierkegaard, and Freud. The year he spent in Europe, he had come to know the great professor-psychoanalyst, and used to call on him on Sunday afternoons in Grinzing. They often discussed the conscious or unconscious use of psychoanalysis in literary art, and the relationship between them. (Freud once told him that "die dichter"—the poets—"have always known it!") Since French had been his field in teaching for so many years, Wilder was steeped in French literature, also; and now he did a "beautiful adaptation" (according to Burns Mantle) of Andre Obey's *Le Viol de Lucrece,* which he called simply *Lucrece.* In 1932, the play was produced and directed by Guthrie McClintic with Katharine Cornell in the title role. The playwright attended rehearsals, broadening his knowledge of the theater, watching Mc-Clintic direct Cornell and her cast, but not venturing to offer any comment. He followed Shaw's custom of noninterference at rehearsals, preferring to avoid verbal arguments or discussions if he could. But immediately after rehearsals, he would send McClintic the "voluminous notes" he had taken, containing "pertinent suggestions, and possibly a few gentle protests." The production was an artistic success if nothing else. Katharine Cornell's Lucrece was as "beautifully realized" as Wilder's adaptation; but the play had only a restricted sale at the box office—"restricted to the more devoted Cornell admirers," unfortunately. With background music by Deems Taylor, who was a friend of Wilder, the production was theater art in the truest sense, but it was considered too "highbrow" for the majority of critics and playgoers. It was published the following year by Houghton Mifflin, and took its place as a literary work in theater libraries.

In 1935, Thornton Wilder met Gertrude Stein when she came to lecture at the University of Chicago, and, like so many others, he could not help being influenced in some degree by her dynamic views, her sweeping exercise of free association and the subconscious. It would be several years before the echo of the word-fugues created by Stein's *Four Saints in Three Acts* would be heard in the chaos scenes of Wilder's masterpiece of fantasy, but the notes were sounded in 1935. During the second term, he accepted an invitation to be a Visiting Professor at the University of Hawaii, an experience which added to his knowledge of Oriental culture. A fourth novel, *Heaven's My Destination,* a half-satiric, half-serious character study of a young man, appeared at the end of the year.

The plays that Thornton Wilder had seen in his youth had left a strong impression, particularly the productions of Ibsen. After he read Ibsen in the original, however, he had wanted to do his own translation of one of the major dramas; and now he chose *A Doll's House,* and the result of his study was an adaptation as well as translation—a work which bore the Wilder stamp in its "well-made" lines and structure. The unusual presentation of Ibsen was produced and directed by Jed Harris, whose erratic genius was then startling Broadway. With Ruth Gordon in the role of Nora, it was first performed in Central City, Colorado, in July of 1937, and opened in New York at the Morosco Theatre in December. The Wilder-Harris interpretation received uniformly good notices, and its success led to the continuation of the author-director combination the following year.

Wilder had been working on a playscript which sprang from the deep emotional ties he had felt toward the small-town life in Peterborough, and he sought to put into simple dramatic terms the sense of timelessness, the eternal value of daily living, all too often overlooked in the rush, the ever-increasing speed of a scientific age. His title, *Our Town,* expressed the mood, the large and beautiful light in which he pictured "the smallest events in our daily life." He wrote the play carefully, slowly, taking his own time, paring the dialogue down to essentials. Fancifully, he used the "Stage Manager" as Narrator for his play, having him set the scene as he spoke, as in the classical or ancient Chinese theater. (Contrary to the accepted impression, Thornton Wilder never saw a Chinese or Japanese play while he lived in the Orient. Not until Mei Lang Fang came to America on his famous tour did the playwright see Chinese acting or plays, although he had known of the forms through his reading on the Oriental theater long before he witnessed that particular performance.)

Our Town was produced and directed by Jed Harris, working in close collaboration with the playwright. At first the play was conventionally staged, with full scenery and props. It was tried out in Princeton, January 22, 1938, and went from there for a two-week engagement at the Wilbur Theatre in Boston. The notices in Princeton had been mildly favorable, but in Boston they were downright bad, and the second week was canceled. A conference was held immediately after the last performance to decide what could be done to save the play before it moved into New York. For a long time Thornton Wilder had felt that most settings of plays were so cluttered with scenery and infinite detail in properties that the larger meaning of the play was lost, or at best limited to one locality in place and time. "I began writing one-act plays that tried to capture not verisimilitude but reality," he wrote twenty years afterward in the Preface to the publication of his three most important plays. "In *The Happy Journey to Camden and Trenton* four kitchen chairs represent an automobile, and a family travels seventy miles in twenty minutes. Ninety years go by in *The Long Christmas Dinner*. In *Pullman Car Hiawatha* some more plain chairs serve as berths and we hear the very vital statistics of the towns and fields that passengers are traversing; we hear their thoughts; we even hear the planets over their heads." At that crucial conference in 1938, he presented his ideas to Jed Harris, who was quick to see the point. (When Burns Mantle reported at the time, "Jed Harris took away the scenery and other props except a few tables, chairs, a ladder, etc.; played on an essentially bare stage, *Our Town* was much more successful," he neglected to mention that Wilder was initially responsible for the important change in presentation.)

The pared-down production opened in New York the following week (February 4) at the Henry Miller Theatre, and while some critics thought the staging was rather severe, most of them found it a refreshing departure from the usual overstuffed Broadway shows. Almost all praised the play itself enthusiastically, without reservation. Few realized that much of the eloquence of the simple lines emerged because of the simple staging. *Our Town* was called "a tender idyll"; "an antidote for anxiety"; and "an American classic." It settled down for a long run, eventually winning the Pulitzer prize.

In September, Frank Craven, who was playing the Stage Manager, came down with an illness so serious he could not go on. Wilder himself was "deputized" to act the part. He knew the lines almost by heart, and he felt a sympathy and kinship toward the town itself—"Grover's Corners, New Hampshire, just across the Massachusetts line"—which was patterned after Peterborough. The citizens there have always taken great pride in the play written about their town. For many years the Peterborough Players, one of the most professional of summer theater groups, gave a performance of *Our Town* once every season, several times with Wilder in the role of the Stage Manager. He found that he enjoyed acting, and occasionally has taken parts in the productions of other playwrights. In his early one-act, *Pullman Car Hiawatha*, in which he first employed the Stage Manager as narrator, he had used the place name "Grover's Corners" as an Ohio town. It seemed to him better than any to represent the typical American name for a small town.

The play has been produced countless times all over the country. Its first major revival was at the City Center Theatre in New York in 1944. Two years later, an American production directed by Jed Harris opened in London at the New Theatre.

Before the end of the original run, the playwright had launched another play on Broadway—a "free adaptation" of Johann Nestroy's *Einen Jux will er sich Machen,* a Viennese play of 1842. (The Austrian playwright in turn had based his great comedy on *A Day Well Spent,* by the British writer John Oxenham, in 1835.) Wilder's version was entitled *The Merchant of Yonkers, A Farce in Four Acts.* His primary intention was to parody the stock company plays he used to see at Ye Liberty Theatre in Oakland in his high school days. By making fun of nineteenth-century staging, he could perhaps "shake off the nonsense of it," as he wrote in the Preface to the publication of his second version, called *The Matchmaker.* But before he was through, the comedy was more than a spoof. It said something in addition to entertaining the public. In his Preface, he noted the bewilderment of German "theses" which compared his play with the "great Austrian original."

He went on, "There is most of the plot (except that our friend Dolly Levi is not in Nestroy's play); there are some of the tags; but it's all 'about' quite different matters. My play is about the aspirations of the young (and not only of the young) for a fuller, freer participation in life. Imagine an Austrian pharmacist going to the shelf to draw from a bottle which he knows to contain a stinging, corrosive liquid, guaranteed to remove warts and wens; and imagine his surprise when he discovers that it has been filled overnight with very American birch-bark beer."

In 1938, *The Merchant* was produced by Herman Shumlin, directed by Max Reinhardt, and performed by an excellent cast, featuring Jane Cowl. Wilder had great admiration for Reinhardt, who fled Nazi Germany and joined the staff of the New School for Social Research in New York. The playwright, as a matter of fact, had written *The Merchant* specially for the famous director, and during rehearsal weeks made little comment or suggestion, either vocally or on paper. Reinhardt went ahead in his usual style, directing the piece as he would have for European audiences. He was not familiar enough with American theater custom to realize that such a comedy, full of slapstick, using old stage devices like mistaken identity, quick leaps for hiding places in closets and under tables, must be kept moving or its humor falls flat. The production, which opened on December 28, had a short run of only 28 performances, a bitter disappointment to both author and director. Almost fifteen years later, in 1954, when Thornton Wilder was invited to contribute to the Edinburgh Festival in Scotland, he rewrote the script "only slightly," and retitled it *The Matchmaker* (thus giving the play to the character he had created, Dolly Levi, instead of the Merchant, who was in a sense the "villain" of the plot). With Ruth Gordon in the title role, Tyrone Guthrie, who directed the play for the Festival, kept the action moving at the rapid pace it requires. Festival audiences were so enthusiastic that the production toured England for seven weeks afterward, and opened in London at the Royal Theatre in November, 1954. After running for almost a year, it reached New York in October of 1955, and was received with open arms by critics and American audiences; considered a hit, *The Matchmaker* was filmed, and latterly was adapted for musical comedy under the title *Hello, Dolly!*, a tremendous box office success.

(As *The Merchant of Yonkers,* the play was published in 1939, by Harper & Brothers; and as *The Matchmaker,* in 1957, by the same company, in a volume with Wilder's two Pulitzer prize plays. For publication, he wrote a telling dedication: "This play is a rewritten version of *The Merchant of Yonkers,* which was directed in 1938 by Max Reinhardt and is again dedicated to Max Reinhardt with deep admiration and indebtedness.")

As a dramatist who became a public figure, Thornton Wilder has been second only to Robert Sherwood, and in the field of literature he stands alone as cultural ambassador. He traveled for three months in the spring of 1941 through three South American countries as a lecturer for the State Department. He had been passionately interested in the writings of James Joyce for several years, and in many of his speeches he discoursed on *Finnegans Wake,* as well as *Ulysses* and the earlier works. He met with students and teachers in South American universities, and the talk would frequently center on Joyce. After the tour, he went to England as a special guest of the British Government, and a delegate to the International P.E.N. Meeting. Before the end of the year, his "Essay on James Joyce" appeared in *Poetry: A Magazine of Verse*. Directly after publication, the devastating raid on Pearl Harbor took place, precipitating the Second World War.

It was not surprising, therefore, to those who were aware of Wilder's proclivities, his scholarly essays and profound spiritual beliefs, that his next play should be a fortuitous fusion of his gifts for fantasy, humanism and high comedy. He himself wrote of it fifteen years later in the Preface to the three plays published in 1957: "*The Skin of Our Teeth* begins, also, by making fun of old-fashioned playwriting; but the audience soon perceives that he is seeing 'two times at once.' The Antrobus family is living both in prehistoric times and in a New Jersey suburb today. Again, the events of our homely, daily life—this time the family life—are de-picted against the vast dimensions of time and place. It was written on the eve of our entrance into the war and under strong emotion and I think it mostly comes alive under conditions of crisis. It has often been charged with being a bookish fantasia about history, full of rather bloodless, schoolmasterish jokes. But to have seen it in Germany soon after the war, in the shattered churches and beer-halls that were serving as theaters . . . was an experience that was not so cool. The play is deeply indebted to James Joyce's *Finnegans Wake*. I should be very happy if, in the future, some author should feel similarly indebted to any work of mine." His work also owed certain of its concepts to the playwright's knowledge of Freud, Jung, and Gertrude Stein.

At the time the original production burst upon Broadway, how-ever, few people seemed to know of its literary and intellectual antecedents, or, if so, did not take them into consideration. The play was performed by a superb cast, including Fredric March and Florence Eldridge as Mr. and Mrs. Antrobus, their children by Montgomery Clift and Frances Heflin (representing the family of man), and Tallulah Bankhead as Sabina, the irrepressible maid-of-all-work, mistress to Antrobus (representing the Earth-mother). Elia Kazan directed the production, which opened in New York at the Plymouth Theatre on November 18, 1942, at a time when the United States had been at war almost a year. First-nighters were somewhat baffled and bewildered; a few left during the last act, and even some of the critics, who understood Wilder's work, his whimsical humor and flair for fantasy, felt that he had taken too many liberties with form in his latest attempt to revitalize the theater. But all agreed, whether they liked it or not, that this was the work of genius, and that some of the truths which emerged from the cosmic, brilliant, semi-satiric tragi-comedy were profound evidence of Wilder's faith in human beings, in their ability to survive, if only by the skin of their teeth, crisis after crisis, war after war. Reviews were generally favorable, and the play won for Wilder his third Pulitzer prize.

This does not mean that controversy did not rage for some time. As early as December 19, a month after the opening, an attack on the playwright's source material for *Skin* appeared in the *Saturday Review*, the first of two articles. Entitled "The Skin of Whose Teeth?", it was written by Robinson and Campbell, who were writing their "Key" to *Finnegans Wake* in 1942; the article sought to prove that the play was "an Americanized re-creation, thinly disguised," of Joyce's novel, implying, if not actually charging, that Thornton Wilder was a plagiarist. (James Joyce's death in 1941 was the signal for a series of critical and commemorative pieces on his life and works.) A literary battle followed, in which a few critics stood up in staunch loyalty to Wilder, outraged at the accusation of plagiarism. The majority, however, including the formidable George Jean Nathan, who gave active support to the charge, were inclined to believe it, or at any rate to look on Wilder with disfavor for drawing so heavily on Joyce. The playwright himself, surprised by the barrage, saw fit to take a neutral position and was quoted in *Time* as stating that all he could do was to suggest that all those who were interested in the argument could "read *Finnegans Wake* and make up their own minds." He would neither deny nor defend his use of Joycean themes; to him the whole controversy seemed petty and irrelevant in the light of the larger meaning he intended, and at a moment when the greatest battle in history for man's survival was raging.

He was far removed, physically as well as spiritually, from the intellectual tempest in a teapot: he had enlisted in the United States Air Force early in 1942, had taken basic training in Miami, Florida, and further training in the Air Intelligence School in

Harrisburg, Pennsylvania, after which he was commissioned a Captain. He was first assigned to an air base near San Francisco, and shortly after *The Skin of Our Teeth* opened in New York, he was in a vastly different "theater": the North African Theater of War, where he was assigned in November of 1942. After serving there for a year, he was sent to the Mediterranean Theater of Operations, and served there until near the end of the war. Small wonder that he could not be concerned with the squabbles and the bickerings over the question of his plagiarizing or not! In his eyes, the answer was perfectly clear when he thought about it. He had borrowed from *Finnegans Wake,* it was true, just as he had borrowed from other works, including his own early plays, *The Long Christmas Dinner,* and *Pullman Car Hiawatha,* for a definite and distinctive purpose—to create a separate and highly original piece of theater art. As such his borrowings were completely legitimate, and it had not occurred to him to offer acknowledgments to any one of his sources. (If he had, he would have to give credit to Olsen and Johnson's *Hellzapoppin* for comic stage effects like the flying scenery in Act I, when the realistic walls of the set go up into the fly gallery to denote "two times at once," as he said when he finally offered an explanation and acknowledgment of indebtedness in the 1957 Preface.) In some of the long talks he had had with Gertrude Stein, she had taught him to ignore the critics and to write "as though no one else were listening," and as her disciple, her admiring friend, he followed her advice.

Before the end of the war, Thornton Wilder had been appointed to the rank of Lieutenant Colonel, and decorated with military honors from several countries besides the United States, an unusual record for the sensitive young man who had difficulty qualifying for service in the First World War. His interest, however, was peace. Like Mr. Antrobus, he had "all sorts of ideas for peacetime," and they were based on the preservation of books. He received the Goethe Plakette and decorations from the governments of Germany, Austria and Peru. He received the Peace Prize of the German Publishers and Book Dealers. He had abhorred the Nazis and the rule of der Führer, but he was the first to grant the German people the chance to see the futility of dictatorship, of all war. He hoped fervently that the productions of *The Skin of Our Teeth* presented in bombed-out German cities right after the war would bring home to the theater-starved audiences a little food for thought as well as entertainment. He hoped some of the speeches in the final act, when the human race is shown emerging from a war like the one in 1942, would help the German people to find the true values in living again. Sabina tells Mrs. Antrobus in her report of Mr. Antrobus' plans: "The first thing he wants to see are his books. He says if you've burnt those books, or if the rats have eaten them, he says it isn't worthwhile starting over again. Everybody's going to be beautiful, he says, and diligent, and very intelligent." Henry, the Antrobus' son, who represents the love-hate complex in the human family, cries: "The first thing to do is to burn up those old books; it's the ideas he gets out of those old books that . . . that makes the whole world so you can't live in it." At the same time, he is sorry for himself, complaining that nobody cares about him. Sabina retorts: "There's that old whine again. All you people think you're not loved enough, nobody loves you. Well, you start being lovable and we'll love you."

It is Sabina who sounds a note of pessimism, however, in regard to the future: "That's all we do—always beginning again! Over and over again. Always beginning again. . . . How do we know it'll be any better than before? Why do we go on pretending? Someday the whole earth's going to have to turn cold anyway, and until that time all these other things'll be happening again: it will be more wars and more walls of ice and floods and earthquakes." Mrs. Antrobus tells her to "stop arguing" and go on with her work, and she says, "All right. I'll go on just out of *habit,* but I won't believe in it."

Mrs. Antrobus, "aroused," will hear no more. She demands: "Do I have to explain to you what everybody knows—everybody who keeps a home going? Do I have to say to you what nobody should ever *have* to say because they can read it in each other's eyes?

"Now listen to me: I could live for seventy years in a cellar and make soup out of grass and bark, without ever doubting that this world has a work to do and will do it. Do you hear me?" And when Sabina, frightened, answers "Yes," Mrs. Antrobus demands if she can see their house at "216 Cedar Street," and goes on:

"Well, just to have known this house is to have seen the idea of what we can do someday if we keep our wits about us. Too many people have suffered and died for my children for us to start reneging now. So we'll start putting this house to rights. . . ."

In the powerful quarrel-scene between father and son, Mr. Antrobus tells Henry ("hard"): "How can you make a world for people to live in, unless you've first put order in yourself? Mark my words: I shall continue fighting you until my last breath as long as you mix up your idea of liberty with your idea of hogging everything for yourself. I shall have no pity on you. . . . You and I want the same thing; but until you think of it as something that everyone has a right to, you are my deadly enemy and I will destroy you." It was of this scene that Wilder wrote, "I doubt whether I could have expressed it that way without the reading in Freud." The conflict between father and son becomes so strong that Sabina has to "stop the play" because the actor who is in the role of the son is so angry he almost strangles the play-father. The actor apologizes and claims that the scene makes him feel like "fifteen years old again," resenting authority. (It may have been that the author was expressing his own resentment against the domineering head of the Wilder family when he and his brother Amos—who had become a theologian and author of religious writings—and their sisters were growing up.)

The final scene rings with the glory of great words from the great minds spoken through the "Hours" of the night, as Mr. Antrobus named them, lying in the trenches during the war, trying to bring forth a faith in human nature from the past. "Nine o'clock I used to call Spinoza," he says, and an actor, bearing the Roman numeral nine, appears onstage, quoting a passage from the Spanish philosopher. He is followed by Ten o'clock, Plato (read by "Hester," a colored girl, wardrobe mistress backstage), whose quotation should have served to warn the German people against another Hitler: "Then tell me, O Critias, how will a man choose the ruler that shall rule over him? Will he not choose a man who has first established order in himself, knowing that any decision that has its spring from anger or pride or vanity can be multiplied a thousandfold in its effects upon the citizens?" Aristotle (Eleven o'clock) and the Bible (Twelve o'clock) closed the quotations with the line:

"And the Lord said let there be light and there was light." The stage directions read, "Sudden blackout and silence, except for the last strokes of the midnight bell. Then just as suddenly the lights go up, and Sabina is standing at the window, as at the opening of the play." In an ironic touch, she repeats the opening lines, and then comes down to the footlights. ". . . We have to go on for ages and ages yet," she tells the audience. "You go home. The end of this play isn't written yet." But she assures everyone that Mr. and Mrs. Antrobus are full of plans and "they're as confident as the first day they began. . . ."

John Gassner, writing of the period of the early forties on Broadway, commented, "The outstanding Broadway play of this period of crisis was undoubtedly *Skin of Our Teeth.* Thornton Wilder's chronicle of man's precarious survival since the Ice Age and the Deluge, with its wonderful *Finnegans Wake* kind of synthesis of time past and present, won little support in New York after it succeeded in confusing its tryout audiences." Eric Bentley, on the other hand, felt that the play was "over-explanatory," and that the use of the "frame" of backstage and proscenium speeches (as Sabina's frequent appeals to the audience) might be called "reach-me-down" to the audience. The European audiences after the war had no objections to his device, welcoming his explanations and asides. His works have always received warm embraces in Germany, France, Italy and, with the Edinburgh Festival, in Scotland.

Wilder was discharged from the Service in September of 1945. Part of his concern during the war had been with Intelligence, information and resistance from within enemy territory; this, and the fact that he had lost a close friend, the Roman poet Lauro De Bosis, who was killed trying to organize a resistance movement against Mussolini, gave him a personal motive for the subject of his next novel, involving the question of living and dying for one's principles. Stationed in the Mediterranean, he probably turned his thoughts to the classic example of resistance to an absolute power— the one that resulted in the assassination of Caesar. *The Ides of March,* based on the life of the Roman ruler, was published in 1948, one of the best American novels in the postwar period. The London *Times* Literary Supplement called it a "short, witty, and extremely serious book." The philosophical content of Caesar's story as Wilder retold it, drawing parallels with events of World War II, combining elements of existentialism and humanism, brought wide discussion of the book and academic honors to the author. In the same year he translated and adapted for the American stage Jean-Paul Sartre's *Morts sans Sepulture,* which he called *The Victors.* A scholarly piece of work from a literary standpoint, it had little appeal except for theater libraries, and has never been produced.

As a mark of recognition, Thornton Wilder was invited to lecture in the Charles Eliot Norton chair at Harvard during 1950–1951. Taking the general subject, "The American Characteristic in Classic American Literature," he chose three New England figures—Thoreau, Melville, and Emily Dickinson—to illustrate his thesis, and spoke to full auditoriums. As much a professor as dramatist, he had the ability to become engrossed in the task at hand, to take pleasure in detailed research and scholarly perfection. There have been those who felt that the quality produces a poorer playwright, while others claim it makes his work the richer. At any rate, he did not return to the theater until the Edinburgh Festival of 1954, when the success of *The Matchmaker* brought him requests for a new play to be presented at the Festival the following year.

For some time he had been interested in the legend of Alcestis and the spirit of self-sacrifice for divine love. He borrowed from Euripides' great original drama to construct a tetralogy of his own, adding a satyr-play after the third act. His "Watchman" serves as Greek chorus and narrator, like the Stage Manager in *Our Town.* He said of the play: "On one level my play recounts the life of a woman—of many women—from bewildered bride to sorely tested wife to overburdened old age. On another level it is a wildly romantic story of gods and men, of death and hell, of resurrection, of great loves and great trials, of usurpation and revenge. On another level, however, it is a comedy . . . about the extreme difficulty of any dialogue between heaven and earth . . . about the misunderstandings that result from the 'incommensurability of things human and divine.'" In his hands, the legend became an allegory, which he titled after the Greek, *The Alcestiad.* The producer of the Festival presentation, however, imposed his own title, *A Life in the Sun,* on it for the premiere at Edinburgh in 1955—to the playwright's dissatisfaction. He usually bowed to the director or producer's judgment with quiet grace, but in this instance, he protested that such a flat phrase lost the classical allusion completely. He was voted down, and the play as presented in Edinburgh was not far from being a total failure. His disappointment was lessened by the production of *The Skin of Our Teeth* sent to Paris by the U.S. State Department for the Salut à la France festivities. Starring Helen Hayes, George Abbott and Mary Martin, it played to packed houses at the Sarah Bernhardt Theatre, and returned to tour several cities before going into New York for a brief run, until the company had to disband because of previous commitments.

Wilder would not give up on *The Alcestiad,* however. He translated the play into German, and in 1957, it was presented at the Schauspielhaus in Zurich, Switzerland, with considerably greater success than in Edinburgh. Later performances in Austria and Germany achieved wide critical attention and popularity. Paul Hindemith composed an opera for *The Long Christmas Dinner,* for which the author wrote the libretto. It was then that he conceived the idea of setting *The Alcestiad* to music. He persuaded the composer Louise Talma, for many years a colleague of his at the MacDowell Colony, to compose an opera for the German version of the play, *Die Alkestiad.* Begun in 1960, the work received its world premiere at Frankfurt-am-Main, Germany, in the spring of 1962, with Inge Borgh singing the role of Alcestis. Both composer and playwright were present, and the production was a source of satisfaction to both, although it has not been presented anywhere since.

Thornton Wilder's most recent productions appeared earlier in 1962, at the Circle in the Square Theatre; called *Plays for Bleecker Street,* they included three one-act plays from his Cycles, *The Seven Deadly Sins* and *The Seven Ages of Man,* which he had been working on for several years, during the summers. He and his sister Isabel live in Hamden, Connecticut, outside New Haven; summers they usually spend at Chillmark, Massachusetts, near Vineyard Haven. (In the summer of 1960, he received the Edward Mac-Dowell Medal for his contribution to letters. He went to Peterborough for the ceremonies and to accept the award, but he had not spent a summer there for some years.)

Two months after the premier of *Die Alkestiad*, in May, 1962, Thornton Wilder retired to the Arizona desert to have uninterrupted time and quiet for several writing projects that were delayed because of his many activities and commitments to public life. Except for a brief period when he was out of the country, and another while he was recovering from an operation, he has been writing steadily. No hint has come as to the nature of the "projects" he is working on; but it is to be hoped that he will return to the playwriting that gave to the theater plays of the caliber of *Our Town* and *The Skin of Our Teeth*. As he himself said, "The theater has lagged behind the other arts in finding the 'new ways' to express how men and women think and feel in our time."

He went on with a summing-up, in a few succinct sentences adroitly encompassing a lifetime of endeavor: "I am not one of the new dramatists we are looking for. I wish I were. I hope I have played a part in preparing the way for them. I am not an innovator but a rediscoverer of forgotten goods and I hope a remover of obtrusive bric-a-brac. And as I view the work of my contemporaries I seem to feel that I am exceptional in one thing—I give (don't I?) the impression of having enormously enjoyed it."

More than most writers, Thornton Wilder has enjoyed the rewards of public recognition of his achievements. His most recent honor came in 1965, when he received the first National Medal for Literature of the National Book Committee, and the award was the first national prize ever to be presented at the White House.

CHAPTER XI

———◆◆◆———

TENNESSEE WILLIAMS

THE FIRST experience that Thomas Lanier Williams could remember as significant in the light of his eventual choice of career was the weekly visit to the poor and ailing, when he accompanied his grandfather, Reverend Edwin Dakin, an Episcopal minister in rural Mississippi, on the regular round of parish calls. Leaving the rectory in Columbus, where small Tom lived from the time of his birth, March 26, 1911, with his older sister Rose; his mother, the former Edwina Dakin; and his gentle, yet strong-minded grandparents, he and his grandfather would drive to the crossroads and nearby farms, where the sick and lonely awaited them. They always made a lengthy stop at a certain house where Laura Young, a thin, wasted woman who never seemed to get any better, greeted them with a sad, patient smile. "There is a shadow on her," his grandfather would sigh each time as they drove away. Then one day they did not go there, and when he asked why, his grandfather told him Laura was dead. But Tom never forgot the wistful, fragile face, the glow of religious faith that shone from her eyes as she talked to her minister. It was she who served as inspiration for the heroine of his first full-length play, *Battle of Angels,* some twenty-five years later.

The playwright (who did not take the pen name "Tennessee"

until he was inching his way along the precarious path that led to the theater) discovered more than one trait of human nature on those rounds with his grandfather, more than one personality that impressed itself on his mind, and later came to people his plays.

On their return, Tom would play with his sister in the rectory sitting room or in the rocky backyard outside. Rose was a delightful companion—spirited, imaginative, fun-loving, she made up stories and games to entertain her brother. He in turn looked up to her all during their childhood in Mississippi and Tennessee, in the various villages and towns of their grandfather's parishes. For the most part, the children rarely saw their father, Cornelius Coffin Williams, during those early years. He was a traveling salesman who came to see his family only for brief visits, and then he paid little attention to the children. Their mother, an only child reared in the shelter of the church, preferred to stay with her parents until her husband found a steady job in one place. She and the children lived in the rectory wherever it might be—Columbus, Nashua, Canton or Clarksdale—until Tom was seven and Rose nearly ten years old.

It was in Clarksdale that Tom was struck by a serious illness which affected his life in a strange way. Diphtheria was a common if dangerous disease, and Tom, at five years of age, suffered a severe case, which left him with weak kidneys and paralyzed legs. He could not run and play outdoors with Rose or other children. For the better part of two years his legs were useless, his body frail. He could not even accompany his grandfather much during all that time, and lived largely in the company of his grandmother, his mother and his sister—three generations of women, all of whom helped to keep him occupied and oblivious of the fact that he was close to being an invalid for many months.

Then, just as he was recovering, regaining some strength in his legs, his father received a promotion as sales manager for the International Shoe Company in St. Louis, a permanent post, and the family had to move to the city to live. Cornelius Williams wanted to set up a home for his wife and children at last, but Edwina was expecting their third child, and did not have the energy to go house-hunting or shopping for furniture, especially since it was summer (in 1918) and St. Louis, as usual, was unbearably hot. So they bought a furnished house, adequate for their needs, but drab and gloomy, with small dark rooms that required electric light in the daytime. It was in an uninteresting, treeless part of town, neither a poor nor a rich neighborhood, but incredibly dull, completely colorless. To Tom and his sister, the house was a tenement, if not a prison. Neither he nor Rose ever liked St. Louis, "from the moment they set foot in it," according to their mother.

Both of them were used to having the run of the towns where their grandfather was the minister, and now they were lost in the vast turmoil of a teeming city, where no one knew or cared who they were. The third child, a boy named Dakin, who was born five months after they moved, accepted the city as a matter of course. But Tom, who started in at the Eugene Field public school that fall, felt terrified and lost in the welter of shouting pupils. Rose was in a higher grade, and he was left to shift for himself. The boys teased him because of his southern (Mississippi) accent and taunted him as a "sissy" because he hung back and would not take part in games. He was too shy to tell them that less than a year before his legs had been paralyzed so that he could not walk, much less run. Even now they were weak and shaky, but he did not want to admit it, and went through most of the eight grades in sheer terror. As he put it, he was "scared of everyone on earth, and particularly public school boys, and public school teachers, and public school principals, most of all." Even in the upper grades, the name *public school* kept "stabbing at his guts" until he wanted to cry, old as he was.

Another adjustment that proved a serious problem to Tom and his sister was the dominant presence of their father. Up until they moved to St. Louis, he had been practically a stranger to them or, at most, an occasional visitor to the rectory, who seemed less a parent to them than their grandfather. Now he was constantly on the scene, directing their everyday lives, commenting on their manners, their tastes, every move they made. Or so it seemed to Tom, who could not get used to a father like Cornelius, who came from an entirely different background from that of the Dakins. In his work he lived in an entirely different world, and made no effort to understand his wife or his two older children. (Between Cornelius and Dakin, who knew his father from infancy on, there was much more common ground.) Tom, forced by his illness to turn to books and the world of his imagination instead of athletics for his recreation, began writing stories by the time he was eleven, and withdrew from the rest of the family except Rose. His father scoffed at his preference for reading or going to movies with his sister instead of playing baseball with the neighborhood team. He often referred to his older son as "Miss Nancy" in humorous contempt. Tom tried to laugh it off, but his face grew hot as resentment burned deep inside him. The friction between the two mounted year by year. His mother, sympathetic to Tom, sided with him against his father, but this only added to the aggravation between them.

Nor could his father get along with his mother, who disapproved of her husband's habits and pastimes, his poker-playing friends among the salesmen, his liking for liquor. Mismated from the start, they disagreed constantly, and would probably never have stayed together if Edwina had not been a minister's daughter, keenly aware that the church disapproved of divorce and would have been doubly critical in her case. She endured the mean-tempered tongue lashings, the stinginess of her husband with even the most essential household expenses but she would not tolerate any drinking or gambling in the house. She insisted that Cornelius go to his club if he wanted to indulge in such pastimes. So he stayed away, but when he did come home, he would roar like an ogre, a tyrant over all of them. As Rose grew older, Cornelius picked on her almost as much as he did on Tom, pushing her toward her eventual mental breakdown.

For several years, Tom and his sister, siding with their mother, stayed close together in staunch league against their father. But when Rose reached adolescence, they were suddenly separated by the fact that she was "growing into a young lady," as her grandmother would say. The few years between them became an unbridgeable gap. Rose no longer wanted to go for bike rides, or make up games, or even stories, as she had before. The only childhood interest she kept up was her collection of glass animals of different sizes, some miniature, some not so small, which she had begun in Mississippi. She did not have many friends at the high school she attended, but she began to ape them in dress and hair styles, and occasionally she went out with older boys. Her father objected loudly to everything she did, but this only made her sullen and withdrawn, although she occasionally flared up and flung a few angry words—or, as her mother said, was "saucy" to her father—at him before shutting herself up in her room to mope, fingering the little glass animals for comfort.

Tom, at first bewildered, then hurt by his sister's abrupt change and apparent loss of interest in him, finally gave up trying to help defend her to their father, and abandoned her for the typewriter his mother gave him on his eleventh birthday. He began to write stories instead of making them up with Rose. He continued going to the movies with her, but her battles with their father were out of his province now, and he felt that, as the oldest child, she could fend for herself.

He wrote principally as a means of escape from the miserable family life, and over his father's objection that he was running up too high an electric bill, pounding the typewriter late afternoons when he came from school and, as he grew older, long into the night. The complaints fell on deaf ears; Tom had an outlet now, a life apart "from the world of reality, in which I felt acutely uncomfortable," as he said. He succeeded in removing himself so well that his first reward came as a result of presenting himself as a sophisticated divorced man and winning third prize in a *Smart Set* contest on the question, "Can a Wife Be a Good Sport?" The check, for five dollars, which arrived a month after his sixteenth birthday, was accompanied by an encouraging letter from the editor, ending, "Try again, won't you?" He cherished the letter and the little check as pure gold. He could not share his joy with Rose, but he showed his treasures proudly to Hazel Kramer, a high school classmate with whom he had become friends. He could confide his hopes and dreams to Hazel, intelligent and talented in her own right. In spite of his father's opposition, she was able to give Tom sympathy and understanding in his struggle to be a writer.

It was not surprising that young Williams' second achievement should be the acceptance of his short story by one of the most flourishing magazines of the time, *Weird Stories*. His imagination and flair for the bizarre made him a promising find, and the story was printed promptly, in the fall of 1927. To celebrate the occasion, Tom took Hazel to the movies; and after that he would often take her to the neighborhood moviehouse on his "writing money." By the time they were seniors, they had become close friends; both had much the same interests, and they enjoyed each other's company. They planned to go to the same college (University of Missouri) so they would not be separated after graduating from high school in January, 1929. The relationship might well have developed into a romance if Tom's father had not interfered.

He had continually disapproved of Hazel (just as he frowned on Rose's boy friends or frightened them away with his boorish tyranny) because he claimed she was not good enough for *his* son—no matter what his private opinion of Tom might be. Her parents had been divorced, and she lived with her grandfather, who worked in the sales department of the International Shoe Company, as one of Williams' subordinates. With Machiavellian intent, Tom's father informed the older man that he would not allow his son to go to the university if Hazel went. Her presence would interfere with Tom's studies. While not actually saying so, he implied that he might have to change the salesman's territory. Hazel's grandfather, feeling that his job was in jeopardy, sent her to the University of Wisconsin.

Tom's fury was monumental, but he repressed it. He wanted mostly to get away, to study and to write without hearing or having to shut out the family squabbles—his mother's nagging complaints about finances, his father's ranting at Rose and his mother, for one reason or another. Once he was enrolled at the university, and settled in his room in Columbia, Missouri, he often thought about Rose and the change that had come over her in a few years as a result of their father's abuse. In one of his letters to his mother, he referred to it as "Rose's long trouble," and expressed the hope that the psychiatrist she had been seeing could help her overcome the listless apathy, broken by violent bursts of angry terror, into which she had fallen. He felt there was nothing he could do now, however, and threw himself into his studies, particularly a course in drama he had elected. He began reading the plays of Chekhov, Lorca, and others, and suddenly felt an urge to write a play himself, although he had never tried, and knew little of the art. He plunged in, however, and was the first freshman at the University of Missouri to win honorable mention in the Dramatic Arts Contest. The slight recognition spurred him to make another attempt, and yet another, until all he wanted to do was to write plays. "My conversion to the theater arrived as mysteriously as those impulses that enter the flesh at puberty," he wrote later. He satisfied those impulses by submitting manuscripts to the drama department. One of them, a sketch called *Beauty Is the Word,* was produced at the university theater and pronounced "an original and constructive idea," but the handling was "too didactic and the dialogue often too moralistic," according to the criticism. His maternal puritan background was evident throughout.

He attended the university for three years. Occasionally during vacations he would see Hazel, but as her grandfather was uneasy about it, they did not meet often. Tom's consuming interest was writing, and he concentrated on it to the exclusion of all else, but he never failed in any subject except ROTC. (His legs had never regained normal strength, and he cut military training more often than not.) Unfortunately, his father considered it of prime importance; having attended military school himself, and proud of having served in the Spanish-American War, he was furious with his son. He swore he would take Tom out of college and put him to work; it was the depths of the depression and he could not afford to pay tuition for a son who could not pass ROTC. He carried out his oath and got Tom a job for $65 a month at the International Shoe Company. "Designed for insanity, it was a living death," the twenty-one-year-old poet-dramatist described the drudgery that lasted two and a half years—his "season in hell," he called it.

He entered his father's world as a menial—dusting shoes, typing out factory orders, hauling around packing cases for eight hours a day. He went through the chores in tight-lipped silence, and every evening after supper he shut himself up in his room to write. He would be clicking away at the typewriter long after the blast of the radio had been turned off and his parents' arguments had died down. Rose was in a state of vague melancholia at the moment; she had been in the hospital twice during Tom's absence, the second time after a broken romance with a widower, who was killed in an automobile accident. She went around depressed; even Tom could not get through to her except by taking her to the movies, and most nights his compulsion to keep on with his career as a creative artist overrode all other impulses. With the aid of black coffee and cigarettes he held up through half the night, writing and rewriting with fierce concentration. (Once his mother tried to bring him a tray of food, but he only glared at her with, "I *did* have an idea!" and sent her away.) He slept no more than a few hours before starting the treadmill again at the office in the morning. It was a grim existence, but he was determined to become a professional writer.

Such endless driving eventually took its toll. Young Williams, although lean and wiry, possessed of boundless nervous energy, was never strong after his childhood illness. He was of medium height with fairly broad shoulders, but the lower half of his body was never robust. His face, with its prominent, striking features, only showed his suffering in his deep-set, dark eyes; and in spite of everything, he had an explosive sense of humor that kept bursting out unexpectedly; but he did not have the physical stamina to continue the grueling schedule indefinitely. About the middle of 1935, he heard that Hazel Kramer was married, and although he said little, the news was somehow a deep blow to him. A month later, when he was coming home from a movie with Rose on a night he could not work, his heart began to pound, his legs gave way under him, and he collapsed.

Rose was able to hail a cab and help him into it, but on the way to the hospital his old paralysis set in, and he had to be carried into the emergency room. Brief examination showed that he was in a state of physical exhaustion, and the doctors agreed that he would have to be under their care for some time. Rose managed to keep her head in the moment of crisis, telephoning their mother with the news, but reassuring her that all Tom needed was rest and care. That night at home, however, the full impact of his breakdown struck his sister with crashing force, and destroyed the frail thread of her grasp on reality. She wandered from one room to another in panic, and woke her father up, screaming, "You're going to be murdered! We're all going to be murdered!" Shortly afterward, she was committed to a sanitarium once more; various treatments were tried, both psychiatric and surgical, but she was not able to return to normal life again.

Tom had to be in the hospital at least a month, and on leaving, he went to stay with his grandparents in Tennessee until his strength was fully regained. In the harmonious atmosphere of the rectory, he was soon healed, and with his returning health came the desire to resume writing, but he had no intention of going back to his job at the shoe company. He wanted to complete his college education, but his father still refused to pay for it, even though Tom suggested going to Washington University in St. Louis to save living expenses. His grandmother, who understood the deep urgency Tom felt for knowledge and self-expression, offered to pay his tuition.

Enrolling in the summer session in order to earn the credits he needed to enter the senior class the following year, he became engrossed in literature, reading avidly and writing with renewed ardor. One of his classmates was the future poet, Clark Mills, whose family name was McBurney; the two struck up an immediate friendship that proved rewarding to both. They exchanged ideas on their favorite authors—Chekhov, Lorca, Wilde, Faulkner, Melville, Stephen Crane. They discussed all these and more in the basement of the McBurney home, where they could read, talk and write as they pleased, to Tom's delight. Through Clark, he discovered the poetry of Hart Crane, for which he had a great feeling of rapport. The lyric quality of Crane's lines as well as the poet's brief tragic life struck a responsive chord in Tom Williams (whom his classmates dubbed "Tennessee" because of the accent he had picked up while at his grandparents'), the vibrations of which were to echo in more than one of his plays. Under Clark's urging, he tried his hand at poetry; and his friend in turn sought to create drama. In moments of practicality, they banged out stories for "the pulps." Both boys wrote a great deal in "the literary factory," as they called it. They usually fortified themselves with a pint of inexpensive liquor with which they spiked the lemonade that Mrs. McBurney brought down, and munched the sandwiches she furnished while they worked. All during the hot St. Louis summer they sat in "the stifling cellar, contentedly scribbling away."

It was perhaps the feverish activity of that summer that enabled him to win the Webster Grove Theatre Guild contest—and his first production—the following year. His mother noticed in the paper that they were offering a prize for the best one-acter, and suggested that he try his luck. The deadline was three weeks away. Although he declared he would "never make it," he began pounding the typewriter and got the script off in the nick of time. Several weeks later came the announcement that he had won by the unanimous decision of the judges!

"*The Magic Tower,* the prize-winning play, is a poignant literary tragedy with a touch of warm fantasy," the review read when the play was produced by the Guild. "Exquisitely written by its poet-author, and beautifully directed by David Gibson, this play evoked the emphatic response of the audience throughout. . . ." When he read those words, the new-found playwright in Tom Williams cried out for full expression of his talent for the theater. He decided to get his degree at the University of Iowa, where he could attend the seminar in playwriting conducted by Professor E. C. Mabie, whose course was patterned after Baker's drama workshop at Harvard.

In spite of his success in the contest, Tom's father still felt he was wasting his time, and refused to take care of the tuition, so his grandmother again came forward to help him. By waiting on tables in the cafeteria of the university hospital, he earned enough to keep him in the drama course until he completed it. He enjoyed being in the company of others who were striving to write plays, who understood the struggle for self-expression in the drama, and were willing to forgive mistakes. He plunged into work and within a short time had written two full-length plays. One of them, entitled *Spring Storm,* a play "all about love," he read aloud to the class one day. When he finished, there was a long, embarrassed silence. No comment, no criticism was offered by any of the students or the professor. Mabie looked, indeed, as if "he had drifted into a trance," but he finally remarked in a kindly voice, "Well, we all have to paint our nudes."

The second play, *Not About Nightingales,* dealt with a prison riot that took place in the South during the thirties. Setting out to be realistic, Tom drew the picture in full scale and never wrote anything to compare with it in violence and horror. Before he had completed a satisfactory draft, he received his B.A. degree from Iowa (in 1938) and went home to work on it. The Mummers, a semi-professional group in St. Louis, expressed interest in the script, offering to produce the revised version; they had no money to take an option, but he was heartened by the mere prospect of production. However, the depression—or, more accurately, the "recession" of that year—forced the Mummers to disband, and his hopes were dashed.

Tom now felt that he had reached a turning point in his life and his career. He was too far along the thorny path that every creative person must tread—as he called it and was to know it more intensively in the next five years—"a life of clawing and scratching along a sheer surface and holding on tight with raw fingers to every inch of rock higher than the one caught hold of before"; he could not accept a routine job writing for the WPA or, like so many college graduates, take an interim post as a social worker investigating relief cases. He was earning a little money by selling an occasional short story, but it was not enough to be considered his board and keep at home. His father, who took pride in his younger son's athletic prowess and military training record (twenty-year-old Dakin, the complete opposite of Tom, eventually became an Air Force officer), continued to regard his older son as a weakling, a hopeless struggler, even a wastrel; and Tom, in turn, looked on his father with a kind of cold, humorous contempt, beneath which the fires of resentment still burned. He felt a certain pity for both his parents, for he knew they were beset with guilt about Rose. It was at this time that the doctors performed a lobotomy on his sister, in the hope that the operation would relieve some pressure on her brain and so improve her mental condition; but the move had proved a grave mistake, and they were all saddened by the negative, nearly disastrous result. Later Tom was to feel that he, too, had been responsible for his sister's condition, but at the moment he knew only that he could not stand to live in the house in St. Louis any longer. The time had come for him to strike out on his own.

Much as she dreaded to see him go, his mother, always sympathetic toward his talent, if somewhat fearful that he might fail, agreed that if he felt impelled to travel, to taste another sort of living, he must leave St. Louis. He had had a hankering to see New Orleans ever since he had heard and read stories about the Mardi Gras city, so in the early fall of 1939, he set off, although he had "not one cent in his pocket," as his mother said.

The scene he discovered for himself opened his eyes and his heart to humanity. Here the must-be playwright met up with the "shadow people," creatures without roots, who lived in utter loneliness. Like Eugene O'Neill, he felt a certain kinship with them, for he realized that the grim emotions he had been suffering were shared by a whole segment of human life. These lost souls would go to any lengths to dispel their despair; and at first their explosive, wild, frenzied existence overwhelmed him with its excesses. A kaleidoscope of drinking, sex and revelry danced before his eyes in crazy prisms of color. Sauntering wide-eyed through the streets of the Latin Quarter, he rubbed shoulders with panhandlers, prostitutes, procurers, homosexuals and dope addicts, "living a fringe-area life fraught with desperation and wild despair." Unlike O'Neill, however, young Williams did not let himself sink to the precarious pit of dissolution that could have permanently damaged his health. He reveled in the abandon he found, but he did not let it drag him as close to destruction as O'Neill did. For one thing, he had no wealthy actor-father to rely on, and he was determined never to set foot in St. Louis again until he was successful. Starting as an elevator operator in a small hotel, he had a series of odd jobs to keep him going, and outside working hours, he lived with greater license than he had ever known. He said, "I found the kind of freedom I had always needed. And the shock of it against the puritanism of my nature, has given me a subject, a theme, which I have never ceased exploiting." In New Orleans, the puritan and the bohemian clashed and fused in the future playwright.

No matter how much he might mingle with the ragged fringe of society, some part of him remained solely the observer, and he wrote a series of one-act plays concerned with the individual struggle for freedom against hopeless emotional and material odds. Published later as *American Blues,* under the name "Tennessee" Williams, which he decided to call himself professionally at this time, they came as close to being plays of social consciousness as any he ever wrote. Sending three of them off to the Group Theatre, he set out for California with a clarinetist he had met, the two of them joining the westerly pilgrimage of hitchhikers, hoping to find work in Hollywood.

To his astonishment, Tennessee Williams' one-acters made him the winner of a citation and $100, which was forwarded to him in California. No manna from Heaven was ever hailed with greater joy. He managed to live off of it all season long at Laguna Beach, then an undeveloped stretch of sandy shore below rugged cliffs. He took his typewriter out on the beach and began to write more one-acts and sketches which became scenes in full-length plays. It was in 1939 that he met the poet Donald Windham, the two soon discovering their mutual admiration of Faulkner and D. H. Lawrence, and not long afterward began writing a play together based on Lawrence's short story, "You Touched Me."

In New York, meanwhile, Mollie Day Thatcher of the Group Theatre convinced Audrey Wood that such a promising playwright should be under the agency's protective wing, and the next thing he knew, young Williams received word that the Rockefeller Foundation had awarded him a grant for playwriting. He was in St. Louis at the time, convalescing from surgery on his left eye, which had developed a cataract some months before. (He had reached a lull in his work, and decided to attend to the condition.) When the announcement came, his mother shed tears of joy—the first time he had ever seen her cry. He himself was "numbed with happiness," as he described his feelings. Coming as it did after an eye operation that was not very successful, and when he had begun to doubt his ability as a playwright, the news brought him out of the darkness of discouragement. "I knew how Lazarus must have felt when he sat up and saw daylight again," he said.

He also received a scholarship to an advanced playwriting seminar at the New School in New York City, beginning in February, 1940. The course was conducted by Theresa Helburn and John Gassner, both of the Theatre Guild. Williams did not like New York much better than he had liked St. Louis, but he made the most of the months spent at the New School. At the end of the semester he was able to hand in the first draft of a full-length play, *Battle of Angels,* a drama of the South, the one that included the portrait of Laura Young, the sick, faded Southern belle, helpless and repressed, which he drew from his recollections of those childhood days in Mississippi, when he made the rounds of parish calls with his grandfather. Gassner and Miss Helburn, feeling they had made a find, rushed to show the script to the Theatre Guild. Before their student-playwright quite realized what was happening, the play went into rehearsal with Margaret Webster as director and Miriam Hopkins as leading lady! The next few weeks he lived in a bubble of suspense, a mixture of joyous hope and apprehension.

The play opened in Boston in the fall (of 1940), but was doomed to sorry disaster, principally because an overzealous stage manager rolled up great billows of smoke in the "conflagration scene" which closes the play, nearly suffocating both actors and spectators. The audience, according to Gassner, "already outraged by the unsparing presentation of repressed sexuality in a Southern community, was literally *smoked* out of the theater." Coughing and gasping, a few people offered a slight trickle of applause for Miriam Hopkins, who had to push through waves of smoke to take a bow. As might be expected, reviews were less than lukewarm, the play was banned immediately because of its subject matter, and the Guild withdrew the production. A letter of apology sent to subscribers included a paragraph on the remarkable talent of Tennessee Williams, but that did not do much to alter the fact that the *Battle of Angels* went down to defeat.

Williams found himself "once more a rootless, wandering writer," trying to eke out a living by occasional acceptances and odd jobs, pushing steadily onward in spite of all obstacles. Soon after the debacle, he went to Florida, where he landed a job as teletype operator for engineers in Jacksonville. In the course of the months he stayed there, he picked up enough material and local color for several one-act plays, among them the one enigmatically titled *Twenty-seven Wagons Full of Cotton*, under which these one-acts were eventually published, and which was the basis for his screen play *Baby Doll.*

He investigated various sections of Florida, including Key West, where he ultimately bought a house, but on his first visit, he had barely enough to buy food and typewriter paper. During this peripatetic period of his life, usually when his funds were at the lowest ebb, he would receive a letter from his Grandmother Dakin, in which he would find, carefully stitched to the paper, a five- or—once or twice—a ten-dollar bill. The money not only encouraged, but touched him deeply, sent as it was, so neatly sewn, unsolicited, and completely without comment. He drifted west again—Texas, New

Orleans, Mexico. The primitive country south of the border charmed and soothed him with its slow pace and its hundreds of carefree vagrants among the natives, as well as travelers like himself, seeking truth and genuine feeling in a callous, competitive world.

In the spring of 1941, he had another eye operation, again with little success, and a third, in the spring of 1942, brought scarcely any more improvement. For a while he wore a patch over his left eye, which gave him the appearance of a bold desperado, but did not help his vision. He and Donald Windham finished their dramatization of *You Touched Me* and decided to try for production of their script in New York. Neither the Group nor the Guild were interested in Lawrence's short story as dramatic material; it was in fact intimated that *Battle of Angels* had suffered from too great an influence of D. H. Lawrence. Still hoping to find a producer, the young playwright stayed in New York, maintaining himself by taking more odd jobs. At one point, he recited verses and waited on tables at a Greenwich Village night spot. He was ushering in a movie theater when Metro-Goldwyn-Mayer made one of its periodic roundups of young hopefuls, and offered him a six months' contract in Hollywood. As usual, the Studio left him to his own assignments, and when he submitted the outline for the plot of an original screen play which bore the simple title *The Gentleman Caller*, the executives promptly dismissed him from their minds and neglected to renew his contract.

He was not sorry. He wanted to work on the script of *The Gentleman Caller* in his own way, taking his time. It was, in his words, "a memory play," the memory of the past he had put behind him when he left for New Orleans the first time—or, rather, it was his remembrance of the one portion of the past he could not forget, and that was the sad fate of his sister Rose. In 1942, he had written an autobiographical sketch of his "season in hell" at the International Shoe Company, called *Stairs to the Roof*, with the revealing subtitle, "A Prayer for the Wild of Heart That Are Kept in Cages." Recalling the grim battle of those miserable months inevitably brought Rose vividly to mind. From hindsight he could see that in locking his bedroom door and pounding his typewriter every night to shut out the sight and sound of bickering and violence, and, later, the melancholy of his sister's face, the sad whine of the old victrola records she used to play, he had been closing the door to her. He had given full sway to his strong instinct for self-preservation, but now he felt it had been at the cost of his sister's sanity. He blamed himself as much as their parents for her pitiful state at the end, when the once spirited and imaginative child who had grown into a beautiful girl had become a vague-eyed and passive creature whose only outside interest was her collection of miniature glass animals or an occasional movie. It was true that in one light no one was to blame for Rose's emotional imbalance, but in another, he felt that he, as well as others, had contributed to her madness, by default.

He hoped that this play in some dim way would make it up to her—at least, in his own mind. Even though she might not hear it, the work would be his cry to her for forgiveness and understanding.

The plot line of the tender drama was far from the Williams family history or situation at the time it took place—the late 1930s, just before the playwright left home. He chose only elemental details of similarity. The brother, also the narrator of the play, is a poet of unknown, and, as implied by his nickname "Shakespeare," of questionable quality; he works in the warehouse of a shoe company for sixty-five dollars a month, and bears the playwright's real name, Tom. His wisdom is the wisdom of retrospect, in his capacity as narrator, looking back after a number of years in the Merchant Marine. During the action of the play, he is by turns affectionate and concerned toward his mother and sister, and again he is bitter, selfish, given to harsh humor, perhaps to cover his gentler feelings. He has been the breadwinner of the family for some time, the father having left home never to return, sixteen years before. This was perhaps wishful thinking on Williams' part. The play could almost be called a fantasy of what might-have-been if Cornelius Williams had left home, as his son must often have wished he would. The photo on the wall seems to symbolize the image of the father Williams knew as a visitor when the children were small.

Amanda Wingfield, the mother and central motivating character of the play, although she may have certain resemblances to the playwright's mother, was obviously not intended to be a portrait of her. Edwina Dakin Williams must have had both intelligence and stoical courage to champion her son's artistic ability in the face of her husband's blind opposition. And, while she may have been helpless, nagging, and rigid on the subject of his drinking and gambling, was far from the fishwife and faded Southern belle of the mother in the play. Amanda, both a comedic and tragic character of Tennessee Williams' creation, seems to have been molded with the intent of teasing and taunting his mother about her shortcomings, and her share in his sister's decline.

The widest difference between reality and art was in Rose. In dealing with his sister's character and story, Tennessee Williams chose to present her psychosis as deriving from a physical defect, significantly one very similar to his own: "A childhood illness has left her crippled," reads the description of Laura Wingfield, "one leg slightly shorter than the other and held in a brace. . . . Stemming from this, Laura's separation increases until she is like a piece in her own glass collection, too exquisitely fragile to move from the shelf." Rose, on the contrary, was a handsome, rather robust girl, according to Mrs. Williams: high-spirited to the point of being hypersensitive and subject to moodiness, but physically perfectly normal.

In revising his script, which he eventually gave the more poetic, meaningful title, *The Glass Menagerie*, Tennessee Williams consciously or unconsciously was making a plea for himself—for the artist, and the quality of spun glass that makes him "different" from all the other people in the world. That "difference," of which the poet Robert Frost wrote so eloquently, and which the Gentleman Caller, Jim O'Connor, senses in Laura and fumblingly tries to express in the play, is vital to the artist, whether his work is ever recognized or not. Williams found he had written a play of tremendous appeal in its aching nostalgia, mournful humor, and fragile dream of unfulfilled romance.

The Glass Menagerie was first tried out by Margo Jones in Dallas, with the result that Miss Jones insisted that it was a play for the "big time," and when Audrey Wood (still Williams' agent) showed the script to Eddie Dowling (fresh from his huge success in Saroyan's *The Time of Your Life*), he fell in love with its touching drama. He not only produced it with Louis Singer, and staged it with Margo Jones, but took the part of Tom Wingfield, the son and narrator in the play. They decided to open in Chicago, and the first performance took place at the Civic Theatre on December 26, 1944. It received rave reviews from all the critics, but in spite of their praise for both the play and the actors (particularly Laurette Taylor, whose superb interpretation of Amanda Wingfield came as a happy surprise to both playwright and producers), audiences seemed to shie away from *The Glass Menagerie*. People may have suspected it of being "arty" because of the "screen device" in the original production whereby titles and images were projected on a screen at given moments to accent the point of the scene. (Williams had borrowed the device from Erwin Piscator, German director of the "epic" theater, with whom he worked at the New School; but now, because of "the extraordinary power of Miss Taylor's performance," the visual means of communicating emotion and drama was unnecessary, and it was dropped in the Broadway production.) Whatever the reason, Chicago theatergoers did not respond at first. The producers were ready to close, when Claudia Cassidy, most intrepid of drama critics, led her colleagues in a daily barrage of columns urging people to see the play. Within a week, attendance had doubled, and the next thing they knew, *The Glass Menagerie* was playing to full houses.

The Broadway production opened on March 3, 1945, to instantaneous, unqualified acclaim from critics and audiences alike; the thirty-four-year-old playwright, after struggling so many years, found himself hailed as an "overnight success." He was besieged by admirers, autograph seekers, offers from stage and screen producers. Even before the play left Chicago, he was overwhelmed, and now he felt awash on the gigantic wave of success. He moved into "a first-class Manhattan hotel," and "lived on room service," as he says in the brilliant and penetrating Preface to the published version of *The Glass Menagerie*, a piece which first appeared in the *New York Times* under the title "The Catastrophe of Success." But the luxury did not dispel his disturbing sensations of letdown and gloom. In desperation, he decided to have another eye operation—his fourth on the same eye, this time on the muscle—principally to put him "behind the gauze mask," out of touch with the world. The enforced physical stillness that any eye operation requires brought with it the quietude he needed to reassess the value of success, the conditions it imposed, the losses it could easily entail of far more enduring elements of life—friendships, and, most important, the creative impulse. The first thing he did when the gauze mask was removed was to check out of the "handsome hotel suite." The final operation on his eye may not have improved his eyesight any more than the others, but it gave him a clear view of the action he must take if he was to survive. Before *The Glass Menagerie* had received the already scheduled Drama Critics Award, and before rehearsals began for the production of *You Touched Me* (the play he and Donald Windham had written, which opened in the fall of 1945), Tennessee Williams left for Mexico, where he settled in the remote spot of Chapala. Here he began to work with steady concentration on a play destined to bring him far more fame than his first success. Based on the scenes and personalities he had observed in New Orleans, the locale of the play, he created composite characters for a skillfully structured, emotional drama, to which he initially gave the naturalistic title *The Poker Night,* later changing it, as he had done with *The Gentleman Caller,* to the imagistic—or surrealistic—*A Streetcar Named Desire.*

Two years later, on December 3, 1947, the play with the odd yet compelling title opened on Broadway and assumed its proper role as the most significant, powerful, and artistically wrought dramatic work in many a season. Playing to capacity houses from the start, *A Streetcar Named Desire* won both the Drama Critics Award and the Pulitzer prize for 1947–1948. A great deal has been written about *Streetcar,* from the time of its premiere on, most of the criticism on the credit side of the ledger. Praise has run all the way from Eric Bentley's grudging admission that Williams' play was "on the borderline of really good drama," to David Sievers' proclamation that the playwright "must be credited with a psychological masterpiece," and that Blanche Dubois is "no less a tragic figure than Antigone or Medea."

The Christmas of 1947 was a joyful one for Williams, not only because of his stunning success (which he now could take in stride), but also because he received the welcome news that his mother was at long last obtaining a legal separation from his father, who was going to Tennessee to live with his sister. It was with mingled relief and sadness that the playwright read his mother's letter. The bitter resentment he had felt toward his father had abated with maturity and the financial security that came with success; on the rare occasions when he had returned briefly to St. Louis, there had been an unspoken truce between the two men, an uncomfortable silence. Now he could go home if he wished, but he had no desire to do so. "A tragic situation has worked itself out too late," he wrote to a friend. "As for the old man—he has probably suffered more than anyone, and it will be a bitter end to his blind and selfish life." He could not forget the pain and suffering that Cornelius inflicted on his family because of his own loneliness and lack of understanding.

Rose was beyond the playwright's help, except for seeing to it that she had the best possible care in a good sanitarium, and visiting her when he could, getting permission to take her for drives or short trips. His mother, however (in her sixties in 1947), was in reasonably good health, and he determined to make the rest of her life as serene and pleasant as he could. He had already made her a co-partner in the receipts from *The Glass Menagerie;* the unpublished and published versions of the play were copyrighted by "Tennessee Williams and Edwina D. Williams," so that she shared in all the royalties and could be financially independent. Rather than return to St. Louis and its unpleasant memories, the playwright brought his mother to New York, and in the years that followed, he often took her to Europe or invited her to spend the winter in his Key West home.

Another frequent guest in Florida and on trips to Europe was his grandfather, now retired from the ministry, whose company he still enjoyed as much as he did when they made the parish rounds together. His grandmother unfortunately had died in 1943, just before he could have repaid her for the stalwart encouragement she had given him for so many years. She had shown great fortitude in her life, especially toward the end, when she knew she was dying of cancer. To the last, she had been a mainstay to him. He always regretted that she had not lived a few years more, but he could at least show his appreciation toward his grandfather. (They became good companions, and when his grandfather died of a stroke in 1955, at the venerable age of ninety-eight, Williams felt an infinite sadness and sense of loss; he had a blanket of English violets, his grandfather's favorite flower, laid on the grave.)

Tennessee Williams has traveled much since his triumphant trip to Europe in January, 1948, directly after his permanent place on the theatrical roster was assured, and before the production of his next play, *Summer and Smoke*, which again drew a picture of repressed Southern womanhood, this time the daughter of an Episcopalian minister. The play, full of religious and sexual symbols, failed on Broadway, but had an extraordinary success in an Off-Broadway revival in 1952 because of Geraldine Page's sensitive, suggestive portrayal of Alma, the central figure.

Williams fell in love with Italy, with the Italian people; and the warmth he felt emerged in *The Rose Tattoo*, a tragi-comedy set in the Sicilian colony along the Gulf of Mexico, which he wrote soon after his return from Europe. Produced in 1951, *The Rose Tattoo* revealed a lyric, yet lusty, earthy side of the poet-dramatist, a facet of his talent as yet undeveloped, which could appreciate and depict vitality in people as well as emotional suffering, loneliness, and defeat. In creating Serafina Delle Rose, one might almost say that he has gone too far the other way from his portraits of repression, of the faded Southern belles living in the past. But Serafina is saved from caricature by the playwright's flair for comedy, and by the sense of spirituality one feels in Serafina's sensuality. Similarly, the men in *The Rose Tattoo* are shown as savoring sex as a normal, healthy, systemic function—not without its spiritual aspect, but devoid of the problems it poses for most of his heroes.

Unfortunately, Williams saw fit to follow this refreshing attitude (in 1953) with his most cynical, heavy-handed, symbolistic theater piece, *Camino Real*. Written in free verse, replete with literary allusions, it was apparently intended to be the greatest philosophic and poetic contribution to the theater since Shakespeare, but the playwright left out the most important ingredient—characterization. There are no original personalities, no people one can love or hate in his diatribe against tyranny, sadism, injustice, and the various vices of the world.

The play, a dismal failure, was a bitter disappointment to Williams; but he seems to have profited by his mistake in *Cat on a Hot Tin Roof*, which was something of an emotional bombshell in its honest yet sensitive handling of homosexuality, its grasp of human greed, desire and frustration. Here again, in Maggie-the-Cat, he has created a heroine of tremendous, if obsessive, vitality—a modern instead of a faded Southern belle, not without charm—pitted against the formidable passivity of her husband. Brick himself is caught between warring tendencies that have left him an emotional vacuum, unable to love anyone. In the person of Big Daddy, Brick's father—a present-day, disillusioned Falstaff—and in Big Mama, Gooper and Mae as well, Williams has created characters worthy of Faulkner in depicting Southern folkways. If the play is blatant with vulgarity, it also blares out in praise of the vim and vigor of a healthy sex life—not the conscious breeding of Gooper and Mae, nor the twisted union of Big Mama and Big Daddy, but the soul-satisfying, if unattainable, fusion born of love. Produced first in England, *Cat* was met by official reproof (the Lord Chamberlain's ban), mingled with the mild interest of curiosity seekers. In the United States, however, it received critical approval and amazing popularity on both stage and screen.

For all his success, Williams had not forgotten his first failure, and the acceptance of *Cat* gave him the confidence to rewrite *Battle of Angels,* increasing its symbolism, and changing the title to *Orpheus Descending.* The Broadway production, in 1957, brought little more applause than the original, seventeen years earlier; but the revised version did better in an Off-Broadway staging two years later. In 1959, a new drama, *Sweet Bird of Youth,* a strange mixture of melodrama and striking character study, attracted and startled wide audiences with its macabre machinations. "My corn-pone melodrama is all my own," he said in an interview at the time (1960).

No matter what fare Tennessee Williams has to offer, his works have the richness of a passionate—and compassionate—creative artist. Called a "scenewright" as well as playwright, he is a master at holding an audience enthralled with the throb of human emotion. Among the later plays, *Suddenly Last Summer, The Garden District,* and *Night of the Iguana* all have scenes of great power and intensity. And whether he is successful or not, he has the sensitivity of the poet, combined with the theatricality of the dramatist and the dedication of the artist, to place him among the foremost of modern American playwrights.

CHAPTER XII

ARTHUR MILLER

THE NAMES of Tennessee Williams and Arthur Miller have been linked together so often they seem like the twin stars of Gemini in the theatrical firmament, for they appeared at about the same time, and both shone with equal brilliance in the limelight of the theater. Yet, as all who have tied them together readily admit, the two dramatists are as far apart as the poles—in background, in personality, and in their creative output.

Arthur Miller was born in Manhattan, October 17, 1915, and attended high school in a Brooklyn suburb, a greater contrast to the villages of rural Mississippi than anyone could imagine without a knowledge of the vast difference that still existed between North and South in the first thirty years of the twentieth century. Arthur's parents, Isadore and Augusta Barnett Miller, belonged to the middle-class community in the bustling industrial borough of the sprawling metropolis that had given rise to the term "the melting pot" a generation or two earlier. Mr. Miller was a hard-working businessman, a manufacturer of women's coats, who sought to give his family such advantages as he did not have as a child in Austria-Hungary. His wife Augusta, born in America, apparently had few interests outside her home and children, leading the life of the average Brooklyn housewife. Although she had always longed to go to college, she made a career of looking after her husband's needs and tending to her brood of three. (The playwright has an older brother, now in business, and a sister who is on the stage.)

Arthur, a thin wiry boy, whose hazel eyes looked out thoughtfully from his thin, pointed, sensitive face, was hardly studious, but rather athletically inclined. As a child, he was an avid baseball fan; and by the time he reached high school—a tall, rangy teen-ager—he became a football star, graduating in 1933 as a "hero." He wanted to go to the University of Michigan, mostly because of the nationally known football team, whose fame he had followed all through high school. However, his father, like most businessmen, had been hit by the depression and could not afford to send his son to Ann Arbor or any college. So for two and a half years, Arthur Miller worked as a loader and shipping clerk in an automobile warehouse at Tenth Avenue and Sixtieth Street in Manhattan, saving all he could toward his tuition.

In the process, a profound change took place in the football star —one that sharply altered his aims, his whole outlook on life. Since the warehouse job was routine, it soon became mechanical, giving him a chance to think. He had to take a long subway ride every morning, so he began to read some of the books he had had to put off because of too many outside activities in high school, and once he started, there was no stopping. He read straight through *War and Peace* while hanging onto a subway strap, and he often went to the library on his lunch hour. The direct opposite of Williams, whose career was already carved in outline when he was forced to go to work at the shoe company, Miller did not find the experience like "a season in hell," a "cage," or prison, but saw it rather as a liberating force that released his inner being to the whole wide world of the mind as revealed in literature. He read everything he could cram into his waking hours, discovering for himself the delight in the words that expressed the truths of life—partly in poetry, more in novels, but mainly in plays. Like most New Yorkers, he had always enjoyed the theater, going to Broadway shows, but now he felt an urgent desire to write plays.

After reading a book with the commanding title *Write That Play!*, by Kenneth E. Rowe, of the University of Michigan Drama Department, young Miller wanted more than ever to go to Ann

Arbor to study. When he had saved enough money to pay his tuition, he realized that his marks in high school were not good enough to qualify him for entrance exams, so he impetuously wrote to Clarence Cook Little, the progressive president at Michigan, asking for permission to enter on the grounds that he would prove his merit in the first year of his study. If he did not do more than passing well, did not show true distinction as an embryo playwright, he would drop out. He was granted the opportunity, and went off to the Middle West with his family's blessings. He plunged into playwriting as if he had been born to the theater. He found in Kenneth Rowe the kind of understanding critic and teacher he needed to make him "write that play," following it with another, and another. By the end of a year he did not have to quit, and for two years he succeeded in winning the Avery Hopwood Award, offered annually at Michigan for the best original play. He rapidly gained a thorough knowledge of the theater, from the writing through the producing of plays. The Lydia Mendelsohnn Repertory Theatre had opened in 1929 in the newly built Women's League, and offered a workshop for new as well as seasoned productions. He attended rehearsals, performances, sessions in lighting, set designing. Ideas came to him; words, dialogue flowed from him. When he went to Chicago during one vacation, he saw a performance of Clifford Odets' *Awake and Sing,* and the core of its message, "Life should have some dignity," made a deep and lasting impression on him. (The telling line, "Go out and fight so life shouldn't be printed on dollar bills," seemed to epitomize the attitude of the thirties toward the false ideals of the twenties.) He thought a great deal about the change the depression had wrought in his family, as in so many others. He considered the values that had caused so many Wall Street suicides when men were forced to face financial failure.

He was forming the concepts of moral responsibility within the family which were to furnish the central themes of his plays, particularly the relationship between father and son. Extending from there to the family of man, he placed the responsibility for the general welfare of the masses on the individual; it was, therefore, immoral for one man to amass great wealth at the expense of the many, and it was immoral to hold financial, material wealth the yardstick of a successful life. This in turn led him to an appraisal of the injustices, the sins committed in the name "free enterprise," the tendency to condone any means to achieve success. In his plays Arthur Miller was to question and to sit in judgment against the false values of the past and present, as yet a distant outcome of his college years, but already clearly outlined in his early manuscript plays.

In 1937, one of the Hopwood-award-winning plays received a truly substantial prize of $1250—at that time a small fortune—from the Bureau of New Plays, set up by the Theatre Guild under the directorship of Theresa Helburn. It was cause for great celebration, not only on the part of the fervent young playwright and his mentors in the drama department at Michigan, but his favorite coed on Michigan's largely male campus—one of his classmates, Mary Grace Slattery. Their romance blossomed after that signal event, and by the time Arthur left Ann Arbor in 1938, his B.A. degree in hand, they were engaged.

With his record of prizes, he had little trouble landing a post on the Federal Theater Project, writing plays for a salary of $22.77 a week. He had to report at the Project office every day, and at night he continued playwriting on his own. He completed work on a poetic drama, which he called *Montezuma,* concerning the conquest of Mexico. Seemingly removed from contemporary life, the play was related to the international struggle of the thirties by implication—foreshadowing the technique he was to use to such great advantage much later, in *The Crucible.* With high hope, Miller sent copies of his play to all the organizations that seemed likely to be interested: the Theatre Guild, the Group, the New Theatre League, and others. But nobody wanted to give consideration to an historical drama (according to its title) just then; indeed, Harold Clurman, Managing Director of the Group, recently confessed that he found the script several years later in his files—unread. Disappointed, but not actually discouraged, the young playwright kept plugging away. He tried his hand at radio script writing with some success, to his surprise, and when the Federal Theater Project was abandoned in 1940, he was able to earn a living in a medium he had never seriously considered. Shortly after he was established, he and Mary Slattery were married.

They settled down to a semi-suburban life in **Patchogue**, Long Island, never really joining the suburbia community, for Arthur's most consuming interest was the theater. Within a few years their daughter was born, and, in three more, their son. All the time Arthur was turning out radio scripts, he was also writing plays and trying to get them produced. When World War II came along, he did some scripts for a documentary film, *The Story of G.I. Joe,* based on Ernie Pyle's columns of the war. Miller visited numerous army camps, keeping a diary as his research, which was published in book form, entitled *Situation Normal.* He had also been working on a novel which was his protest against an openly Fascist organization, but thinly disguised by the name Christian Front. Miller's book, *Focus,* revealed the anti-Semitism of such organizations, and pointed to the dangers of religious prejudice. It received notable coverage in the press, provoking varied opinion and discussion of its timely subject.

In the same year, 1945, he was fortunate enough to find a producer for his ninth playscript, *The Man Who Had All the Luck,* a rather contrived tale of a man whose constant good luck is a source of dismay and insecurity to him until he suffers a serious setback, when he feels assured that he will drive forward of his own volition. Except for the fact that it was produced, the play itself had little luck in presentation, lasting only four performances. Nevertheless, his name had been brought to light as well as his work, and no one could deny that Arthur Miller was now a professional playwright. That alone was enough to make him feel that real recognition was in sight. In fact, although reviews had been generally negative, Burton Rascoe had been perceptive enough to point out Miller's potential as a challenging, forceful playwright of the contemporary theater. Of far more significance was Miller's immediate reward in the form of requests for his next play from several top producers, among them Harold Clurman. The course was set for his goal just ahead!

He had already begun to write a realistic drama, to be called *All My Sons,* involving his basic concept of moral responsibility in the family, linking it to the inner struggle of men in authority during the war. With the end of world conflict in 1945, people began to ask the inevitable questions, seeking to place the burden of guilt where it belonged: not only on the enemy, but on the individual who in any way had shown complicity in the slaughter. Taking the hypothetical case of an executive who allowed defective airplane motors to be shipped to the Army rather than ruin his company's business and losing the contract, the playwright sought to show the consequences of the man's dereliction. By the end of the play, Keller realizes that the pilots who flew those planes were, as he says, "all my sons"; and the fact that war is a business to makers of military equipment does not exonerate him. His son Chris, disillusioned in the father he had revered, cries out: "I know you're no worse than other men, but I thought you were better. I never saw you as a man; I saw you as my father." His is a scathing, yet heartbreaking denunciation, because it implies the loss of deep respect, of filial love.

There were certain artificialities of plot (among them the device Bentley called "the time-honored prop of melodrama," the last-minute discovery of a lost letter in which "all is revealed"), but in the main it was a sincere, moving, at times gripping drama of ideas. Harold Clurman was ready to produce it at once; he was joined by Walter Fried and Elia Kazan, who directed—the beginning of a continued, happy association between director and playwright. The play opened on January 29, 1947, a box office success which won the Drama Critics Award as the best play of the season. Arthur Miller had arrived to stay on Broadway and, with Tennessee Williams, to try to lift the commercial theater above the level of the "commodity play."

Miller's next attempt, like Williams', thrust him into the climax of his career. Just fifteen months after the appearance of *Streetcar*, his prize-winning *Death of a Salesman* made its debut and walked away with both the Pultizer and the Drama Critics awards for 1949. The play represented Miller's theory carried one step farther than in *All My Sons* to its logical conclusion. Here the playwright not only placed on trial the moral values of his central character—Willy Loman, the salesman—but a society that by competition compels its individuals to forsake native talents in favor of achieving material success, at the price of human dignity. Willy Loman might have been a superb craftsman, but he is forced by the demands of a mechanized world to run pantingly in search of the will-o'-the-wisp,

financial wealth. He takes on the vapid, superficial life of the salesman, the false heartiness, the emptiness, the loneliness covered up
by colossal bluff, the fleeting pleasure of a sportive fling, and the
anodyne of alcohol.

The irony of Willy's tragedy is that the material goal is a mirage.
Not only does he fail as the father, the head of the family, but he
never comes anywhere near his goal of immense wealth. The implication is that if he had succeeded he would not have been happy,
but he cannot achieve even the Philistine satisfaction of money. He
is in moral and financial ruin by the end of the play, and can only
think of taking his life so his son, Biff, can at least have the benefit
of his insurance policy. In condemning Willy Loman to die by his
own hand, Miller is actually condemning the economic system that
fashioned his fate. Salesmen are the patsies of the industrial ring-
masters whose products they parade; only one out of a hundred
becomes a star, rising to change his status in the world. In creating
Willy Loman, who typifies a large segment of the American population, the playwright also created an unforgettable character in the
theater, an individual personality who somehow arouses sympathy
and love in the spectator. His wife, who, like the wife in *All My
Sons,* is loyal to her husband and sons to the last, arouses pity as
the innocent sufferer, but it is pity not unmixed with annoyance at
her insistence in adhering to the hypocrisies of convention, the
chimeras of society.

The play was hailed as a thought-provoking drama, full of psychological and sociological insight. (Bentley, who had assailed *All
My Sons* as being serious "in intent only," called *Death of a Salesman* "a signal event" in the theater, and most critics agreed that it
gave true dramatic intensity to the theater of ideas.) Miller, strong
in his convictions, was regarded not merely as a skillful playwright,
but as a moralist, and, because of his attitude toward the inequali-
ties of society, a radical. When the forces of reaction, in the form
of the House Un-American Activities Committee, began to repress
the voices of social progress, to persecute as revolutionaries those
who had supported the much-needed reforms of the thirties and
early forties, Arthur Miller was among the first to speak up in protest against the modern witch hunt of McCarthyism.

Between 1952 and 1953 he wrote perhaps his most controversial play, *The Crucible*. Set in Salem, Massachusetts, in 1692, the play is a dramatization of the famous—and infamous—witch hunt that took place in the New England village, drawing the obvious parallel between the hysteria of that day and the present. "It was not only the rise of McCarthyism that moved me," Miller wrote in the Introduction to his *Collected Plays*, "but something which was much more weird and mysterious. It was the fact that a political, objective, knowledgeable campaign from the far Right was capable of creating not only a terror, but a new subjective reality, a veritable mystique which was gradually assuming even a holy resonance. That so interior and subjective an emotion could have been so manifestly created from without was a marvel to me. It underlies every word in *The Crucible*. . . . I saw forming a kind of interior mechanism of confession and forgiveness of sins which until now had not been rightly categorized as sins. New sins were being created monthly. It was very odd how quickly these were accepted into the new orthodoxy, quite as though they had been there since the beginning of time. . . . Above all, above all horrors, I saw accepted the notion that conscience was no longer a private matter, but one of state administration. I saw men handing conscience to other men and thanking other men for the opportunity of doing so." Feeling as he did, he had to show how reprehensible the conduct of the Committee was in his eyes, and in the eyes of all thinking men. Going back into American history, he dug up the records of the Salem witchcraft trials, and created his own characters based on the few facts of "known behavior" of the persons involved. The result was a powerful indictment of mass hysteria and savage fury born of terror and superstition.

   The Crucible had two opening nights of two separate productions six months apart, one in January and one in July of 1953. The first was staged with full sets by Jed Harris, and came close to being a flop because of the rigidity of the production. The analogy was clear enough, the preachment powerful, but the play was considered heavy-handed, lacking in the warmth or passion necessary for good drama. Even a fine actor like Arthur Kennedy (who had scored as Biff, the older son, along with Lee Cobb, as Willy Loman, in *Salesman*) seemed wooden in the role of John Proctor, the chief

protagonist in *The Crucible*. The playwright was deeply distressed
by the reactions of critics and audiences to the play, whose subject
he considered of the gravest import. He determined to keep his
work before the public, to keep his message alive. He decided to
stage it himself, adding a single scene between Proctor and Abigail
(leader of the accusers) to heighten the passion and strengthen the
motivation. In his production he did away with the scenery, using
drapes as a backdrop to the action as well as an effectively lit cyclo-
rama, which gave more flexibility and fluency to his interpretation
of history. It pointed up the timelessness of the tragic situation in
the play, the implication that, regardless of the century in which
it occurs, "the sin of public terror is that it divests man of conscience, of himself."

The revised production, which had a long run in the Martin
Beck Theatre before going on a national tour, came much closer to
evoking the response Miller had anticipated. Audiences were
deeply stirred, and critics agreed that the new version had greater
dramatic and artistic value than before. If his drama did not reach
the heights of true tragedy, it elevated the emotional plane of plays
possessing "broad social awareness," to use the playwright's term.
(His reply to the critics about the lack of warmth in the work was
that in such plays emotion and private feeling should be restrained.
In the second production, however, the checkrein was not so much
in evidence, and as a result, the play was far more effective.)

Arthur Miller, whose name as playwright was rapidly becoming
associated with "moralist," continued to lash out against the betrayal of free speech being perpetrated on the country by the
McCarthy committee, and to delve more deeply into the psychology of the informer. In an interlude of repose, however, following
the strain of *The Crucible*, he recalled with a touch of nostalgia
the days of the depression, when, for all his hours at the warehouse,
he read and studied with a serene mind, uncomplicated by the
complexities of ethical considerations. As an expression of his feeling, he wrote *A Memory of Two Mondays*, a one-act play that
brought to life the scene in the warehouse as he remembered it.
Called (by John Gassner) "a sensitive and admirably uncontrived
genre-piece," it served as curtain raiser to a much longer one-act

play that pushed it into the background—his tense, impassioned drama of inquiry into the soul of the betrayer, *A View from the Bridge*.

Here he was probing for the real motives lurking beneath the surface reasons an informer might claim as justification for his treachery. Taking as his subject the illegal immigrants smuggled into the Brooklyn waterfront from Sicily by the Mafia through friends and relatives—familiarly called "submarines"—Miller presents the case of Eddie Carbone, who, in a passion of jealousy, informs on his wife's relatives. Two recently arrived submarines, they have been staying at the Carbone home, and the younger one has fallen in love with the niece of Eddie's wife, an orphan who has grown up in their house. Eddie, overly protective of the girl, is unconsciously in love with her. His dark, deep, unacknowledged feeling sends him into a jealous fury when she and the younger "submarine" wish to get married. Against the advice of a lawyer, who serves as Narrator or Greek chorus for the piece, and against his own inner voice, he turns the two refugees from an impoverished land over to the Immigration Office. He dies at the hands of Marco, the older man, who comes to claim vengeance paid in full. The meaning of the play seems rather muddled, as Alfieri, the lawyer-narrator, concludes, "Most of the time now we settle for half, and I like it better. But the truth is holy, and even as I know how wrong he was, and his death useless, I tremble. . . ." The impression is that Miller himself could not make up his mind in what measure the informer should be condemned. (And he was not alone in his bewilderment, his alarm at the number of people who apparently had little or no compunction in giving out names to the McCarthy committee.)

First presented on September 29, 1955, on a double program with *A Memory of Two Mondays*, the drama unfolded in *A View from the Bridge* proved so forceful and moving that it demanded single billing. A London production had been scheduled previously, and for this, the playwright expanded the script to two acts, reluctantly shelving the little memory-play that preceded it. The new version of *A View* benefited from the more detailed, realistic staging given it by Peter Brock in London (the opposite of *The Crucible's* stage history!) if it lost certain elements of poetry and classical allusion by the deletion of a verse prologue and epilogue spoken by Alfieri in the original play. British audiences were spellbound by the complex emotions laid bare in the tale of the outwardly simple, hard-working lives of longshoremen. The moral truths may have been overlooked in the pungency of the drama, but whatever the case, the play was tremendously popular in England, and has been presented in the second version in the United States since then (the first time in 1957; the latest, an off-Broadway production in 1965).

Because the theatricality of the play was so great, most audiences failed to grasp its serious meaning, but concentrated on the complexities of its sexual psychology. They did not even try to find its true import. The playwright was deeply disturbed by their attitude, which had been a source of concern ever since the advent of *The Crucible*.

To put it in his own words (given to an interviewer in 1964): "The production of *A View from the Bridge* clinched the growing feeling that the work I was doing was regarded as unimportant. I felt I was a kind of entertainer, succeeding in drawing a tear or a laugh, but it seemed to me that what was behind my plays remained a secret." He was "fed up" with the whole profession. And, so far as Arthur Miller offerings were concerned, the theater was "dark" for the next nine years.

It was not that the well-springs of his creative urge had run dry, but that the flood-tide of events which altered the course of his life, sweeping him into the vortex of public existence and attention, prevented him from seeing the world or himself clearly enough to write a play that he considered worthy of presentation. To begin with, his opposition to the tactics of the McCarthy committee placed him in the forefront of those being attacked, and under suspicion whether guilty or not. He saw its methods at work, incredulous: "Astounded, I watched men pass me by without a nod whom I had known rather well for years"; he recounted in the introduction to his *Collected Plays* in 1957: "and again, the astonishment was produced by my knowledge, which I could not give up, that the terror in these people was being knowingly planned and consciously engineered, and yet that they all knew it was terror."

He was called before the committee a number of times and, in 1956, was convicted of contempt of Congress for refusing (like Lillian Hellman and many other colleagues of his) to give the names of people he had recognized at a certain meeting years before. At the same time, a momentous change had been taking place in his private life, a mounting alteration of feeling between him and his wife that in the same year, 1956, brought about his divorce from Mary Slattery Miller. In the light of his deep-seated belief in the family as the "symbolic cell" of the social structure, the decision to part must have come to Arthur Miller with great conflict. But make it he did; and, once the divorce was granted, he plunged into a second marriage with the movie actress, Marilyn Monroe. Whether or not he had misgivings toward the wisdom of such a match, he must have been aware that his private life, which had been threatened by the McCarthy proceedings and his divorce, would now be almost entirely public, and that the precious seclusion, the solitude every writer needs, would be lost to him—unless Miss Monroe were to give up her career, and this she apparently had no intention of doing. Although he may not have fully realized it, their marriage was doomed to disaster from the start. In addition to the differences over publicity, background, and temperament, Miss Monroe suffered from serious emotional and psychological problems which neither the couple nor her doctors could solve, and which worsened rapidly after their marriage. He wrote a screen play, *The Misfits*, for her, a sensitive, penetrating film, which, on one level, shows the fate that Biff in *Salesman* might have encountered when he flees an industrial society to be a lone rancher out West. On another level, it deals with Miss Monroe's failure to adjust, and probably with their own incompatibility. The playwright admitted that it was "marred by too many cross purposes"; but despite its defects, the film was considered by many an artistic endeavor, of a much higher caliber than the majority of motion pictures. (A macabre note was struck by the fact that both Clark Gable, whose last picture it was, and Marilyn Monroe were dead within a year or so after *The Misfits* was released in late 1960.)

Through the first two years of his second marriage, Miller was completely involved in protesting his indictment in court. He not only pursued his case legally, but he wrote articles and made speeches in defense of the human rights under fire. At the height of his trial (proceedings), he spoke before a large audience at the first National Assembly of the Authors' League, in May, 1957, on the subject of censorship of the press. (Even as he sat in the second row with other speakers in the theater where the meeting was held, waiting his turn and making notes, a messenger came running down the aisle with a telegram, informing him of some development in his court case. He got up and left hurriedly, but came back virtually on cue to accept his introduction; and those who were present will long remember his gaunt face, his anxious eyes as he stood tall on the stage and in a quiet, determined voice admonished his fellow authors to hold firmly to the human right of free speech.) Arthur Miller was absolved of the charges against him by the United States Court of Appeals in 1958.

Soon afterward his domestic cares doubled; and, following a series of episodes paraded in the headlines, he and Marilyn Monroe were divorced. He went abroad for a while, and met Miss Ingeborg Morath, a photographer of Austrian birth, whom he married in 1962.

All during this period of stress, and in spite of being "fed up" with the theater, he had been trying to write plays. He completed five scripts, none of them to his satisfaction. He could not formulate his thinking to compose a play which would reveal its "secret" significance to the spectators. He decided that either the audience was out of step or he was; there seemed to be no resolution, and yet he was sure there must be. In the five unproduced plays, he had attempted to develop a viewpoint toward the world and himself. The plays were searching, but they came to no dramatic conclusion that gratified him. Then, in 1959, he first conceived the idea of writing a play that presented the search itself. The concept grew; he began giving it more body and contour, and by the time he was remarried, a new work was taking shape.

The play, which opened the much-heralded Repertory Theatre of Lincoln Center (housed in a temporary building provided by ANTA), was his emotionally personal *After the Fall*, which, again, was received by a storm of controversy—or, in his words, "a nimbus of myth and hysteria." It was distressing to find that audiences

were still overlooking the meaning of his drama for its theatricality
of subject matter. Certainly it was true that *After the Fall* was the
most introspective play he had ever written, and the first that dealt
with marital relations on so large a scale. But in so doing, Miller
was actually extending the thesis of his other plays. In addition to
stating once again his belief in the responsibility of the individual
to the whole of mankind, he is sitting in judgment against himself
as judge. When Quentin, the central figure, cries out, "I can't bear
to be a separate person!" he is reechoing the poet's belief, expressed
in his plays before, that "no man is an island." Yet ultimately he
recognizes that man must be a "separate person" (an individual in
his own right) and at the same time an inseparable cell in the civilization he has helped to build. That there were Nazi massacres,
McCarthy inquisitions, and suffering in an economic depression
(all of which come into the play as Quentin recalls his life) is to
the shame of all mankind. Quentin, a lawyer, is on the verge of
marrying for the third time. He is talking to a Listener, the audience, or, perhaps, the analyst—the impartial ear outside himself.
And as he speaks, calling up in his mind the different people who
have had the greatest effect on his life—his parents and siblings;
his first wife; his close friends and colleagues caught in the web of
McCarthyism with him; his second wife; his recent client—all
appear, disappear, and reappear in varied sequences before the
spectator. From the kaleidoscopic succession of scenes, the single
pattern of truth emerges: the element of universality in man may
yet be his salvation, the eternal well from which love springs and
hope rises after the fall into despair. Quentin, not absolved, but
accepting and understanding his "guilt," can now go forward to
greet his love.

As presented by the repertory company in the fall of 1963, the
play met only qualified critical approval. This may have been due
to the interpretation of Quentin as portrayed by Jason Robards,
Jr., whose superb rendition of O'Neill roles was no doubt responsible for his miscasting as Quentin. Those who called the work
"maudlin," full of self-pity and self-accusation, might have changed
their minds if they had seen Hal Holbrook, who later alternated
with Robards in the role. As Holbrook played it, Quentin was not

a weak man indulging in self-pity, but a highly intelligent human being engaging in self-analysis.

However, the public being what it is, the playwright observed that "there was more speculation as to whether the play was really about Marilyn Monroe than there was discussion about its intrinsic, artistic merits." He still claims that he saw no resemblance between Barbara Loden (who created the role of Maggie in the play) and Marilyn Monroe. "She doesn't look or act anything like her, really," he protested. "It honestly never occurred to me that anyone was trying for a literal resemblance or that the audience would see one, because I didn't see it." (If such is the case, it is unfortunate that the costume designer and make-up man both chose to pattern Miss Loden's appearance after Miss Monroe.) He pointed out that *After the Fall* was definitely not a literal play, no matter how personal its theme and conclusions were. He added that the production in Paris in 1965 came closer to the emotional truth that he intended than the original New York version.

While traveling in Europe, Miller had attended the trials of Nazi murderers in Frankfurt, and his immediate reaction was to write an impassioned article "re-instating in the public mind an understanding of the dynamics of Fascism." His thoughts then turned toward writing a play which would dramatize the subject, based on an episode that had been in his mind since 1950. Once more his theme was that of guilt and responsibility, which he approached with a viewpoint sharpened by the trials he had witnessed. Although the action takes place in a detention room in Vichy, 1942, recounting the brutal tactics of the Nazis and the sacrifice made by an Austrian prince who gives his papers to a Jewish doctor when he becomes aware of his own unconscious share in the Nazi invasion, the play is also "about today," according to its author. "It concerns the question of insight, of seeing in oneself the capacity for collaboration with the evil one condemns. It is a question that exists for all of us— What is the responsibility of each of us, for example, that the slums of Harlem exist?"

He called the play simply *Incident at Vichy* and declared that no matter what its reception was, it met his own artistic standards. "I'm satisfied that the play exists," he said. "It has a shape, a form, a truth." And although a good many probably missed his larger meaning, playgoers who saw the preview of the long one-acter, performed without intermission, in November of 1964, praised the performance with prolonged applause and cheers. Reviews were generally good, but "mixed" as to the artistic merits and the significance of Miller's latest work.

The playwright himself paid little heed to the pros and cons of the critics toward his canon. "Any body of work is a voyage with ports of call," he remarked. "Each of my plays has carried through some element of an earlier play." (In a facetious moment during a lecture in Poland in February, 1965, he answered a student's question, "What should a critic look like?" by replying, "Small and invisible, deaf and dumb.") He has continued to write more for himself than the playgoers or critics, although he realizes that the audience is an integral part of a play, a fact which makes the theater different from all other arts. Miller was enthusiastic about the Greek design of the ANTA theater "in the round," the curtainless stage, without apron or proscenium arch, but with great depth, so that moments of intimacy, and poetic austerity could both be achieved. He worked closely with the whole company, looking forward to the time when the Vivian Beaumont Theatre, the repertory's permanent theater in Lincoln Center, would be completed; but he was shocked and dismayed at the dismissal of Robert Whitehead, the producer who had conceived and catapulted the ANTA theater into being. He felt it was a disaster and, more than ever, resolved to write for himself first. If he could meet his own criteria for a successful play, he would not worry or fret about the reactions of the public or the journalistic judges. (During the last few years, he has had much wider production of his work abroad than in the United States, perhaps because people in other countries are more concerned with his themes of social consciousness and moral obligation than the majority of American playgoers appear to be.)

Since his marriage to Miss Morath, Arthur Miller has been able to lead the sort of life the playwright needs for the full fruition of his ideas. With his wife and their small daughter, Rebecca, he lives in Roxbury, Connecticut, where he spends most of his time writing in a semi-separate studio, sitting at a huge desk he constructed from an oversized door. (He also built a darkroom in the house for his wife, who accepts a few selected, and brief, assignments in photography.) When he had to be in New York for weeks of rehearsal before *Vichy*, the playwright brought his family with him, although the old-fashioned suite at the Chelsea Hotel—where he chooses to stay when in New York—was "hardly set up for light housekeeping."

Now just over fifty, Arthur Miller has the appearance of the literary ascetic: still lean and wiry, his pointed features sharper with age and a receding hairline; his eyes grave and intent, yet looking out from his dark-rimmed glasses with friendly interest. In conversational exchange, he is at ease, his remarks keen and considered, as if he swiftly weighed his words while uttering them. If he has the aspect of the monk in his face, in his tall lean figure and comfortable loose-fitting clothes, he also has the assurance of a man who has found his place in the world through a maze of agonizing turns. More than any other contemporary playwright, Arthur Miller has assumed the mantle of Robert Sherwood as the public conscience of America. In articles like "The Playwright and the Atomic Age," which he wrote for the *Tulane Drama Review* in 1961, he reveals an international viewpoint and a deep concern for the preservation of world peace. He is a popular playwright because he has the touch of common speech mingled with democratic idealism, poetic expression, and an ancient people's capacity for understanding the anguish of the soul.

CHAPTER XIII

———◆———

WILLIAM INGE

ROM Independence, Kansas, William (Motter) Inge, born two years before Arthur Miller—on May 3, 1913—came onto the Broadway scene two years after the New York dramatist, and by a much more roundabout route. An actor, teacher, and journalist, he became a playwright almost by accident. For years he planned on eventually making the "big-time" stage, and trod the boards in the Middle West with one eye on Broadway, but he never dreamed he would land there in the role of dramatist. His thespic career began when he was about seven years old.

He came by his talent naturally. His mother, the former Maude Sarah Gibson (whose given names of two famous actresses could hardly have been a coincidence), was a descendant of the illustrious family of "acting Booths." Her older brother, William's Uncle John Gibson, went on the stage at an early age, starting his professional career with a Shakespeare troupe, but it came to an end when he was called home to take care of the family harness business. ("My uncle became one of Wichita's leading citizens but remained at heart an unsatisfied actor," the playwright wrote.) William's father, Luther Clayton Inge, was a small-town merchant and traveling salesman, who had to put in long hours on the road to provide a living for his wife and five children, of whom the playwright was the last to be born.

As the youngest by several years, William grew up apart from the rest, but the center of attention, as the youngest usually is in a large family. It was not surprising, therefore, that at the age of seven he began reciting poems—monologues and dialect pieces, popular in the early twenties. He records that none of the other children showed any bent for acting or shared his interest in the theater, so his uncle was no doubt delighted to find someone in the family he could talk to, and his fond memories of his Shakespearean tour were a source of glamour and inspiration to young Bill Inge as he grew up. The boy soon built up a reputation as a talented reader, in demand for recitations at club meetings, church and school programs, and home talent shows. He gave up these appearances for the most part when he began to act in high school plays during his early teens. He graduated from high school in Independence in 1930, and entered the University of Kansas the next September. Still intent on an acting career, he majored in speech and drama, taking leading roles in University productions. He had the kind of countenance that could have made a "matinee idol": his deep-set eyes, classic nose and full, curving lips combined in rounded contour to form, according to Tennessee Williams' description, "the very handsome and outwardly serene face of William Inge." He was tall and well-proportioned, and moved with the easy gait of an actor.

Like Williams and Miller, he was delayed in getting his college degree because of the depression. He lost a year when he stayed out in 1933–1934, but unlike his colleagues, he was lucky enough to find a job in his profession. He went on tour with a tent show, or what was called a "Toby show," in which he was cast as juvenile. The experience was hardly considered an avenue to the Broadway stage, but it taught him a great deal about small-time show business, show people, and the harsh realities of life. The knowledge made a lasting impression on him, and, although he could have used it to better advantage, served him as source material twenty-five years later.

When the Toby show broke up, in June of 1934, he joined a summer stock company, the Maxinkuchee Mummers, at Culver

Military Academy, Indiana. As a popular juvenile lead, he made friends with the faculty and students, among them the head of the speech and drama department, Major C. C. Mather. With the Major's encouragement, he saved enough money to go back to the University of Kansas, taking his A.B. in speech and drama the following June (1935). He returned to Culver that summer to teach, replacing the Major, who was on leave. He planned to save enough this time to make the long-awaited journey to New York and finance his acting career. But somehow his salary slipped through his fingers every week, and he did not even save the cost of his fare to get there.

At this point he was offered a fellowship at Peabody Teachers College in Nashville, Tennessee. Being more or less at loose ends, he accepted, and went to begin work on a Master's degree in English. During the year it dawned on him that if he wanted to become a Broadway star, he should have had the self-discipline to see to it that he got to New York and started trying out. He despaired of ever becoming an actor, now doubting his talent. He tried to accept teaching as his profession instead, but by the end of the year he "developed a sickness of mood and temper" which compelled him to leave for home two weeks before he was to get his degree. After that he "floundered" for a year or so: he spent the summer on road construction with a highway gang, and then went to Wichita, where he worked in a radio station as script writer and announcer. But he soon had his fill, and in the fall of 1937, took a job in a high school in Columbus, Kansas, teaching English, speech and dramatics once more. The following summer he returned to Nashville, finished his Master's, and began teaching at Stephens College for Women at Columbia, Missouri, in the fall of 1938. Here his odyssey ended for a time, for he found friends and a renewed interest in the theater which held him for the next five years.

Two of his friends were Albert Christ-Janer and his wife Virginia, who were just starting to teach at Stephens at the same time as Inge, and the three beginners made their way together, forming a bond that lasted over the years. (In 1958, Christ-Janer, who wound up as Director of Fine Arts at Pennsylvania State University, invited the playwright to participate in the drama festival, that summer featuring the work of prominent contemporary dramatists. For the occasion, "Bill" dug up four early one-acters and arrived a week ahead to be present at rehearsals and visit his friends.) At Stephens, the three beginners discussed their problems and dreams, their ideas for the theater. All of them benefited from the proximity of the celebrated actress, Maude Adams, who retired from the stage to head the drama department at the college. Inge, who spent his last three years at Stephens working with her in the drama, found it deeply rewarding, and felt the lure of the theater drawing him once again. He kept a journal, in which he recorded his reactions and ideas; he wrote short stories (none of which were published) and poetry, but only for his own pleasure and the release of inner tensions. He never considered himself a "writer." And somehow, although his greatest interest was the theater, he never thought about writing plays.

However, he grew restless with teaching, and left Stephens in 1943, when he was given the opportunity to become drama, music and movie critic for the St. Louis *Star-Times,* replacing a friend who went overseas. The idea of a newspaper job appealed to him; he felt sure he could do it, so he took it, and found the work stimulating and enjoyable. He praised the plays or films that had merit, but for the most part he found little to laud in the "attractions" that came to St. Louis. At times he panned the plays mercilessly for being on such a low or superficial level, for showing poor craftsmanship or being too obviously contrived. He became more sure of himself, writing his daily column, developing confidence as he went along. Seeing all the latest plays—some good, but most of them bad or indifferent—he could not help wondering if he couldn't write better ones. He began to try casually, but he still needed a final motivation to go at it in earnest.

His incentive came unexpectedly with the arrival of Tennessee Williams, who fled to his parents' home in St. Louis "as a refugee from the sudden shock of fame" he had experienced in Chicago a few weeks after *The Glass Menagerie* "broke the ice," in December, 1944. With some trepidation, Bill Inge called the Williams' home and spoke to the playwright, asking for an interview for a "sort of 'Home Town Boy Makes Good' article" and suggesting that for a little social diversion, Williams come to his apartment.

"He was living in a housing project, way downtown in a raffish part of the city," Williams wrote later in the Preface to the published version of Inge's fourth play. "But when he opened the door, I saw over his shoulder a reproduction of my favorite Picasso, and knew that the interview would be as painless as it turned out to be." A few weeks after Williams returned to Chicago, the *Star-Times* critic went up to witness a performance of *The Glass Menagerie,* which he found "so beautiful and so deeply moving," as he said, that he "felt a little ashamed for having led an unproductive life." He went backstage to offer his congratulations, and was invited to Williams' hotel in the Loop. On the way there, Bill Inge, to his own surprise, suddenly confided that "being a successful playwright was what he most wanted in the world for himself." At first, Williams thought he was merely being polite, but before Bill Inge left, he had the other's promise to read and advise him on a script he had in mind.

He returned to St. Louis and, while still working on the paper, wrote his first play, *Farther Off from Heaven.* Williams helped him to get it produced by Margo Jones in Dallas (1947) and, as the production came off well, urged him to keep on trying. Bill did. He wrote two more plays in rapid succession, through a change in jobs and other minor upheavals. He hated to give up the newspaper post, but his friend returned from overseas, so he had no choice. He took another teaching job in the English department of Washington University in St. Louis, and spent every spare moment in playwriting. The fourth script he sent to Tennessee Williams made such an impression that Audrey Wood (now agent for Inge also) got busy at once, submitting it to the Theatre Guild, which voted to take an option on it for summer production. The play was *Come Back, Little Sheba,* Bill Inge's first big success as a playwright. He gave up teaching that summer (1949) and came to New York to be on hand for rehearsals of the production, which opened in Westport.

The play, expertly performed by the Guild cast, particularly Shirley Booth and Sidney Blackmer in leading roles, portrayed, like most of his plays, the pathetic lives of lower middle-class people in a small Midwestern town. In the drama of the unhappy marriage of "Doc" and Lola, Inge revealed the unheroic or near-tragedy of neglected souls, those on whom fortune never seems to smile, but whose sad fate is far from noble. Yet, so realistic was the picture he drew of the disillusioned pair—he—the husband—a chiropractor who gave up medical school to marry his girl when she became pregnant, a man so put down by the loss of his dream to be a great doctor that he turns to alcohol for solace; and she—the wife—a once-pretty girl who loved a good time, so heartbroken when she loses the baby and learns she can never have another that she loses her zest for life, becomes a listless slattern who turns to her little dog, Sheba, for solace—so true to life was their suffering that the audience was caught up in their lives, mingling also with the minor characters who figure in the plot. The dialogue was natural, the motivation valid, the feelings genuine, and playgoers embraced William Inge as the third gifted playwright of the postwar period, along with Tennessee Williams and Arthur Miller. He was not as powerful as either of them, but he possessed (in John Gassner's opinion) "a sensitivity to the vibrancies of little lives in the commonplace corners of the world," a kindness and compassion for his characters which gave rise to a homely wisdom and understanding that endeared him to his audiences. *Come Back, Little Sheba,* which some critics still consider Inge's best play, opened February 15, 1950, the beginning of a long run. It received the rather unusual George Jean Nathan and Theatre Time awards, and won for its author the reputation of being a careful craftsman, a perceptive and thoughtful playwright.

During his period of "floundering," he had undergone psychotherapy for a time, and in writing *Little Sheba* he made certain that his premise was correct by having several psychiatrists read and approve the script before it reached Broadway. Now, in the summer following his success, he began to work on his second play, *Picnic,* in the same painstaking way, expanding a one-acter that was part of his experimenting before he was ready for Broadway. The idea for the piece grew out of the tableau presented by a group of women sitting on a side porch gossiping one summer morning when he was out for a stroll in a town the tent show was playing, and happened to walk by the house. Like *Sheba,* the theme of *Picnic* derives from the humdrum lives of small-town people, where little occurs to change the monotonous rhythm except the seasons. In this case, however, he shows the effect of a vagabond soul, in the form of a handsome young drifter who ambles into the village, upon the drab existence of a small segment of its inhabitants. The impact of his presence on a "klatsch" of females living in adjacent houses is immediate and ominous, and accelerates in the course of the action, which takes place during a Labor Day picnic. As might be expected, he seduces the beautiful daughter of the widow who lives in one of the houses, thereby upsetting the apple cart of hope that she will marry the scion of the town's wealthy family. (In the Broadway version, the girl follows him when he moves on at the end, but in the original, he leaves her heartbroken, and she settles back with the others into the repetitious tempo of small-town life.) The repression in the women of *Picnic* is like that in Tennessee Williams' *Summer and Smoke*, but in a minor key. The emotional excitement, however, at one point rises to a higher pitch than at any time in Williams' play because of the understatement; by contrast, the climax is unexpected, more explosive and effective.

Picnic opened almost exactly three years after *Sheba*, on February 19, 1953; and, like Williams' and Miller's second plays, received the signal honors for the year—the Pulitzer prize, the Drama Critics Circle Award, and the Outer Circle Award. It has been called (by Gassner) a "pathetic pastoral," but it also possessed the richness, the earthiness of an al fresco bacchanale, in terms of American folkways in the Middle West. In a slightly more comedic mood, Inge followed *Picnic* with *Bus Stop*, a different slice of Americana from the plains. Constructed in the pattern of *Petrified Forest* (but without the melodrama or social significance in depth), *Bus Stop*, as the title indicates, takes place in a shabby roadside cafe, one of the "rest" stops for passengers on cross-country buses, and brings together an assortment of characters, among them a wistful wraith of a nightclub singer, Cherie, fleeing her last "spot"; also a big, handsome, rough-spoken but kindhearted cowboy, "Bo," short for Beauregard; and several others in various circumstances. For the most part in a light key, *Bus Stop* has serious overtones and moments of sadness, and in its way is a commentary on the haphazard lives of those who try to live by their talents, beauty, or wits, without a penny in the world, homeless, rootless. (When Cherie says gropingly, "Ya gotta have a direction . . ." she expresses the longing for some kind of order, or goal, besides the daily struggle for existence.) The play, which, like the others, made its appearance in February, after only a two-year interval (in 1955), was greeted with great enthusiasm, and proved to be a matching success to the playwright's previous offerings.

His fourth, *The Dark at the Top of the Stairs,* was a revision of the first script he had shown Tennessee Williams (then called *Farther Off from Heaven*). Produced in 1957, the play broke theatrical precedent by being the fourth consecutive hit and only the fourth produced play of any writer for the Broadway theater. Since the dominant theme is the adjustment of adolescents to the problems of adulthood, and since the play was written under the immediate influence of *The Glass Menagerie* and was Inge's first serious effort, it seems likely that *The Dark at the Top of the Stairs* is also "a memory play." Certainly the salient details are autobiographical: the time and setting, the early 1920s in a small Midwestern town, must have been similar to Inge's surroundings when he was ten years old, the age of Sonny Flood, the boy in the play. Sonny gives recitations, in the second act delivering Hamlet's first soliloquy, and it is his uncle who compliments him afterward by saying, "That was a fine recitation, Edwin Booth." Sonny's sister Reenie is a teenager, four or five years older than he, and his father is a traveling salesman in the harness business. While the action concerns the marital relations of the adults in large measure, its primary purpose, one feels, is to show the overattachment between the boy and his mother. The resolution of the problem (involving an extraneous teen-aged character who befriends both children and later commits suicide, as well as the renewed marital relations of the parents after an estrangement) is not quite satisfactory; but the play as a whole had wide appeal, and was one of the outstanding hits of the season.

Whether the mother-son relationship was autobiographical or not, William Inge was sufficiently interested in the subject to develop it in his next play, *A Loss of Roses,* unfortunately to the detriment of the drama he might have created. The story, set in a small town outside "Kanz City" in 1933, deals with Kenny Baird, twenty-one (Inge's age that year); his mother Helen, a widow who works as a nurse in the local hospital; and Lila Greene, an unemployed actress, a refugee from a tent show that has had to close because of the depression, who, many years before, took care of Kenny when he was a small boy. An antagonism between mother and son, born of unconscious overattachment, is somehow resolved when Kenny has an affair with Lila, ten or twelve years older than he. With the realization that marriage with Lila would not work, comes the intuitive knowledge that the emotional interdependency between his mother and him is destructive, and that he must leave. *A Loss of Roses,* which opened November 28, 1959, was a total loss —artistically and financially—and its failure was a deep disappointment to the playwright. In the Foreword to the published version, he tries to account for the fiasco, and states that he feels his most serious mistake was to permit the New York production to end with the parting scene between mother and son, instead of concluding with Lila's departure, as he originally conceived it. He adds, "for it is really Lila's play," and there he may have revealed the true mistake of the work. Even with the original ending restored, as it is in the published version, one has the impression that it is just as much, if not more, Kenny's play. One cannot help wondering why William Inge could not have written a truly dramatic play based on Lila's background and experiences with the tent show. He gives tantalizing glimpses of that particular field of show business (which he knows first-hand) and introduces a number of interesting characters, only to whisk them offstage. A good play still has to be written about tent-show life, or about a resident stock company in a middle-sized Midwestern town; and Inge seems admirably suited to the task. However, he seems preoccupied with the mother-son constellation, which entered into his next offering, *Natural Affection,* a second failure (in 1963), concerned with a hodge-podge of sex—depravity, violence, and most *un*natural affections.

Inge's latest vehicle, which he calls a "meaningful comedy," entitled *Family Things, Etc.,* is about young theater people in New York, and after a tryout in Westport in 1965 summer stock, was being revised at this writing.* But whatever the future brings, William Inge remains a master of the genre-piece, depicting, with honest affection, the little lives of small-town folk.

* The revision, entitled *Where's Daddy,* opened on Broadway February 28, 1966, to mixed reviews, with high praise for Betty Field and Hiram Sherman in the featured roles.

CHAPTER XIV

EDWARD ALBEE

AND

THE CURRENT SCENE

Iᶠ WILLIAM INGE seems to have an obsessive interest in the adoration between mother and son, Edward Albee, by contrast seems constantly haunted by hostility toward "Mommy," thereby exhuming a deep-set anger toward women in general and one in his own life in particular. To discover ample justification for his attitude, one has only to turn to his beginnings. The story of Edward Albee's early life might almost be called—to employ the cliché form he is so fond of using—"The Poor Little Rich Boy."

Born in Washington, D.C., on March 12, 1928, he was adopted, at the age of two weeks, by Reed Albee, owner of the famous chain of Keith-Albee vaudeville theaters, and his second wife, Frances, twenty-three years his junior. Presumably it was Frances' idea to adopt a child, for she apparently had rigid notions about child-rearing, which she unceasingly if always unsuccessfully tried to carry out with Edward. As a baby, he learned to walk in the nursery of a luxurious Tudor house in Larchmont, New York, cared for by nurses and maids. He grew up in a world of servants, tutors, riding lessons (which he loathed), winter sojourns in Palm Beach, and summer sailings on the Sound. He had a profusion of toys surrounding him, and no one to share them with (or to fight over them with). He had a variety of pets, from a huge St. Bernard, who pulled his sled in the winter, to cats and a penful of guinea pigs. His clothes amounted to an extensive wardrobe, hung in a closet as large as a room. When he was slightly older, a Rolls-Royce with a liveried chauffeur used to bring him into the city for matinees. (The Albee empire evidently did not fall or even tend to topple during the depression or the decline of vaudeville.) If loneliness had been Edward's only cause for suffering, his childhood might have been bleak, but not acutely unhappy.

However, within his adoptive family circle, the fates had conspired to bring together a monumental mismating of temperaments. Reed Albee, a small, silent man, eager to please his second wife, had fallen into a habit of continual agreement with anything she said or did in order to avoid argument or harangue. He was so taciturn that he used to announce his presence by jingling coins in his pocket when he came into a room (a symbolic touch worthy of an Edward Albee play). Frances Albee, who stood a foot taller than her husband, was extremely vocal, on the contrary, always ready to express her opinions in ringing tones of approbation or denunciation, as the case might be. Where Edward was concerned, it was usually the latter. A large, good-looking woman, Frances was fond of horseback riding, and tried to force Edward to become an expert. She would stride around in her riding clothes and derby, carrying a riding crop. Edward did not care for riding— or riding crops. Indeed, he had no enthusiasm for any sort of athletics. He was introspective, fond of reading, inclined to fat, indifferent to sports that might harden up his muscles.

From the beginning, he found himself besieged with demands to become something he was not, and it required both skill and cunning on his part not to be overcome. By the time he was eleven, the Albees shipped him off to Lawrenceville in the hope that boarding school would "knock him into line." But here he cut classes, ignored assignments or any reading related to formal study (though he would sit up all night writing weird stories or lurid poetry, a practice he had started in Larchmont a year earlier); he ducked out of obligatory sports and deliberately behaved so badly that he was "bounced" in a year and a half. His tactics only worsened his fate, for his foster mother decided that military school would make him learn to toe the mark. The mere thought of the nightmare period which followed was enough to make him see red years later, but he managed to live through it and went on to Choate. Here, like O'Neill at Betts Academy, young Albee was happy for the first time with the kind of education offered him, the flexibility of outlook. Though his teachers were not impressed with his creative ability, he wrote continuously, sometimes up to eighteen hours a day. He finished a 538-page novel, dabbled in poetry, and turned out short stories by the dozen. None of these were published, and most of them were bitter discourses born of disillusion and anger. They recalled Thomas Kyd—"chronicles of violence and sudden death, or adolescent philippics against the monstrous regiment of women."

He graduated from Choate, after which he attended Trinity College in Hartford for about a year and a half. With his adolescent years, Edward lost the tendency to fat, and stretched up, becoming pencil-slim. His face, with neat, straight features, was immobile, and his eyes, curtained by a fringe of thick lashes, added to the masklike expression he usually wore, a mixture of detached amusement and disdain for the world in general. While at Hartford, he cultivated a mocking mustache and an "Orson Welles manner" to heighten the effect. He rarely laughed aloud, but smiled mysteriously. His wit, which was quick and sharp, early showed signs of the sardonic and cynical.

Perhaps because he felt fortified by the hard sheath of misanthropy, he spent another year at home in Larchmont, trying to lead the life of the liberal literati in the midst of the country-club set, writing continuity for a New York radio station, and running around with a group of artists and young intellectuals whom Mrs. Albee could not understand or abide. The struggle between them went on, as it always had when he was home from school on holiday. The battle raged without a letup, from "minor skirmishes" over his taking a volume of Turgenev from the library shelves, thereby marring the effect of the décor, to "major engagements" over his selection of friends, his peculiar aim to be a writer, his behavior in general. In an effort to conform, he got engaged to a sub-deb named Delphine, but they were soon disengaged, which did not improve the atmosphere in the Albee mansion. The mounting tension and misunderstanding finally became insupportable. One morning in 1948, after a bitter argument over a petty misdemeanor, Edward packed his books and records and left home for good.

So began the era the playwright calls his "pudding years." ("One year was so much the same as another, I remember the whole decade in a haze," he said.) They started hopefully enough in an apartment on lower Fifth Avenue, which he shared with a boyhood friend. He was still getting $250 a month from a legacy left by his paternal grandmother, so he could concentrate on writing plays, poems and stories to his heart's content. (He continued in the "Spanish tragedy" tradition of macabre tales in which a slain body lies decomposing in one room while a light conversation chatters on in the next.) But after a year or so, the legacy ran out, and he was forced to look for a job and another apartment.

At about this time, he met William Flanagan, the composer and musicologist, with whom he roomed for the next nine years, and who brought him into contact with the near-famous and a few famous figures in the music and literary worlds. Through Flanagan, Albee spent a summer at the MacDowell Colony, where Thornton Wilder gave his poetry some encouragement. (Whether the future playwright had the temerity to show any of his scripts at that time is doubtful.) W. H. Auden suggested his writing pornographic verse as an antidote to his high-flown style. It was discouraging, to say the least. Moreover, since he had to earn a living, he was variously a record salesman, a waiter, and a Western Union messenger, all of which prevented him from doing as much writing as he had done before. As months went by and nothing moved in the direction he sought, he began to feel the burden of "unused days." He and Bill Flanagan lived in a succession of cold-water flats smelling of dampness (and reeking of cat food because of Albee's fondness for picking up stray kittens), so that he never had much inclination to write at night. Instead, the sordid chronicle of his "Village decade" includes pointless nightly prowls through the crooked streets and alleys with the growing army of banjo-playing poets; muted literary discussions in coffeehouses on Macdougal Street, and more blatant, all-night bull sessions in somebody's dirty rooms. There were innumerable nameless relationships, some rewarding, but most of them dismal. When he first came from Larchmont, just after his twentieth birthday, the nocturnal shenanigans were a novelty, but after a while they became tedious. Toward dawn, Albee would start a bizarre game, the asssassination of his friends: one must go because he was a private nuisance, another because he was a public bore, a third out of friendly feeling, to spare him a hot, lonely summer in New York—a pastime suggestive of the devastating "fun and games" in the opening section of his first full-length play.

By 1957, his existence took on the quality of a nightmare. He wandered aimlessly, wrote little, and drank a lot. Recalling this period, he said, "I felt like a glass dome had dropped over me. Everything was terribly black." There came a night when he did not even want to go out.

He sat hunched over his typewriter at the kitchen table and started writing a play about a desperately lonely boy who meets a man on a park bench. In a struggle over which one shall have the bench, he at first cajoles and then terrifies the man into giving him the point of contact that he needs on the blade of a gleaming knife. The boy shouts: "A person has to have a way of dealing with someEthing. If not people, Something!" The script became *The Zoo Story*, Albee's initial bid for recognition as an avant-garde playwright. He must have known that he had spoken out at last, telling the truth in a sweeping indictment of the world as he had found it —a world that made conformity a virtue and nonconformity a vice, a disease. He showed the script to Flanagan, who was sufficiently impressed to send it to a friend who had connections with a theater in Germany, mailing it after rejection by New York producers, who were interested, but considered the one-acter too explosive, too experimental. In Berlin, producers were not only impressed, but loudly enthusiastic, and a presentation was arranged for 1959.

Heartened, Edward made a fresh start on his career as a writer, concentrating now on plays. In March, 1958, when he passed his thirtieth birthday, he came into a comfortable inheritance, so he did not have to sustain himself financially any longer and could devote himself full time to becoming a professional playwright. He had no more need of nightly prowls, and started going to bed at a reasonable hour so he could begin working early in the morning, a habit he has maintained. (He is usually up at about six-thirty, goes at a rapid pace for three or four hours, and then must stop. After that he often takes a long walk to think out what is to follow, or the revision that must be made in the scene he has written. In writing a play, he spends no more than three or four months at the typewriter. The rest is "walking-around time," when the characters take shape and grow.)

He began thinking about a new play based on an idea that had come to him from reading the liner notes on the sleeve of a record album of blues songs sung by Bessie Smith, famous colored singer of the thirties. The notes contained a brief account of the auto accident she had been in and her horrifying death in 1937 from bleeding outside a "white" hospital which would not admit her. In those stark facts Albee found the basic line of a powerful theme—the destructive force of blind prejudice—which expanded as he went along.

In the writing, the story "turned into an autopsy of other deaths —the death of idealism, ambition and hope among the people in the white hospital," who squabble over personal matters while the singer bleeds to death outside. Here, in the character of the nurse, the young playwright's deep-seated hostility toward women burst into full fire. She is the most bigoted, and, although unmarried, as one critic said, "the meanest of the Mommies," whose "neurotic and anti-intellectual political attitudes add a sinister dimension to the composite Mommy portrait." She seems to epitomize the bitch in woman, the most horrid of his harridans, yet she is acutely unhappy, and capable of hysteria: "I am *sick*," she cries. "I am sick of everything in this hot, stupid, fly-ridden *world*. . . . I am sick of going to bed and I am sick of waking up. . . . I am tired of the truth and I am tired of lying about the truth. . . . I am tired of my skin. . . . I WANT OUT!" But she is trapped, as all are who allow themselves to be ruled by prejudice, the play implies.

The dialogue throughout is stinging, acrimonious; the action is rapid-fire, a series of short, staccato scenes, shifting between the nurse's home life (where her father, an arch segregationist, provides motivation for her behavior) and the hospital. The whole piece is dominated by the dying of Bessie Smith, offstage, whose slow fatal bleeding is reported intermittently by her companion, Jack. He rushes in time and again, pleading frantically for her admittance, only to be refused or sent someplace else, where he is also refused. Her death in the end suggests the sublimated spirit that finally brought about the civil rights movement twenty years later. Bessie's death will haunt them all—the nurse; the Negro orderly; and the intern, a doctor with liberal leanings, in love with the nurse, who tries unsuccessfully to convince her to break the white supremacy rule for once. (A sparring love-duet between them runs through the play like counterpoint to the central theme.)

Entitled realistically *The Death of Bessie Smith*, Albee's second long one-act play was first presented in Berlin also, following the 1959 production of *The Zoo Story*, which was a tremendous success with German audiences. It was acclaimed and presented in other European cities as well, and the attention that Albee received as the newest and most promising of avant-garde playwrights caused a quick about-face among American producers. Richard Barr and Clinton Wilder set him up in a series of off-Broadway productions, starting with *The Zoo Story*, which, significantly, opened at the Provincetown Playhouse in January, 1960, trumpeting in the new decade. It was featured intentionally with Samuel Beckett's *Krapp's Last Tape*, emphasizing the similarity between the two playwrights—a double bill that was revived at the Cherry Lane Theatre in 1965, when the differences between the two became more apparent. (Both are prophets of doom caused by despair over the rise of physical instead of spiritual culture, and both employ variants of the same technique; but Albee is less abstract than Beckett: his characters, though they may represent ideas or segments of civilization, are nevertheless real people.) *The Zoo Story*, while received with reservations by some critics, established the young playwright in his native land. Experimental theaters across the country sought to present his one-acts, and aspiring neophytes of the theater of the abstract and the absurd took new hope.

Albee, meanwhile, had been industriously adding to his impressive beginning. He was commissioned to write a play for the Festival of Two Worlds at Spoleto, for which he fashioned *The Sandbox*, which in turn was the forerunner of his far more notable *The American Dream*. The former, no more than a skeletal sketch, contains the same characters as the latter—"Mommy," "Daddy," their son (in the first play, "the young man" or "athlete"; in the second, the "Cipher"), and "Grandma," representing the past generation. In the first piece, Grandma is summarily relegated to the sandbox, to live out her second childhood—a device akin to Beckett's in consigning the parents in *Endgame* to the ashcan. For some reason, *The Sandbox* was never performed in Spoleto, but was produced later by Henry Lutz at the Jazz Gallery in New York with other short pieces; it was also on television, with Sudie Bond in a superb rendition of "Grandma." Performed as it was after *The American Dream,* critics tended to regard it as a lesser repetition of the longer play, a parody of a parody, and hence dull.

The fact is, however, that *The American Dream* grew out of *The Sandbox,* and is a further budding of the same idea. The playwright wrote that it is "an attack on the substitution of artificial for real values in our society, a condemnation of complacency, cruelty, emasculation, and vacuity; it is a stand against the fiction that everything in this slipping land of ours is peachy-keen." In taking his stand, Albee has not only torn down the false framework, but has sketched a zany, imaginative caricature of the traditional American family portrait. And the resemblance to his own family picture is unmistakable: "Mommy," a large, handsomely turned-out woman, dominates the scene and towers over her husband much as Mrs. Albee must have. "Daddy," a drained little man, is acquiescent but ineffectual, sterile. Their "son," a big, cheerful, athletic Cipher is actually the identical twin of an *adopted* son whom Mommy had ordered years before but had dismembered after a few months because he was "too wild" and would not conform. "Grandma," the least cartoonlike of the characters, who faces facts and is always preparing for the "moving van" to come and take her away, may have been drawn after Albee's paternal grandmother. (Her "pioneer-stock" values are discounted, her pleas to be put to use ignored.) The boy has one defect: he cannot love; when Mommy cut off the vital organs of his twin, the sterility was naturally transferred to him. "Mommy" is a wildly exaggerated study of the emancipation of women, as is "Mrs. Barker," the afternoon caller, who represents the "professional woman." But in Mommy's mean-tempered, immoderate, insincere and carnivorous attitude, the playwright seems to be recklessly discharging all the resentment of his early years. The play is satire with a vengeance, particularly in the character of Mommy, which prompted one critic to ask whether Albee's representation of her really suggested some important truth or was "the distorted revenge of an injured man." Undoubtedly there is a personal element in his delineation, but it is also true that in the harsh light of ridicule he has illuminated the artificiality of our civilization as no playwright has since Elmer Rice in *The Adding Machine*. (Albee carries the effect of mechanization one step further, resulting in sterilization of the emotions. As the Cipher says, "I cannot touch another person and feel love. . . . I have no emotions. . . . I can feel nothing.")

The American Dream opened Off-Broadway with a one-act opera, *Bartleby*, with libretto by Albee, based on a short story by Melville, which his friend Bill Flanagan had composed at about the same time Edward was "composing" his play. (He has said, "Plays are constructed rather the way music is," and his long association with the composer undoubtedly had its effect in his brilliant use of duet and contrapuntal dialogue, particularly in the work that followed. At present, Flanagan is composing a longer opera, *The Ice Age*, for which Albee is to do the libretto.) When *Bartleby* failed to win approval, *The Death of Bessie Smith* replaced it, to provide the first full evening of Albee's plays.

Although reaction to *The American Dream* was in the main favorable but mixed, the double bill proved extremely popular, enlarged the circle of Albee fans, and provoked a good deal of discussion regarding the merit and the meaning of his sensational one-acters.

He had already begun writing his first full-length play (in 1960) by way of reply to those who questioned his talent. Here the idea the playwright had nurtured through his four pieces came into full flower. Here the negative aspects of a mechanized, science-ridden world—loss of individuality as a result of uniformity, and emotional, sexual sterility as a result of conformity—are viewed under his microscope with brilliant yet blinding and terrifying clarity. (His lens does not penetrate too deeply, but brings out surface detail that is startlingly, shockingly clear.) Moreover, the playwright was canny enough to choose educated people, even quasi-intellectuals as his characters, with the result that their dialogue seems logical, rational (or mad only in the playful sense), and their condition highly believable.

He gives the audience Martha and George (suggestively the last remnant of the ideal couple from Revolutionary days), respectively, the daughter of a college president, and her husband, a history professor in the college. Martha is a few years older than George, and, like other Albee Mommys, somewhat larger physically; both are attractive, bright, evenly matched in devastating wit, though Martha is the more vulgar and earthy, George the more intellectual and inventive of the two. Approaching middle age, they have no children except the one of illusion. Their lives and broken dreams are unfolded during the pre-dawn hours of a drunken orgy enacted with a younger couple, new to the faculty: "Honey," the simpering novice-Faculty Dame, full of her own neurosis, fear of child-bearing; and her husband Nick, the biology professor, working toward the goal of altering the human genes "to order," to produce a perfect scientific baby of the future (the "American dream"). The examination of these prototypes (but very real people) of the modern academic world takes place in "The living room of a house on the campus of a small New England college." No details are described in the published version of the play, perhaps to imply that the over-all effect of the set should be that of the New York production: a room of good taste, combining traditional with modern décor, early American furniture in juxtaposition to a hi-fi record player and portable bar. Well-filled bookshelves and a fireplace set off by an abstract painting over the mantel—in other words, the home of upper-middle-class, up-to-date intellectuals. Martha's opening line (after her blasphemous entrance), "What a dump!" is in startling contrast to an apparently charming and gracious environment.

Her words sound the note of decay that Albee intends to show in the honored institutions of the family and the halls of learning, and sets in motion the round of scintillating repartee and violent invective that continues between Martha and George for three acts and ends only in mental homicide. Honey and Nick, although far from their equals, are drawn, bewildered, into the "fun and games," the ghastly gallows humor of the older couple. In countless variations, the theme of the play is expanded and expounded, with mounting cadence rising to a deafening drumbeat from Martha, the "earth-Mother," and inspired inventions on the part of George. In retaliation to George's barbs, Martha gleefully relates the suffocating of his only brain child—a novel—by her father; and at the outset of the evening's hostilities she had broken the prime rule of their marriage by mentioning their combined brain child: the fantasy of their union, a son they invented twenty-one years before—to be exact, it is the eve of his "twenty-first birthday." They have kept their marriage alive by the secret bond of keeping alive the child of their imaginations, the son they were incapable of producing physically; but once Martha has betrayed their solemn oath of secrecy, has made "public" the most private sector of their lives, she has forfeited the right to continue the fiction. George's revenge is complete: he murders their son by inventing a telegram announcing his death in an auto accident; but first he prods Martha into speaking at length about the child (as long as she has mentioned him in the first place), and in a stunning duet he recites the Requiem mass as she recounts the "past." When it is over, he breaks the news of the death telegram to her, which at first brings forth her rigid fury and then her collapse, as with a pathetic cry of terrible loss she moans, "You have no right . . . no right at all." When he tells her (tenderly now, seeing her sorrow) that, although they never spoke of it, he could kill the boy any time he wanted to, she asks brokenly, "But why? Why?" And he reminds her, "You broke our rule, baby. . . . You mentioned him . . . to someone else." As the others go, George, with quiet acceptance, tries to show his wife that it is better—"maybe"—for the family to be "just us." They are both bereft, but one has the feeling that George has found a certain confidence in the fact that truth is better than illusion as a means of coping with life's problems.

Albee divided his drama conventionally into three acts, but unconventionally gave them titles, like the sections of a novel: "Fun and Games," the first act, is followed by "Walpurgisnacht," and finally "The Exorcism." He had intended to use the last as the title of the play, but instead chose the principal "fun" device—a pun on names, to the tune of "Who's Afraid of the Big, Bad Wolf?", which serves as the leitmotif of the action throughout *Who's Afraid of Virginia Woolf?* Devotees of the British writer have devoutly wished that Albee had kept his original title. The derisive connotation inherent in *Who's Afraid of Virginia Woolf?* is painful to those who have found in the author of *The Waves, To the Lighthouse, Mrs. Dalloway* and the other incomparable novels, a true artist who has made a lasting contribution to English literature. However, it cannot be denied that *Who's Afraid . . .* was a much more intriguing title than *The Exorcism,* and undoubtedly drew many more playgoers to the box office than the original. And in the final scene, it is used with sympathetic effect, as George sings the refrain softly, and Martha confesses that *she* is afraid. He nods slowly as the curtain falls. (One critic has suggested that there may be a reference to Miss Woolf's famous essay, "The Separate Room," which in turn relates to Martha's fear, but that seems to be stretching the point too far.)

The play was first produced on Broadway by Richard Barr and Clinton Wilder, in a presentation directed by Alan Schneider, which opened at the Billy Rose Theatre, on October 13, 1962, with Uta Hagen in the role of Martha. It received dynamic reviews, rife with phrases like "shattering drama"; "brilliantly original work of art"; "excoriating theatrical experience"; "articulately and terrifyingly among the quick," and "a crucial event in the birth of a contemporary American theater." The drama deservedly received every award of the season except the Pulitzer, which was withheld only because the judges could not agree. This reaction in itself was proof of the effectiveness of Albee's thesis in the play, and the fact that Pulitzer gave no award that year indicates clearly that Albee's work "towered over the common run of contemporary plays," as Taubman remarked in the *Times.*

Foreign productions were sought, the young playwright was lionized, sent on tour by the State Department, and was probably the most talked-about writer on the theatrical scene since Tennessee Williams. Publicity stories multiplied; when Edward Albee bought a house on Montauk Point so he could work in peace and quiet, it was news; and when he moved into an elegant Tenth Street apartment in the Village, there were descriptions of his handsome, long-windowed living room, with its brown cork walls, white couch, and modern paintings. (He has become an art addict since buying several oils of Milton Avery, his latest acquisition being a couple of Picasso drawings.) The apartment on Tenth Street houses the offices of Pesces Productions, an enterprise set up by Albee and his associates to provide an off-Broadway platform for embryonic playwrights. Predictions were proffered as to his ultimate place on the top rung of the theatrical ladder, and while he was denounced as the dramatist of decay by some, he was hailed by many as a genius who was "a physician to the sick soul."

Unfortunately, Edward Albee has not lived up to the promise of his first full-length play or the prognostications of his admirers in regard to his rising star. His dramatization of Carson McCullers' *Ballad of the Sad Cafe*, produced in 1963, was more of a theater-reading of Miss McCullers' novel than a creative contribution on Albee's part, and served mainly to strengthen the playwright's concern with the physical and emotional sterility of modern man. Furthermore, his most recent essay into the field of physical fruitlessness and erotic psychosis, *Tiny Alice*, which opened December 29, 1964, was a hopelessly muddled and mystifying extension of his thesis. Indeed, he has called this denunciation of present-day materialistic values and the resultant vacuum "a mystery and a morality play." It concerns one "Brother Julian," who is induced by his Cardinal to let himself be seduced by "tiny Alice," the world's most powerful woman, who has propositioned the church with a subsidy of vast amounts of money in return for Julian's presence in her boudoir. When he, like other Albee heroes, fails to give satisfaction, he is shot to death by Miss Alice's lawyer. He thus becomes a martyr, but just why this is so remains a "mystery." (Some critics have offered the theory that the whole play is a sexual revery in the mind of Julian, but if so, it nullifies the message—granted that Albee intended a message; and if he did not, then the play is a "hoax," as it was labeled by Robert Brustein.) Moreover, if it is to be regarded as a morality play, it seems highly sacrilegious.

The only flaw in Albee's hypothesis of present-day sterility is that he apparently overlooks the population explosion prevalent in the world today. However, in spite of the gross discrepancy between theory and fact in Mr. Albee's thinking, his premise is surprisingly convincing within the framework of his plays. The dialogue and action, especially in *Who's Afraid . . .* , are so skillfully wrought that the spectator does not question the validity of his sociological statement in regard to man's loss of power to propagate as well as his diminishing creative ability in art. With the exception of *Tiny Alice*, the plays speak out with bold clarity in regard to the false values of a mechanized civilization, the vapidity of man grown soft with the comforts of modern invention, the destructive force of unvaried, encroaching uniformity, and the decay beneath the shiny surface of a neon society.

Presently at work on a new play entitled *The Substitute Speaker,* Edward Albee pursues his course calmly in the face of the fury his work provokes. Among the American playwrights of the sixties, his name stands out brightly, a beacon of challenge.

With each new decade, the theater, like some imperishable phoenix, rises from the ashes to confound those who are predicting —or announcing—its demise. In and around the orbit of Albee's star, at least a dozen lesser lights shimmer and gleam. Like him, most of them emanate from Off-Broadway theaters and travel to the commercial stage from there. Others issue from television or the printed word. One of the brightest of the latter is Gore Vidal, whose plays sparkle with penetrating wit and satiric humor. His first title (appropriately) was *Visit to a Small Planet,* an adaptation of his widely acclaimed television comedy about a man from Mars who lands on earth in a flying saucer. In his realistically done fantasy, he points out the folly of American foreign policy and militarism in a nuclear age, accomplishing his aim with such aplomb that the play was a long-run hit and was followed in 1960 by the playwright's equally brilliant political satire, *The Best Man.* Here the target of his rapier thrust was the "dog-eat-dog" system of electing government officers, the hypocrisy of our morality code in regard to public servants.

Gore Vidal is well qualified to present the political scene in his plays. Seven years after his birth in 1925, he became the youngest member in the household of his distinguished grandfather, Oklahoma Senator Thomas P. Gore, in Washington, and from that early age on was exposed to politics, attending his first national convention at the age of fourteen. After his school days in Washington, Gore went on to Phillips Exeter Academy, where he developed a passion for the novels of Henry James, and three years after he graduated, published a novel of his own, *Williwaw*. It was the first of many notable works by Mr. Vidal as a writer of varied facets: novelist; television dramatist (he has written numerous network shows, one of the most impressive being, *The Indestructible Mr. Gore*, a memoir of his famous grandfather, in which he appeared as narrator); screen-play writer and producer (including Tennessee Williams' *Suddenly Last Summer*, and the most recent, award-winning remake of *Ben Hur*, as well as the film version of *The Best Man*); and playwright. He has been criticized as "limited" by his conventional form, the "well-made" play. But for those who view with alarm the increasing formlessness in the theater (which may be one reason why Broadway is rapidly becoming a music-hall show place), it is a relief to find a playwright capable of strongly structured drama. He said in the Foreword to the published version of *The Best Man*: ". . . I do not write beautiful plays. I use the theater as a place to criticize society, to satirize folly, to question presuppositions . . . in such a way that the audience is led . . . to new perceptions." Handsome, polished, twice a candidate for Congress himself, Vidal is a unique figure in the contemporary theater.

Another recruit to the theater from the world of fiction and (in this case) article writing, is James Baldwin, the bold, eloquent champion of the civil rights movement in the South. Born a year before Vidal, in a Harlem hospital in 1924, he lived in New York "all the years except those between 1948 to 1957; I spent those years in Paris and saved my life," he said in an interview in 1964. Although he received sporadic help and encouragement through those years from teachers and one social worker in particular, his life was a constant struggle for existence and for recognition until he began to publish short stories and articles in Paris, then in the United States. He first turned from the printed page to the stage in 1952, when he came home from France to publish his novel, *Go Tell It on the Mountain*. The one-act play, which he called *The Amen Corner*, a picture of the plight of a small Negro congregation, was produced at Howard University, in 1955, and received very good reviews. But Baldwin was told that Negro plays could not succeed in America, so he put the script away and went back to Paris for another two years. He returned for the civil rights movement, when he took the play out of the trunk and tried to find a legitimate stage for it. *The Amen Corner* was finally produced in Los Angeles in 1964, a hit that gave him heart to attempt full-length plays. He dramatized his second novel, *Giovanni's Room,* as a project for Actors Studio, and for a time was apprenticed to Elia Kazan, carrying the director's clipboard, taking notes for the production of *J.B.* and *Sweet Bird of Youth.* ("It was very useful training," he said afterward. He learned the inner mechanics—how a play works, how essential it is to get along with crew and stagehands.)

In April, 1963, he started writing *Blues for Mr. Charlie,* in Paris once more, but had to fly home for the march on Washington in May, and remained here, taking an active part in the movement while working on his play. He wrote between meetings and public appearances, in all sorts of places—on paper pads in planes, in trains, waiting rooms and gas stations. In the middle of it, Medgar Evers, his good friend and colleague, was cruelly, fatally shot, and Baldwin knew he had to complete the play. He was afraid if he did not, he would not be a writer anymore. *Blues for Mr. Charlie,* the result, was literally a handwritten play. He typed the script, editing it in the process, and wrote it again. The rewriting went on until the week of production in the fall of 1964, at the ANTA theater. A harsh, realistic picture of the life of the Southern Negro and the bitter antagonism between colored and white, *Blues for Mr. Charlie* had much of the fluidity of form of *After the Fall,* with scenes shifting between past and present, with characters appearing or leaving the stage as various incidents are recalled, following the brutal killing which opens the play. Although no one denied the power and impact of the drama as propaganda, reviews were mixed as to its merits as theater art. Mr. Baldwin is perhaps a better speechmaker and essayist than dramatist. Physically a slight, scrawny, frail-looking man, he has a quiet but forceful way of speaking, and his round, rather bulbous eyes are singularly alive with the fiery light of the zealous thinker, the devoted worker in a cause.

The list of Off-Broadway luminaries includes a host of firecracker playwrights, whose talent sparkles in a single burst and is gone; others continue to shoot off repeatedly, and a few burn with steady light. Among the names that stand out are Frank Gilroy, Arthur Kopit, Jack Gelber, Jack Richardson, LeRoi Jones, Alan Davis, William Hanley, Thomas LaBar, Murray Schisgal, and William Gibson. (The last was first recognized for his Broadway successes, *Two for the Seesaw* and *The Miracle Worker;* the second, an emotional drama dealing with the psychological problems of Helen Keller's famous nurse, Anne Sullivan, moved audiences to tears for more than two years.) Frank Gilroy, born in 1926, is perhaps the oldest of the group. His Off-Broadway *Who'll Save the Plowboy?* had the charm of the Irish playwrights; it was no doubt responsible for the production of his full-length *The Subject Was Roses,* at the Helen Hayes Theatre. This was a far less felicitous vehicle (revealing the vicissitudes of an Irish-American family in the Bronx), reviews of which were mingled; but with extra backing, the play hung on until it caught on, and wound up winning the Pulitzer prize for 1964–1965. Arthur Kopit, perhaps the youngest, who graduated from Harvard with Phi Beta Kappa honors in 1959, won fame at the age of twenty-four with his wild burlesque of murder mysteries, entitled enchantingly *Oh, Dad, Poor Dad, Mamma's Hung You in the Closet and I'm Feelin' So Sad.* His weird melo-comedy with its long, intriguing title was almost as much of a conversation piece for theatergoers as Albee's plays, and promised much from the brilliant young Harvard grad who started out as an engineer, but found writing for the theater-of-the-absurd much more fun. However, his next sortie, *The Day the Whores Came Out to Play Tennis,* instead of skyrocketing, fizzled out after four performances.

Jack Gelber is best known for *The Connection,* his play concerning dope addiction among teen-agers, which shocked and excited Off-Broadway audiences into action against dope peddling in general. His follow-up, *The Apple,* failed to live up to the promise of his earlier work. Jack Richardson, considered by his colleagues one of the sturdiest talents, has written a number of arresting, acrid plays, particularly *The Prodigal* and *Gallows Humor.* His Broadway debut came with *Xmas in Las Vegas,* starring Tom Ewell. LeRoi Jones, the angriest among the rebel playwrights, won an "Obie" award for *The Dutchman,* his first claim to fame. Like

Baldwin, LeRoi Jones is a stern interrogator on the question of race relations, and his other offerings, *The Slave, The Toilet,* and *The Room,* are too steeped in harsh feeling to be objective or appealing to most audiences. (Although one of his colleagues quipped that *The Toilet* works, the majority of playgoers found it clogged with unnecessary obscenity and ineffective.) Murray Schisgal, the clown of the lot, and the most lightweight, captivated his spectators with *The Typists* and *The Tiger,* which won for him the Broadway production of his zany "triangle" story of three most confused characters who are in *Luv.* With the skillful handling of the actors, *Luv* became one of the long-run hits of the 1964–1965 season.

A small cluster of playwrights specialize in light comedy for the commercial theater, including two women currently popular on Broadway: Jean Kerr, whose innocuous comedies are saved by clever dialogue, and Muriel Resnik, whose *Any Wednesday,* an up-to-date version of the bedroom farce, is a fresh-minted penny from an old coin. Neil Simon, a Bronx playwright who stands by himself as a comedic writer for the commercial theater, has made four successive hits with his Manhattan folktales: *Come Blow Your Horn,* the first, made use of his family background in the Bronx; *Barefoot in the Park* deals with the trials and tribulations of a young couple living in a West Side walkup; and, *The Odd Couple,* which the *New Yorker* described as "an utterly beguiling comedy about a pair of marital rejects trying to make a go of it in the lonely reaches of a Riverside Drive apartment." The fourth play, an adaptation of Patrick Dennis' novel, *Little Me,* while not as successful as the others in this country, has been a smash hit in England.

The theater may well be in a state of flux, still seeking, as O'Neill did, beginning with his sea plays nearly fifty years ago, a happy medium between the traditional and the modern (the abstract) in playwriting. The drama must have form in order to be art; and as long as there are playwrights to experiment, the theater, though it may disappear from Broadway to rise in the provinces, will never die.

A SELECTED BIBLIOGRAPHY

Bailey, Mabel Driscoll. *Maxwell Anderson: the Playwright as Prophet.* New York, Abelard-Schuman, Ltd., 1957.

Bentley, Eric. *The Dramatic Event.* New York, Horizon Press, 1954.

Block, Anita. *The Changing World in Plays and Theatre.* Boston, Little, Brown & Co., 1939.

Brown, John Mason. *Broadway in Review.* New York, W. W. Norton & Co., Inc., 1940.

Clurman, Harold. *Lies Like Truth.* New York, The Macmillan Co., 1958.

Gassner, John. *Masters of the Drama.* New York, Dover Publications, Inc., 1945.

——. *Theatre at the Crossroads.* New York, Holt, Rinehart & Winston, Inc., 1960.

——. *The Theatre in Our Times.* New York, Crown Publishers, Inc., 1954.

Gelb, Arthur and Barbara. *Eugene O'Neill.* New York, Harper & Row, 1962.

Glaspell, Susan. *The Road to the Temple.* New York, Frederic A. Stokes Company, 1927.

Hamilton, Clayton. *Conversations on Contemporary Drama.* New York, The Macmillan Co., 1924.

Hellman, Lillian. *The Autumn Garden.* Boston, Little, Brown & Co., 1952. (Book Jacket)

Krutch, Joseph Wood. *The American Drama Since 1918.* New York, Random House, Inc., 1939.

Lewis, Allan. *The Contemporary Theatre.* New York, Crown Publishers, Inc., 1962.

Mantle, Burns. *American Playwrights of Today.* New York, Dodd, Mead & Co., 1929.

——. *Contemporary American Playwrights.* New York, Dodd, Mead & Co., 1938.

Matthews, Brander. *Playwrights on Playmaking*. New York, Charles Scribner's Sons, 1923.

Miller, Arthur. *Collected Plays,* with Introduction. The Viking Press, 1957.

Miller, Jordan Y. "Myth and the American Dream: O'Neill to Albee," *Modern Drama,* vol. 7, no. 2, September 1964, pp. 190-198.

Nathan, George Jean. *The Theatre in the Fifties*. New York, Alfred A. Knopf, Inc., 1953.

Nelson, Benjamin. *Tennessee Williams*. New York, Ivan Obolensky, Inc., 1961.

Oppenheimer, George. *The Passionate Playgoer*. New York, The Viking Press, Inc., 1958.

Rice, Elmer. *The Living Theatre*. New York, Harper & Row, 1959.

——. *Minority Report*. Simon and Schuster, 1963.

Saroyan, William. *Here Comes There Goes You Know Who*. New York, Simon and Schuster, Inc., 1961.

Sievers, W. David. *Freud on Broadway*. New York, Hermitage House, 1955.

Spewack, Samuel and Bella. *"How to Write a Musical Comedy,"* Introduction to *Kiss Me Kate,* New York, Alfred A. Knopf, Inc., 1953.

Weales, Gerald. *American Drama Since World War II*. New York, Harcourt, Brace & World, 1962.

Williams, Tennessee. "Forward" to *Camino Real*. Norfolk, Conn. New Directions Pub. Corp., 1953.

——. "Person-to-Person." In *Cat on a Hot Tin Roof*. New Directions, 1955.

——. "The Catastrophe of Success." In *The Glass Menagerie*. New Directions, 1945.

——. "The Past, the Present and the Perhaps." In *Orpheus Descending* with *Battle of Angels*. New Directions, 1958.

——. "The Timeless World of a Play." In *The Rose Tattoo*. New Directions, 1950.

INDEX